Information Superhighways

Multimedia users and futures

Computers and People Series

Edited by

BR GAINES and A MONK

Monographs

Communicating with Microcomputers. An introduction to the technology of man-computer communication, *Ian H Witten* 1980
The Computer in Experimental Psychology, *R Bird* 1981
Principles of Computer Speech, *IH Witten* 1982
Cognitive Psychology of Planning, *J-M Hoc* 1988
Formal Methods for Interactive Systems, *A Dix* 1991
Human Reliability Analysis: Context and Control, *E Hollnagel* 1993

Edited Works

Computing Skills and the User Interface, *MJ Coombs and JL Alty (eds)* 1981
Fuzzy Reasoning and Its Applications, *EH Mamdani and BR Gaines (eds)* 1981
Intelligent Tutoring Systems, *D Sleeman and JS Brown (eds)* 1982 (1986 paperback)
Designing for Human-Computer Communication, *ME Sime and MJ Coombs (eds)* 1983
The Psychology of Computer Use, *TRG Green, SJ Payne and GC van der Veer (eds)* 1983
Fundamentals of Human-Computer Interaction, *A Monk (ed)* 1984, 1985
Working with Computers: Theory versus Outcome, *GC van der Veer, TRG Green, J-M Hoc and D Murray (eds)* 1988
Cognitive Engineering in Complex Dynamic Worlds, *E Hollnagel, G Mancini and DD Woods (eds)* 1988
Computers and Conversation, *P Luff, N Gilbert and D Frohlich (eds)* 1990
Adaptive User Interfaces, *D Browne, P Totterdell and M Norman (eds)* 1990
Human-Computer Interaction and Complex Systems, *GRS Weir and JL Alty (eds)* 1991
Computer-supported Cooperative Work and Groupware, *Saul Greenberg (ed)* 1991
The Separable User Interface, *EA Edmonds (ed)* 1992
Requirements Engineering: Social and Technical Issues, *M Jirotka and JA Goguen (eds)* 1994
Perspectives on HCI: Diverse Approaches, *AF Monk and GN Gilbert (eds)* 1995
Information Superhighways: Multimedia Users and Futures, *SJ Emmott (ed)* 1995

Practical Texts

Effective Color Displays: Theory and Practice, *D Travis* 1991
Understanding Interfaces: A Handbook of Human-Computer Dialogue, *MW Lansdale and TR Ormerod* 1994 (1995 paperback)

EACE Publications
(Consulting Editors: *Y WAERN and J-M HOC*)

Cognitive Ergonomics, *P Falzon (ed)* 1990
Psychology of Programming, *J-M Hoc, TRG Green, R Samurcay and D Gilmore (eds)* 1990

Information Superhighways

Multimedia users and futures

Edited by

Stephen J. Emmott

In collaboration with
David Travis

ACADEMIC PRESS

Harcourt Brace & Company, Publishers

London San Diego New York Boston Sydney Tokyo Toronto

ACADEMIC PRESS LIMITED
24-28 Oval Road
LONDON NW1 7DX, UK

U.S. Edition Published by
ACADEMIC PRESS INC.
San Diego, CA 92101, USA

Chapter 7 has appeared as an earlier version in CSCW journal 1/3 (1993) *Why do Users Like Video? Studies of Multimedia-Supported Collaboration* pp.163-197 (published by Kluwer Academic Publishers).

A catalogue record for this book is available from the British Library

ISBN 0 12 238360 5

Transferred to digital printing 2005

Printed and bound by Antony Rowe Ltd, Eastbourne

Contents

Contributors

Professor Vicki Bruce, Department of Psychology, University of Stirling, Stirling, FK9 4LA, Scotland.
<vb1@uk.ac.stir.forth>

Professor Peter Cochrane, Head of Research, BT Laboratories, Martlesham Heath, Ipswich, IP5 7RE, England.
<pcochrane@bt-sys.bt.co.uk>

Dr Stephen J. Emmott, AT&T Bell Laboratories, 101 Crawfords Corner Road, Holmdel, NJ 07733-3030, USA.
This book was edited whilst the editor was Director, Big Think Ltd, 100 New Bond Street, London W1Y 9LF, England.
<sje@bigthink.demon.co.uk>

Professor William H. Dutton, Director, ESRC Programme on Information and Communication Technologies, Middlesex, UB8 3PH, England, and Professor of Communications [on leave] Annenberg School for Communication, University of Southern California, University Park, Los Angeles, CA 90089-0281, USA.

Dr Christian Heath, Department of Sociology, Kings College London, WC2R 2LJ, England.
<christian.heath@kcl.ac.uk>

Dr Ellen Isaacs, Sunsoft Inc., 2550 Garcia Avenue, Mountain View, CA 94043, USA.

Dr Allan Kuchinsky, Hewlett-Packard Laboratories, 1501 Page Mill Road, Palo Alto, CA 94304, USA.
<kuchinsk@hpl.hp.com>

Dr Robert Leichner, Hewlett-Packard Laboratories, 1501 Page Mill Road, Palo Alto, CA 94304, USA.
<leichner@hpl.hp.com>

Dr Paul Luff, Department of Sociology, University of Surrey, Guildford, GU2 5XH, England.
<paul.luff@soc.surrey.ac.uk>

Dr Robin Mansell, Science Policy Research Unit, University of Sussex, Brighton BN1 9RF, England.

Dr Andrew Monk, Department of Psychology, University of York, York, Y01 5DD, England.
<AM1@tower.york.ac.uk>

Dr Bonnie A. Nardi, Apple Computer Inc., 1 Infinite Loop, Cupertino, CA 95014, USA.
<nardi@.apple.com>

Dr Heinrich Schwarz, Program in Science, Technology, Society, Massachusetts Institute of Technology, E51-017 Cambridge, MA 02139, USA.

Dr Robert Sclabassi, Department of Neurosurgery, University of Pittsburgh, Pittsburgh, PA 15213, USA.

Dr Abigail Sellen, MRC Applied Psychology Unit, Cambridge, UK and Rank Xerox EuroPARC, 61 Regent Street, Cambridge, CB2 1AB, England.

Professor Noel Sheehy, Department of Psychology, Queens University, Belfast, Northern Ireland.

Professor Roger Silverstone, Department of Media Studies, University of Sussex, Brighton, BN1 9RF, England.

Dr John Tang, Sunsoft Inc., 2550 Garcia Avenue, Mountain View, CA 94043, USA.

Dr David Travis, BT Laboratories, Martlesham Heath, Ipswich, IP5 7RE, England.
<dtravis@bt.hfnet.co.uk>

Professor Roger J. Watt, Centre for Cognitive and Computational Neuroscience, University of Stirling, Stirling, FK9 4LA, Scotland.
<watt@cs.stir.ac.uk>

Dr Steve Whittaker, Lotus Development Corporation, 1 Rogers Street, Cambridge, MA 02142, USA.

Foreword

Rarely have hype and understatement been companions to the degree they are with regard to information superhighways. Amidst all the press attention and fanfare, little is said about the potential magnitude of change before us. Furthermore, even less is said about how little government has to do with the information superhighway either in terms of incentives or deterrents. It is happening from the roots and it is unstoppable.

Since bits are bits, it makes no difference if they represent video, sound or text, they are all the same. They don't stop at customs. They know no difference between going next door or from Tokyo to New York. Like never before, the planetful of bits is the head of a pin.

The media industry has been pushing information at people. With the support of advertising, bits are hurled into the ether or printed on dead trees, to catch as catch can. Now suddenly, users will pull on information, directly or through the aegis of their intelligent agents. The media kingdom just turned inside out.

Copyright law will disintegrate. Digital money will be issued by mom and pop organizations. The very purposes of the nation-state are in question. Countries are an artefact of the industrial age.

All of a sudden the 'have-nots' are not those you assume. Many are affluent members of the first world. In fact, the third world can, and is, leap frogging the telecommunications infrastructure of developed nations.

What is going on? A lot more than you think. Read on.

Nicholas Negroponte

Media Lab
MIT
Boston MA, USA

Part 1   Overview

1

Introduction

Stephen J. Emmott

> . . . the creation of a network of networks, transmitting messages and images at the speed of light across every continent, is essential to sustainable development for all human family. It will bring economic progress, strong democracies, better environmental management, improved healthcare. . . To this end, legislators, regulators, and business must now build and run a Global Information Infrastructure.
>
> United States Vice-president, Al Gore (1994)

A remarkable revolution – an information revolution – has begun. The potential scale of its social, economic and political impact is unprecedented; its effects are likely to be greater than those of any previous technological change, leaving almost no-one untouched. The foundations for this revolution are *information superhighways*: global information infrastructures of convergent communications, information and media technologies. It is a marriage of information, creativity, technology and empowerment – enabling people across the world to electronically access, create, control and communicate any information at any time, anywhere and in any way via *multimedia* applications combining digital video, graphics, sound and text.

The key to what is going on in this information revolution is held by the *users* of information superhighways. This is a revolution that will be driven by users (consumers) rather than by media corporations. It will be users – individuals, groups and organisations – as the critical drivers for the development of multimedia and interactive applications who will determine the value and the impact of information superhighways. It will be this impact that will ultimately shape, in a profound way, the political, social and economic future of the increasingly digital world in which we will live.

This book is the first to introduce and examine a range of key issues which focus on the users of information superhighways. The issues are important. For example, the book explores the potential magnitude, and the potential benefits, of the changes we face; it considers the potential dangers in the inequity of a society of information haves and have nots, and it discusses the failures of media hype and industry expectations. The issues are significant for the communications, computing, consumer electronics, media and entertainment industries currently racing to develop applications upon which their future, and the success of the alliances they are forming, is becoming increasingly dependent. Further, the book outlines a number of applications – interactive multimedia products and services – that emerge when development is user-centred rather than driven by media corporations.

One of the aims of this book is to serve as an introduction to some of the key information superhighway issues. As such, the remainder of this chapter provides an introduction to, and overview of, some of the topics and concepts which are covered in detail throughout the rest of the book.

1.1   Networks and information

'Information' is, in the context of this discussion, simply a technical term which refers to 'bits' of data representing the combination of multimedia content such as video, graphics, text and sound. 'Superhighways' are the key enablers of our use of this information, as the broad bandwidth networks capable of carrying, in real time, the high volumes generated by multimedia content.

Throughout the industrialised world much of the network infrastructure required for a superhighway is already in place. In the UK, for example, around 90 per cent of the communications network is composed of a broadband optical fibre network. Like much of the rest of Europe and North America, it is only the part of this network that directly connects users (at homes, offices, laboratories, schools, universities and hospitals) to the network – the 'local loop' – which remains to be converted to 'superhighway' capability. The copper wire-based local loop has insufficient bandwidth to carry the levels of multimedia-based data in real time, and although it is possible to provide some forms of multimedia content over the local loop via either compression or ADSL (asynchronous digital subscriber loop) technology, these techniques pose limitations. A key limitation of ADSL is that it works in one direction only; it offers only very limited interactivity – the ability to exchange and control information in both directions – which is a key feature of superhighways. The drawback of current compression techniques for real-time use over networks is that they are limited in the visual quality of the end result, the speed at which the technique or the algorithm can be performed, and the amount of compression achieved. Such issues have led to the increasingly accepted concept of information superhighway infrastructures based primarily on optical fibre, and augmented by satellite, radio and optical wireless technologies.

Importantly, the developing and Third World is now beginning to plan and build superhighway network infrastructures. Information superhighways may be the best chance to date many such countries have for radical positive economic and social change, enabling their participation in the information revolution as 'information haves', and providing real benefits for the citizens of those nations.

1.2   Applications

There can be little doubt that the applications are one of the most critical components of information superhighways. Information infrastructures will reach and connect homes, places of work, hospitals, schools, libraries and vast information storage and exchange sites via multimedia-based interactive information products and services. Such infrastructures will be capable of delivering innovative applications which could radically transform the nature of work, finance, healthcare provision, and the educational process as our access to, and use of, information undergoes a fundamental transformation in itself. The effect would be to create profound social and economic change (see Cochrane, Chapter 2).

From information push to information pull

The media industry currently controls access to information primarily through the transmission of broadcast television. The key word here – broadcast – provides a clue to understanding the importance of information superhighways. The small number of channels transmitted (due to the limited available broadcast spectrum) are 'thrown' into the air indiscriminately, leaving the 'users' of this information as passive consumers of the broadcast content, with little choice, and little control, of the information received. We have to take what we can get.

Contrast this with the ability information superhighways provide to truly interact with, create, control and communicate any information, in any format, any time, anywhere and with anyone. The convergence of computing and communications technologies is already beginning to have a significant impact on how many of us work and communicate, and use or exchange information. Financial institutions are beginning to realise the opportunities, and the implications, of digital money – something which will revolutionise banking, retail and trading in the near future, and has far-reaching global political and economic implications in the longer term.

Networks are allowing organisations to re-engineer their business processes in order to increase their performance and gain competitive advantage. Increasingly, as business organisations re-structure themselves and their processes, they are requiring groups of people located at different sites, perhaps even in different countries, to work together using computer-mediated communication. Local- and wide-area networks (LANs and WANs) connected to computers support, to an extent, group working and information sharing via 'groupware' applications. Tens of millions of people are already using local, national and global communication networks for information access and for electronic communication via personal computers (PCs). This is the basis of an existing information highway – the *Internet*.

The impact of the Internet has yet to be fully felt or understood. It is estimated to be currently growing at a remarkable rate of 10 per cent per month. It is now clear that the Internet is profoundly affecting both the way in which individuals and organisations communicate, and also the availability, access, use and exchange of information across the worldwide web (this term is usually reserved for an Internet protocol for information access) of networks and computers. Within the next five years, possibly more than 500 million people worldwide may be using the Internet for electronic communication (via e-mail) and information exchange and access; every individual able to contribute to and interact with the information available. The Internet is a model of how users are critical drivers for both the impact and the application of the convergence of computing and communications technologies. It is successful and important because it enables, as far as it can, people to access and exchange information, independently of space and time, free of corporate control.

In addition to the impact that the Internet is having on commerce and communication, we can only begin to speculate about the potential impact generated by the border-blind nature of such information networks on political systems and on the integrity of nation states. Their impact on the future of governments, currencies and copyright laws, to name a few, is unknown but it seems certain that it will be profound.

The increase in the use, and the value, of the Internet is due, in no small part, to the fact that information has been made more accessible, and easier to find, use and exchange by the development of multimedia-based 'browsers' for the World Wide Web, such as *Netscape* and *Mosaic*. Notwithstanding this fact, a significant drawback is that the application of the Internet is limited by the bandwidth of the existing networks over which it must currently operate, a consequence of which is that real-time multimedia-based information use and communication is impossible.

In many respects, information superhighways are a widening of the 'lanes' of this existing information highway, increasing the speed of information access, and with it, the ways in which communication can take place. Their construction will support and facilitate more effective and more natural communication and collaboration between individuals and groups over networks. They will permit access to, and exchange of, information in real time, in multimedia formats most appropriate to users' needs, and assisted by intelligent agents able to roam networks to find, carry and organise what is required from the mass of information, and stop that which is not wanted. Information superhighways, and the applications they support, will almost inevitably radically change the way in which individuals, groups, and organisations communicate and work. Their development will be *evolutionary*, but their impact *revolutionary*.

'Killer' applications

Given the importance of information superhighways, it is surprising that media attention has focused on little more than the 'benefits' of ordering a pizza or a movie from a television 'set-top box'. Indeed, it is the case that a primary focus of development is on applications which will make relatively poor use of the computing and bandwidth capabilities afforded by information superhighways. Even more surprising is that these are called the 'killer' applications – products and services perceived as generating the greatest demand and therefore revenues, and often cited as a basis for justifying the cost of building the remaining infrastructure. However, their development seems to be driven more by the strategies of media corporations than by user demand or need. The most common of these applications – video-on-demand and home shopping – do not in any case require a superhighway broadband network: they are possible to provide using ADSL technology because the concept of 'interactivity' is limited to choosing from an 'electronic store' a video, bank statement or similar.

1.3   A revolution driven by users

Despite industry assumptions and media hype, it is unlikely that any one 'killer' application will realise the value of information superhighways. Rather, the value – and the impact – is more likely to be in the development of a range of applications which are driven by the needs of users; products and services which make what Negroponte (1991) called 'imaginative' use of the computing and network capabilities. Certainly, applications which meet the needs of users rather than the desires of media corporations will be those which make more imaginative use of the computing and network capabilities of information superhighways than do video-on-demand, home shopping, or 500-2000 cable/fibre television channels.

Whether or not video-on-demand, home shopping and greater viewing 'choice' are eventually successful (in terms of dollars generated per dollars spent in development) is an open, but relatively unimportant question. Their impact on corporate revenues may pale by comparison to the impact that information superhighways may have on the way in which people will be able to communicate, use and exchange information, and the enormous economic, political and social implications that this will have.

1.4   Information haves and have nots

Usability

Attention is often given, quite rightly, to the potential risks of Third World countries and developing nations being left out of this information revolution as information have nots. In developed nations, the risks are of low-income groups becoming the have nots. Of course, information societies will need to ensure that all have equal access and opportunities for participation as 'information haves.' However, on this vitally important issue, little or no attention is given to the critically important fact that large sections of even developed countries, many among the most affluent members of society, face being left out of the picture altogether because of difficult to use technology. The problem is one of increasing technological complexity versus usability. The challenge for those involved in the design process (psychologists, industrial designers, computer scientists and engineers) will be to make increasingly complex technology accessible – easy and intuitive to use – for everyone. This issue will be as important as any other in determining who will be information haves rather than have nots.

The diversity of multimedia applications and the user populations they are intended for will preclude current common approaches to designing the interface between the technology and the user. These typically rely on the user having to learn to adapt to the constraints of the technology, or having some knowledge of computing. Design will have to focus on users in ways it has never done before – it will have to be really *user-centred*. Designers will have to develop applications and devices that have truly intuitive interfaces. It is possible: multimedia – combined vision, sound, text and even touch – is, after all, the basis of human communication.

Further, as fully interactive multimedia applications emerge to meet the needs of users as groups and organisations – 'groupware' applications – user-centred design will require the construction of appropriate 'social interfaces', which facilitate both the task of the group and the important social communication elements which are essential to group working.

A key feature of the multimedia applications discussed in Chapters 8 to 10 of this book is that they have emerged from focusing on the needs of users; their development has been *user-centred*. They are applications which enable the creation and exchange of information, and support communication and collaboration in formats most suitable to the needs of the information users, and the ability to *virtually* work and collaborate, unbounded by the separations of time and space. These might even be considered as alternative forms of 'video-on-demand' (Buxton, 1994). Among the first attempts at user-centred design for social interfaces are those outlined by Heath, Luff and Sellen in Chapter 8 and by Travis in Chapter 9.

Equity, efficiency and regulatory innovation

The potential importance of information superhighways, and the scope they offer for new services and new revenues, is generating much debate and controversy about who should build the final part of the superhighway infrastructure (the local loop), who should carry multimedia services over it, and to whom they should be delivered. There seems little doubt that the only industry with the financial and technical ability to complete the construction of a superhighway is the telecommunications industry. However, the telecommunications operators are increasingly in confrontation with current regulatory policy that restricts who is permitted to carry multimedia services and to whom they should be carried.

Public policy needs to be geared to promoting fair competition to ensure continued technological innovation and encouragement of investment. Public policy must also ensure equitability of access. This has been a central component of the US Government's outline of a National and Global Information Infrastructure plan. However, technological innovation and telecommunication operator strategies are moving at such a pace as to be beyond the capabilities of present policies to regulate effectively. Development strategies, and investment, in both services and infrastructure of the telecommunications operators are bound to reflect not only commercial interests but prevailing public policy, and the telecommunications operators are unhappy about what is seen as increasingly interventionist regulatory approaches. As such, they are seeking changes in policy which would free them from existing constraints. Confronting governments, policy makers, telecommunications operators and service developers is the problem of who should and who will address these issues, and how (Mansell, Chapter 3).

1.5   Organisation of this book

Information superhighways explores a range of key issues which focus on the users, and on the impact of information superhighways. The contributors explore, from different perspectives, a range of key issues which focus on the users of information superhighways. The book is organised into three parts: Part 1: Overview; Part 2: Issues; Part 3: Applications. Part 1 is this introductory chapter.

Part 2   Issues

Part 2 considers, from several different perspectives, the potential impact of information superhighways. In Chapter 2, Peter Cochrane outlines the potential magnitude of the social, economic and even environmental change posed by information superhighways. This Cochranesque vision is one in which commerce, work and society itself will be radically changed. Organisations will become increasingly 'virtual'; the effective status of national and international boundaries will change as governments and industry find themselves unable to regulate the flow of information. The power of the media industries will be challenged and eroded. Opportunities will be created to improve and change the way in which healthcare, education, and work is performed. Cochrane makes the very salient point that change is likely to be limited not by technology, but by our inability to subsume the technological advances to positive effect.

In Chapter 3, Robin Mansell considers how the prospect of universal access to information superhighways, and the ability of regulators to ensure equity in a multimedia future is being severely challenged by the speed of technological changes and global changes to the information network industries and corporations. Mansell suggests that innovation in regulatory policy is urgently needed to control supplier power and to ensure universal access to information networks and services.

Roger Silverstone, in Chapter 4, suggests that the process leading from technological revolution to change in people's everyday lives is not necessarily one of equivalent revolution. Drawing on evidence from studies of the introduction and use of primarily entertainment technologies in the home, Silverstone makes three points. Firstly, and the main point, is that rather than acting as a catalyst for change in domestic structures, the introduction of technology applications in the home is more likely to be 'domesticated' into those structures. Secondly, that change at all is unlikely to occur for many sections of society, including low income families who may be denied access to the networks and technologies, if regulatory policy is unable to ensure universal access, or if the cost is prohibitive to these groups. Thirdly, that other sections of society see, in any event, new technology as inaccessible.

In Chapter 5, Will Dutton considers what lessons, if any, previous attempts to introduce interactive and multimedia technologies may have for the development of applications of information superhighways. Dutton shows that many trials of multimedia applications, such as the 'killer' applications of video-on-demand, home shopping and even video telephony have failed to meet the hype of marketing, industry and press expectations. Dutton makes the important point that one of the primary reasons for these outcomes appears to be the failure to consider properly the needs of users.

Noel Sheehy examines, in Chapter 6, how new technologies and networks for communication can have a profound impact on the structure and function of organisations given, as Sheehy suggests, that organisations are created and maintained through the way in which people choose, and are able, to communicate.

Part 3 Applications

Part 3 outlines the development of a range of multimedia applications whose development has focused on the needs and requirements of users – it has been *user-centred*. This section concentrates on multimedia applications which support enhanced electronic communication and virtual collaboration in a variety of real world settings, including medicine, education and commerce. It could equally have been devoted to a number of other interesting and potentially important applications. The applications are also of interest because they are not just ideas about how, for example, pointcasting will change our lives at some point in the future, important though this issue is. They are real applications that illustrate just one aspect of how multimedia technologies are beginning to transform how we work, communicate and use information right now. Each author discusses the use of multimedia technologies to support communication and information exchange in ways and formats best suited to the needs of the task and users. The applications are alternatives to the simple, and (as Dutton's chapter suggests) perhaps flawed, approaches to the use of multimedia technologies as simply a face-to-face or 'talking heads' adjunct to conventional telephony-based communication. Additionally, many of the chapters in Part 3 outline the diverse, but interdependent, methods used to examine and understand the relationships between people and technology.

In Chapter 7, John Tang and Ellen Isaacs consider how multimedia can be used effectively to support collaborative working. Their discussion relates to current video technology and bandwidth capabilities, and raises some issues which make the case for broadband networks. Tang and Isaacs' chapter centres around an examination of what it is about multimedia that users prefer.

The use of multimedia technologies to support the activities of remotely located groups in working environments is discussed in Chapter 8 by Christian Heath, Paul Luff and Abigail Sellen. They outline the benefits and the limitations of the development of a Media Space to support both 'foreground' and 'background' activities.

In Chapter 9, David Travis introduces a form of multimedia-mediated communication which aims to overcome some of the limitations of current media space environments. The Electronic Agora is based on the advantages of supporting 'social proxemics', (what is sometimes called 'telepresence') in the execution of functional aspects of tasks, which are themselves also multimedia-mediated.

It is worth mentioning that the applications described in Chapters 8 and 9 are purely concept- or evaluation-based, rather than being proprietary products. As a consequence, their physical construction may appear rather unwieldy to some readers unfamiliar with prototyping and experimental models. However, these readers should not be distracted from the importance of the concept by the laboratory-like implementation.

In Chapter 10, Bonnie Nardi and her colleagues examine the use of video as data. The chapter illustrates the future potential for developing video in complex collaborative tasks in order to increase the efficiency of the task completion, and how the use of video as data may also provide a powerful tool as a 'remote expert'. The example given, neurosurgery in a teaching hospital, is an interesting one. Surgery is a skill which (a) relies on the effective collaboration of many people in the operating theatre, and (b) is difficult to learn without being interactively involved in the process. The use of multimedia to more effectively support the process and to facilitate a sense of presence remotely – telepresence – is potentially very significant.

Chapters 11 and 12 consider perceptual aspects of visual communication. In Chapter 11, Vicki Bruce considers the salient perceptual and cognitive aspects of faces that are important for face-to-face communication, and their relation to video communication. In Chapter 12, Roger Watt discusses how the brain may encode the visual aspects of the important facial gestures which convey so much communicative information.

These two chapters are pertinent for a number of reasons. First, as the use of bandwidth-guzzling multimedia applications becomes an essential and expected part of computing and communications, users will, as the popularity of mobile computing increases, want availability of multimedia capabilities on mobile devices. Thus, the bandwidth problem will simply be shifted to a different domain (radio or microwave) for a period. Knowledge about the perceptual aspects of images for communication is vital for determining threshold criteria for bandwidth-shrinking image coding and compression algorithms to ensure that such algorithms do not lose salient or critical visual information. Second, image coding schemes smarter than current DCT (discrete cosine transform)-based codec (image compression-decompression) algorithms used in the JPEG (joint photographic experts group) and MPEG (motion picture experts group) standards will be desirable because the visual quality of images using such 'lossy' algorithms, particularly real-time motion images, is poor. Third, whatever the bandwidth capability of any of the networks, there remains the need to store all of the information. Because multimedia content requires vast amounts of data storage, image compression is still necessary. Several alternative image processing algorithms to the DCT-based approach, such as those based on fractal coding, do exist and are under development. However, although Watt does not discuss it in his chapter, image processing algorithms based on a model of visual processing in the brain, such as that of Watt's model, may offer a far more efficient way of coding images than present DCT-based algorithms, and at the very least, may merit consideration. Watt's chapter discusses visual coding of faces, but the model of human vision outlined works equally well for any visual scene.

One of the things that Part 3 illustrates is that multimedia application development requires people with diverse skills to work together in interdisciplinary teams. In Chapter 13, Andrew Monk examines how design teams, involving people from different disciplines including psychologists, computer scientists, engineers, social scientists and industrial designers, need to share the techniques, vocabulary and perspectives of each other's disciplines in order to work together. By doing so, we will more effectively meet the challenges we face in developing multimedia products and services for the next millennium.

References

Buxton, W. (1994). Integrating periphery and context: a new model of telematics. In: S. J. Emmott & D. S. Travis (Eds.) *POTS to PANS*, Hintlesham, Suffolk.

Gore, A. (1994). Plugged into the world's knowledge. *Financial Times,* September 19th, 1994.

Negroponte, N. P. (1991). Products and services for computer networks. *Scientific American*, **265** (3), pp. 76–83.

Part 2   Issues

PART A   ISSUES

2

The information wave

Peter Cochrane

Our ability to generate information and transport it about the planet on super highways of optical fibre is about to change the way in which we communicate, work and live. There is not a single aspect of our future that will go untouched by the communication and computing revolution that is now upon us. The change we are about to witness will overshadow the impact of the printed word, industrial revolution, and physical transport. How will we view this future, and increasingly virtual, world? Perhaps we will consider that:

> Home is where the heart is
> Business is where the brain is
> Office is where the user is
> Value is where the information is.

The next major wave of IT development will focus on the delivery of information and experience on demand, in the right form, at the right time, at the right price to fixed or mobile terminals anywhere, over networks of optical fibre, radio, satellite, and optical wireless. Bandwidth, distance and time will no longer be significant cost elements as service and access become the dominant features of the changing demands of an information focused society.

2.1   The human condition

From about the year 1600 onwards the human race has been consuming raw materials at a compound rate ~7% per annum (Drexler, 1992).   If the vast majority of these resources were not renewable, then at this rate of growth the whole of planet earth would be consumed within the next 450 years, there would be no planets in the solar system left within 550 years and the sun itself would be consumed in only 650 years. This simplistic extrapolation of growing consumption, which will increase as the third world industrialises, serves to illustrate that the prognosis of the Club of Rome in 1972 is ever more certain (Meadows et al., 1972). Within 100 years we can expect to see severe global difficulties due to the continued burning of hydrocarbons resulting in increased pollution levels and the denuding of raw material stocks (Kennedy, 1993). Exponential growth by humanity based on accelerating raw material consumption is clearly impossible – there are 'limits to growth'.

The average American currently consumes a continual average of 8kW for heating, air conditioning, physical transport, lighting and other services (Cartledge, 1993). If mankind is to live and prosper whilst maintaining the planet in a habitable state, then a much lower level of consumption is necessary. As the sun's energy falling on earth amounts to 1 kW/m^2, and given the available area for solar collectors, and their electrical conversion efficiency, we might assume a reasonable target to be 1 kW per human (Anderson, 1977).

Physical travel constitutes a primary destructive, and perhaps largely unnecessary, activity with almost 100 billion (Bn) passenger miles (costing over £15 Bn) consumed in the UK alone just to get to work (CSO, 1993a). Much of this could be avoided today, and should be negated by information technology before the turn of the century. Not only is travel expensive in raw materials and energy, it also consumes vast amounts of time, with over £15 Bn per year in traffic jams for the UK – and £10 Bn of this in London alone. Similarly we might anticipate large gains in medicine, health care (£35 Bn), care, education (£25 Bn), training (£35 Bn), and entertainment (£31 Bn) in the UK (CSO, 1993b). The cost equation for each of these sectors is largely dependent on people, material, energy and transport. The application of new technologies is long overdue with the potential for substantial savings in raw materials, energy, time and productivity.

2.2   Where is the money?

Broadly speaking, the money devoted to the development of a future information-based society can only grow substantially at the expense of established industries and modes of operation. Looking at the distribution of wealth available in the UK, for example, we see four major target areas depicted in Figures 2.1 and 2.2 that lie outside the established IT industry. Health, education, entertainment and physical travel represent key opportunity segments, which are, in turn, augmented by publishing, shopping, surface mail, and other peripheral activities.

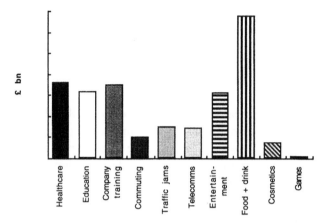

Figure 2.1. Total UK costs in specific service/product categories.

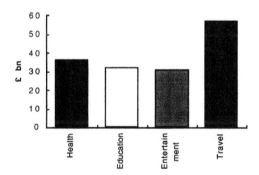

Figure 2.2. Total UK (government and consumer) expenditure on health, education, entertainment and travel.

From the history of earlier industries, it is clear we can expect dramatic reductions in human involvement in manufacturing and services, with subsequent cost savings. This change will be predicated by new generations of robots, materials and manufacturing processes, releasing human and financial resources for a new wave of society. Interestingly, the financing of the information wave looks to be relatively minimal when compared to all previous waves of change since the printing press. In the information wave everyone should have access to the technology, and everyone should be able to participate. All the key technology elements to make this happen are to hand.

2.3   The magic of IT

Information technology (IT) is the only sector delivering an exponential growth in capability whilst reducing raw material and energy costs. Since 1960 our ability to transport information over any distance has doubled each year whilst the use of raw materials and cost has reduced (see Figures 2.3 and 2.4). Today, optical fibre transports over 90% of the UK telephone, fax and data communication. The packing density of electronic circuits, information storage and processing power has nearly doubled every year with power consumption, raw material and cost falling exponentially (Hadenburgh, 1994). We now enjoy a computing and communicating capability that was unimaginable in the 1960s. In ten years we might expect to see computers a $10^3\times$ times more powerful than those of today. Within 20 years (Pearson, 1995) the power could increase by $10^6\times$, and there is a distinct possibility that in 30 years time the power will have increased to $10^9\times$. Machines of such power and capability will see computing and communications infrastructures accessible by entire populations. IT will no longer be the preserve of an elite who have the opportunity, access and skill sets that are necessary to drive today's user-unfriendly devices. Talking to the machine, having hands in the screen and being able to see people and information in electronically generated environments will become the norm.

2.4   Cost reduction – capability growth

In 1956 the cost of a transatlantic telephone call was £2.80/minute, today (1995) it is £0.4/minute (see Figure 2.4). Computers in the home were unthinkable and the storage and transport of information was almost wholly conducted by paper. Today, we have a rapidly expanding global network of optical fibre already transporting 65% of all the telephone calls world-wide (Cochrane, Heatley, Smyth & Pearson, 1993; Cochrane & Heatley, 1994). The first pocket calculator on the market in the early 1970s cost over £80 for just four functions. Today superior technology is given away with petrol! A low-cost electronic wristwatch now has more processing power than a mid-range computer of the 1960s, whilst the personal computer is realising a processing, storage and display ability for the office and home that completely surpasses the mainframe computers of only ten years ago. This is all characterised by an exponential growth in ability, and a correspondent fall in cost – exponentially more for exponentially less.

The scale of change is perhaps best exemplified by the reduction in raw material usage. In the UK there is now an installed base of over 3 million km of optical fibre supporting the communication needs of a 57 million population.   The entire fibre infrastructure was manufactured with just 90 tonnes of sand (silica) compared to the thousands of tonnes of copper cable it replaced!   Similarly, the latest desk top computers are being designed to use materials that are over 95% recycled.   In both cases the performance and capability are vastly superior, power consumption increasingly minuscule, and production cost far less than previous technologies.   Instead of using watts of power for a telephone call we now use mW.

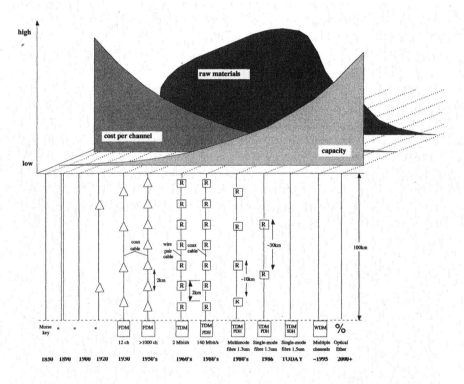

Figure 2.3. History and principal trends in cable telecommunications.

2.5   No frontiers – no barriers

The digital revolution in computing and communication has,
so far, mainly impacted the office and place of work. Before the year 2000 it will have entered the home.   Information will become a commodity item, accessible across the planet at insignificant cost.   This will be made possible by continued advances in chip, satellite, radio and optical fibre technology that will also reach out to the home, car, and/or computer you wear.   This information world will see the barriers between work, play, home and office breached (Negroponte, 1991). The nature of commerce and society will change

(Negroponte, 1991). The nature of commerce and society will change radically with no effective national and international boundaries. This could pose significant political problems with governments and regulators seeing control slip through their fingers. A bit, is a bit, is a bit – there is no difference between a telephone call, CATV, broadcast or data. Regulating the flow, distribution and access to information could be like trying to regulate the rain (Branscomb, 1991).

Organisations themselves will become increasingly – and in some cases totally – dispersed. They will be virtual and organic with people contributing in an electronic rather than physical space. People will work when and with whom they choose, as appropriate, having access to machine intelligence and information. This will revolutionise the way business is conducted and economies are driven. Already we see those at the forefront establishing group environments where work packages are passed around the globe, like a baton, from one daylight zone to another. Programmes, projects, developments, creativity and collaboration can then be non-stop, non-national, but virtual, fast and far more productive and effective than today.

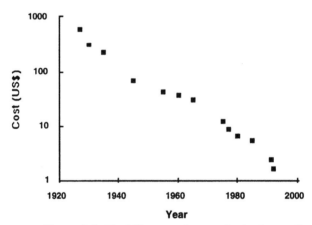

Figure 2.4. The falling cost of a transatlantic phone-call.

2.6   Interfaces for people

The realisation of a global information network presents a major challenge. Its impact will span education, medical applications, leisure, entertainment, business and commerce. The move to the information society presents substantial technological and human interface problems for all IT-related industries as the ideal is to deliver information on demand, in the right form, at the right time, at the right price to a fixed or mobile terminal anywhere.

However, today's IT industry has a multiplicity of hardware, software and interfaces, mainly designed to promote customer lock-in, and it is clear that this presents an immediate challenge. In addition, a combination of technophobia, natural or economic inability, and bad interface design has frozen out over 80% of the human race from using the technology. The move away from MS DOS towards the GUI (graphical user interface) and mouse-based systems has seen the latent ability and demand beginning to be realised. Perhaps the most important next step will be the advent of the really friendly and effective Personal Digital Assistant (PDA), shortly to be followed by computers you wear, with voice I/O systems allowing an even greater number of people access to the technology (Crane & Ritschev, 1993).

Interestingly, the miniaturisation of technology will ultimately preclude the use of a standard QWERTY keyboard and predicate a move to verbal interaction. However, the real breakthrough will be technology that realises the human ability for a co-ordinated combination of sight, sound and touch – 'multimedia'. When augmented by artificial intelligence that is anticipatory, and able to fine tune responses in sympathy with the characteristics of the individual user, then we will have a really powerful and user-orientated interface.

2.7   Physical travel

Why do we travel vast distances just to cluster together to work in offices? The answer to this question is complex, but reasonably obvious: we come together to communicate, interact and organise ourselves in a rather tribal and ritualistic way. With IT this is no longer necessary nor relevant in the strict sense. Many already go home to do real work. The office has become an information exchange, an area of interaction, meetings and high chemistry. Solitude, isolation and concentration have to be sought in new places. Moreover, the chemistry of interaction can be achieved using an electronic medium and we face the prospect of increasing numbers of home, or dispersed, workers away from any centralised office (Lyons, Cochrane & Fisher, 1993). This is not in the far future; it is happening now, and is evidenced by the number of empty office blocks and buildings throughout the western world. It has been estimated that the empty office space across North America is equivalent to that occupied (or not) in San Francisco. In London it appears that a similar availability is being generated. Numerous UK companies are already moving to 'hot desking', with the provision of fewer desks than people, as changing habits release people from being in the office every day. This is a trend that can be expected to increase, and accelerate in concert with IT.

2.8   New capabilities

It is evident that developments in artificial intelligence, visualisation, virtual reality and telepresence will realise new capabilities. Humankind was never designed to cope with spread sheets, the written word, keyboards and small screens that only present a partial picture of a wider activity. Imagine a virtual reality interface with your visual cortex flooded by information from spectacle-mounted or active contact lenses augmented by directional audio input, tactile gloves and prosthetic arms and fingers that give you the sensation of touch, resistance and weight. Imagine also the prospect of a surrogate head that is either machine or human that can allow you to be teleported into environments anywhere on the planet with great accuracy and reality (Cameron, 1992). This might lead to the euphemism: 'what you see I see, what you hear I hear, what you feel I feel'! Alternatively contemplate the convenience of large visual displays with high definition in two or three dimensions. People could appear in full proportion, with the right colour, a voice that emanates from the lips and not from a box at the side in a distortion-free and convincing manner. All of these technologies lead to a feeling of being there. What is more, they are already available today, at various stages of research and development.

Virtual office experiment with the user immersed in the information world – able to interact with the information and objects.

Perhaps the greatest challenge is the creation of a machine that can understand and augment the human mind. It has taken us some 50 million years to evolve, whilst electronic computers have emerged in less than 100 years. If we could converse with machines in the way we interact with each other, then we would have a true interface. However, this dream may be some way off, as generalised machine cognition is not easy to realise. In the short term we can expect to see voice I/O with a 'constrained cognition' for specific fields of application. Today it is command and control, within a decade it might be communication, law, cookery and architecture, etc.

Hands in the screen environment allowing the manipulation of a two-dimensional – electronic – space.

2.9   Past industry

Quite understandably there is great concern over the decline of manufacturing industry and the changing work patterns already evident. In the short term the drive for greater efficiency, improved output and migration from a manufacturing to an information society will involve some hardship and trauma for society. In the long term, however, it has to be seen as part of a general migration that started a thousand years ago.

Ever since we diversified from hunting to farming we have been on a path that has seen 80% of the UK population involved in farming only 700 years ago reduced to less then 1% today (CSO, 1993b). The same is true for clothing production, the industrial revolution with its smokestack industries, and more recently the electronic revolution followed by the present dominance of software. As each new wave of technology has peaked and been made increasingly efficient it has been replaced by new and more beneficial alternatives. Today we are poised to see the emergence of information itself becoming a raw material – something we manufacture, prize, sell and perhaps most importantly of all, network. The number of people involved in this industry can be expected to rise rapidly, and hopefully it will utilise much of the wasted human talent overlooked in previous revolutions.

All of this does not deny the continued existence of farming, the manufacture of clothing, or hard and soft technologies. Quite the reverse. All of these activities are required, but our expectation is to make them far more efficient and less intensive in human terms. A net result will be an increased percentage of the population working in an information space that need not be location-specific (Lyons, Gell & Cochrane, 1993).

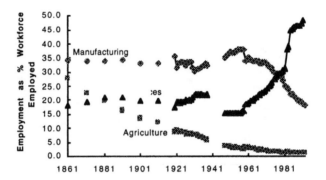

Figure 2.5. Percentage of UK workforce employed by agricultural, manufacturing and service sectors.

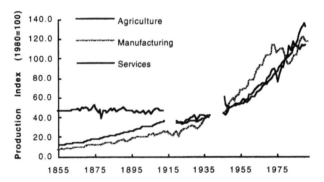

Figure 2.6. UK productivity indices for agricultural, manufacturing and service sectors.

2.10 Information

In Europe there are over 6 million photographs of church windows on record, and within five years we may have video-on-demand (VoD) systems offering a choice from 10,000 videos. The Library of Congress requires 3.5 km of new book shelving every year to accommodate all the new publications. It has also been estimated that the total of mankind's published material – and this is sometimes equated to knowledge itself – doubles every three years. It is also clear that a huge amount of information becomes irrelevant and out of date and represents a largely meaningless clutter.

It is interesting that when addressing a problem, the finding and assembly of all the related information represents the major task and the least interesting one. It is the manipulation of the information, its preparation and presentation that require a great deal of human input, and perhaps the former can be overcome by artificial intelligence realised as autonomous software agents. It has been estimated that professionals can spend up to 80% of their active time trying to find information, and as little as 5% formatting it and making decisions. These proportions are probably true of students, researchers, and much of the creative population. Apart from serendipity, the chancing upon items that are not of immediate interest, or items filed under an obscure but indirectly related category, the looking for and finding of information is no fun. It is generally frustrating and a waste of time and energy.

What we need are technologies to help us navigate through the growing field of information, find what we want, and access and manipulate data so we can get down to the kernel – decision and action! The necessary technologies are all under development with artificial intelligence (AI) for navigation and location, plus Hebbian decay mechanisms (Russell, 1980) for filing, and automatic text summarisation (Preston & Williams, 1994). However, there are still significant problems associated with the complexity and size of systems, data bases and connectivity expected by the year 2000. At this juncture much of the display, software, hardware platforms and interfaces will be available to a wide proportion of the population (Cochrane, Fisher & Taylor-Hendry, 1993).

2.11   Publishing – more for less

In the 15th century the Vatican library had fewer than 400 books and it was one of the biggest libraries on the planet. Today most of us own more books as individuals and the Library of Congress has an estimated 22 to 24 million volumes on 500 km of shelves. To access and keep up to date in an information space so vast is clearly impossible. We cannot afford the trees, the paper, the energy and, most of all, the sheer inaccessibility. Already we see CD-ROM technology delivering 650 Mbytes of information. Such a medium is capable of holding all the classics and most of the specialist books we could desire in a few tens of discs. Indeed a staggering 2,000 classics have recently been published on one CD-ROM. At the present rate of progress we should each have enough storage capacity at work and home to hold the contents of the Library of Congress within 15 years. But this is not the whole story: we only need access, we do not need copies of everything. The first book store on Internet has opened with 50 volumes selling at US$5 each. At this price our purchasing algorithm changes. Buy it and try it. Who cares? It is so cheap I can afford to throw it away if I don't like it!

The publishing industry is thus about to undergo a revolution far greater than the move from the scribe to the printing press. We might recall an old Chinese proverb:

I hear and I forget

I see and I remember

I do and I understand.

To date well over 20,000 volumes are already in digital form and will sell at a fraction of their paper predecessors. Some publishing houses are already predicting that they see the end of paper publishing in sight. For technical and reference volumes this is credible. For the rest it might not be – paper is very user-friendly. The extent of this difference is embodied in the riddle: what is the difference between a laptop and a newspaper? The answer is: no one takes a lap top into the toilet! For general reading we need liquid crystal paper: high resolution, definition, contrast, and flexibility. And compact. Then we might see novels and light reading transformed also, but then again there are alternatives such as talking books.

A further small advance could see custom information on line. Instead of buying a complete newspaper, magazines, books and databases, to discard large sections that are of no interest to us, we may have the option to pay more for less. The focused news, articles, detail, data and information would be far more beneficial. Barring serendipity that is. The future retailing, supply, updating, validation, security, charging, copyright, and format of publications thus pose some major challenges.

2.12   Technology – positive feedback

Why is all of this so exciting and why does it offer such tremendous potential? Twenty years ago the measurement of the amplitude and phase characteristics of an electronic amplifier took a whole morning. Today the same measurements take less then 15 seconds with an automated network analyser. Similarly, the original lathe was made from wood and was extremely crude, being powered by a man or a boy. Soon it was possible to make an even better lathe using the original to produce components to a better accuracy. At some point the wooden lathe reached its height of perfection and it was necessary to use metal to realise further improvement. To this day the lathe story continues. Granted the improvements are now incrementally smaller, but it is now possible to manufacture new forms of machines. The same is true across the broad front of technology, and positive feedback continues to power the IT industry.

From a work perspective it means that research that took over three years to complete just ten years ago, might now be completed in less than three months. In short, far more work can now be completed by far fewer people. Or more positively, the human race can achieve far more in a shorter time. The standard working lifetime of the previous generation was about 100,000 hours. We can now achieve their output in less than 10,000 hours or more impressively do ten times the work and get ten times the results! The next generation looks set to overtake us in a similar manner, provided it can keep pace with the technology.

2.13   Telepresence – infomatics

The developed world's population is getting older and it is highly unlikely that there will be the resources to provide the care that is necessary. In Japan programmes are underway to manufacture robots to take on the task. Other alternatives involve the teleportation of expertise, experience and presence itself. The technologies that allow surgeons to be positioned inside the human body through an endoscope or through the use of a surrogate head peering into an incision are already with us. The prospect of remote diagnosis, inspection and surgery is real and initial experiments are underway. Before long we may see surgeons in California performing operations in London (McCrone, 1993).

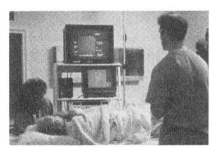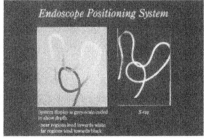

Endoscopy translated into a three-dimensional world for remote operations.

Robots are already being used in hip replacement, brain and eye surgery. The trip to a doctor's surgery or the hospital outpatients' department could soon become an automated and remote activity. Further developments include the remote monitoring of patients through electronic interfaces mounted on the body. For the diabetic, drug and medicine dependent people it is already possible for them to be monitored at a distance by remote computers that can administer and optimise dosage. So far experiments have been confined to hospital wards, but there is no reason why this use of video-as-data cannot be realised globally (Cochrane & Hobsley, 1993).

All of these concepts can be extended to other disciplines including the repair and maintenance of oil rigs, electronic and power installations and even activities in the home. Being able to call experts, teleport them to your location, and then have them guide you through the necessary steps to affect a solution is only a short step away, and is already being tested.

2.14   Remote education

We might also anticipate that the very process of education will have to change. The vast majority of universities are small, with small departments increasingly stretched by a widening curriculum. Staff have to cope with larger numbers of students and teach a wider range of courses in a shorter time. Why then do we have fifteen lecturers giving the same lecture on different days to different groups of students? It is possible for all the students to attend any one of the lectures, or indeed, for the one lecture course to be prepared and delivered by a small team at one university. This would allow specialism by the departments, an increased efficiency and depth of understanding, a real opportunity to conduct meaningful research and perhaps most valuable of all, an ability to allow students to mix and match modules and create their own degrees at a distance (Cochrane, 1994). The distributed degree among five or six key universities would then be a real possibility.

The nature of teaching and education can also be expected to see radical change. Since the ancient Greeks we have hardly strayed from scratching in the sand. Moving to the blackboard, to the white board and overhead projector is hardly revolutionary given the technology at our disposal. Might we expect experiments on the screen to become as respectable as experiments in the laboratory? On-line tutorials, lectures and interactive teaching packages for the rapidly expanding science and technology based curriculum would seem a necessity. Packages are already being introduced in medicine and other professions. The dismantling of high tech structures; simulation of air flow across an aircraft wing; current flow in an electronic circuit; or the dissection of a frog or human organ are already available on trial systems. In many European universities it is becoming impossible to get a degree qualification without your own personal computer.

Perhaps in the not too distant future we will be able to cruise the world's institutions, virtual or real, and drop in for a refresher course presented by an internationally recognised expert – anywhere, anytime!   Perhaps project reports and theses will become active, and interactive documents and high quality visualisation will offer immediately informative representations of physical or other situations, rather than the traditional erudite and oft confusing prose.   Most radical of all, mathematics and the physical sciences may be opened up to all.   Those who have found the traditional long haul of 15 educational years of the tough, difficult, or plain indigestible might find that visualisation or virtual reality puts them in the picture.

2.15   Our children

Already we see our children exhibiting tremendous willingness and ability to move into this new world of information.   The challenge has to be the rigid mind sets of the over 30s who will have to be weaned off the motor car, physical travel, the mass use of paper and dependence on ancient modes of working.   In the remaining years of their life these people are likely to see more change for mankind than has been experienced in the previous 100 years. A major challenge therefore will be the finessing of the technology to make it wholly acceptable to the greater part of the population.   This will require some adept engineering to create new interfaces that are humanised and present a natural mode of immersion for the vast majority of the human population.   If it is to work, the technology has to be available and accessible to all people of all ages.   This probably represents the major challenge and is a vital one if we are to succeed.

A three year old child interfaces and operates a computer as if it were a friend, a tool to be used and experimented with (left).   Being introduced to a computer for the first time at the age of sixteen produces a certain apprehension and a "what's in the box" mentality (right).

2.16   Limits to change

All the technology we have briefly considered results in a reduced need to travel, a positive contribution to preserving the resources of, and reducing the alarming current deleterious environmental effects on this planet, and offers a wider choice of experience for all concerned.

In the information society the need to travel vast distances from home will be drastically reduced. New forms of short distance transport need to develop, and perhaps we might even see the demise of the internal combustion engine and its deleterious effects on humanity and the environment. A further outcome is likely to be the restructuring of conurbations. As fewer people need to travel into cities and increasing numbers of office blocks become vacant there may even be a move to ruralise the environment, remove many of the buildings and return them to their former state. The distributed society working in an information world will create new environments, new cities of the mind, new places to meet and work. Again prototypes are already in the research laboratories and every day new ideas and formats emerge. The rate of change is unlikely to be limited by the evolution rate of the technology, more the inability of mankind and society to subsume these advances and make use of them in a positive and economic way.

The information wave might just be the ultimate challenge, and opportunity, for humanity. We can opt out, but we cannot escape. We have to rise to the challenge, solve the problems, and access the power of information.

References

Anderson, B. (1977). *Solar Energy: Fundamentals in Building Design*. McGraw-Hill: New York.

Branscomb, A. W. (1991). Common law for the electronic frontier. *Scientific American,* **265** (3) pp. 112–115.

Cameron, K. (1992). CamNet: the first telepresence system. *Interlink 2000*, (Aug), pp. 38–41.

Cartledge, B. (1993). *Energy and Environment*. Oxford University Press.

Central Statistical Office [CSA] (1993a). *Social Trends 23*, HMSO, London.

Central Statistical Office [CSA] (1993b). *Annual Abstract of Statistics 1993*, HMSO, London.

Cochrane, P. (1994). Education, technology and change: a personal view. *IEE Computing & Control Engineering*, **5** (2), pp. 52–54.

Cochrane, P. & Heatley, D.J.T. (1994). Modelling change in telecommunications. *British Telecom Technology Journal*, **12** (2).

Cochrane, P. & Hobsley, M. (1993). Visions of a perfect diagnosis. *The Times Higher Education Supplement*, 19 Nov 93, p. 8.

Cochrane, P., Fisher, K., & Taylor-Hendry, R. (1993). The office you wish you had. *British Telecommunications Engineering*, **12** (2), pp. 91–96.

Cochrane, P., Heatley, D.J.T., Smyth, P. J., & Pearson, I. D. (1993). Optical telecommunications: future prospects. *IEE Electronics & Communication Engineering*, **5** (4), pp. 221–232.

Crane, H. D. & Ritschev, D. (1993). Pen and voice unite. *Byte*, Oct. 93.

Drexler, E. K. (1992). *Engines of Creation*. Oxford University Press.

Gregory, R. L. (Ed.) (1992). *The Oxford Companion To The Mind*. Oxford University Press.

Hadenburgh, H. W. (1994). CPU performances: where are we headed? *Dr. Dobbs Journal*, **19**.

Kennedy, P. (1993). *Preparing for the Twenty First Century*. HarperCollins, London.

Lyons, M. H., Cochrane, P., & Fisher, K. (1993). Teleworking in the 21st century. *Computing & Control Engineering Journal*, p. 170.

Lyons, M. H., Gell, M., & Cochrane, P. (1993). Companies and communications in the next century. *Proceedings. of Telecom '93*. Canadian Business Telecoms Alliance (CBTA), Toronto.

McCrone, J. (1993). Computer chaos at medicine's cutting edge. *New Scientist*, 25th Sept, 93.

Meadows, D. H. et al. (1972). *The Limits to Growth: a report for the Club of Rome's project on the predicament of mankind*. New York.

Negroponte, N. P. (1991). Products and services for computer networks. *Scientific American*, **265** (3), pp. 76–83.

Pearson, I. (1995). When I'm 64. *British Telecommunications Engineering Journal*, **14**, (1), (In Press)

Preston, K. R. & Williams, S. H. (1994). Managing the information overload: physics in business. *Newsletter of the Institute of Physics*. July 94.

Russell, P. (1980). *The Brain Book*. Routledge: London.

3

From telephony to telematics: equity, efficiency and regulatory innovation

Robin Mansell

3.1 Introduction

Innovations in telecommunication and computing technologies have reverberated upon the structure and organisation of the telecommunication service industry in recent years. The move from an era of public telephony to one of diverse telematics services has challenged institutions of governance to create innovative regulatory environments. The goals are generally two-fold. One is to ensure equity in the evolution of the public network infrastructure and services for both suppliers and customers. The other is to stimulate efficiency in the supply and use of existing and new infrastructure and services.

This chapter examines innovations in telematics service markets and in regulatory institutions in terms of their implications for equity and efficiency in the marketplace. It raises the question as to whether regulatory institutions are coping with the challenges presented by technical innovations in the telematics field. Questions as to who has the power to take decisions with regard to the new electronic communication environment are fundamental to the changing balance between co-operation and competition in the telecommunication industry, to the economic prospects of the major and smaller suppliers, and to the ways in which new telematics services will alter the ways people can use and control information in their business and everyday lives

The determinants of the transformation of the electronic communication environment on both the supply and demand side of the industry have been marked by a general mystification of the forces contributing to change. For example, market restructuring is often attributed to the 'impact' of technical innovation and the associated 'globalisation' of the industry.[1] This argument camouflages the conflicts and contradictions inherent in the 'globalisation' thesis. The predominant assumption is that the transformations in public and private institutions which are interwoven with technical change are beneficent. Many proponents of the 'globalisation' thesis argue that this process will produce a gradual balancing and redistribution of wealth generating enterprises. These benefits may be accompanied by temporary distortions in the structure of economies and a need for structural adjustment, but the end result will be a 'galaxy' of services and products available to all those who choose to participate in the networked economy.

This chapter suggests that it is not sufficient simply to recognise that the components of the telematics network system, like other technological systems, are 'both socially constructed and society shaping' Hughes (1987). There is a need to link institutional perspectives on the determinants of innovation in technical systems with those focusing upon the capacity for change in governance institutions. This chapter represents one step in that direction.

3.2   Equity, efficiency, technical and institutional change

In so far as equity and efficiency considerations are central to the evolution of the telematics infrastructure, there is a need to consider the ways in which the interpenetration of markets and regulatory institutions carries implications for the evolution of the technical infrastructure and the services that are available. As Freeman has argued:

> The socio-institutional framework always influences and may sometimes facilitate and sometimes retard processes of technical and structural change, coordination and dynamic adjustment. Such acceleration and retardation effects relate not simply to market 'imperfections', but to the nature of markets themselves, and to the behaviour of agents (that is, institutions are an inseparable part of the way markets work).
>
> Freeman (1988)

In the 1990s, a new era of telematics services has been widely acclaimed in the technical and marketing literature. These services integrate telecommunication and computing technologies and their increasingly widespread application is expected to transform the ways individuals, firms and the public sector engage in the production, communication and use of electronic information. Telematics services, such as electronic data interchange and electronic funds transfer, are affecting the speed, control and geographical distribution of productive activities in the late 20th century, but there has been little research which is framed in such a way as to link the determinants of innovation in public and corporate governance structures and processes with the determinants of technical change.

How, to what end, and for whom, do we develop and use the potential of electronic communication? This question is centrally concerned with equity and efficiency considerations. The underlying issue is whether decisions taken by public and private sector actors can ensure a reasonable balancing of equity and efficiency as the electronic communication environment unfolds. For example, will access to telematics services approach the 'universality' of conventional public telephony?

The transformation of telecommunication markets has been marked by growing investment in digital transmission and switching equipment. From the early 1980s to 1990, capital investment in public telecommunication networks in the OECD area increased from some US$68 billion to $90 billion in constant prices.[2] Network modernisation accounted for an average of 80 per cent of total capital investment. There were clear variations among countries such as in Greece and Portugal where investment for network modernisation accounted for only 35 and 52 per cent, respectively, of total investment over the period.[3] Improvements in the information processing capacity of the telecommunication infrastructure have come to be perceived as essential if the challenge to achieve regional coherence and, in many cases, regional dominance of international trade is to be met.

The goal of forging integrated regional markets, e.g. the Single European Market, has been coupled with the opening of national markets to competitive entry. The internationalisation of markets and experimentation with advanced telematics services have created a strong stimulus for reform in the sector and this is reverberating throughout most industrialised and developing economies. The belief that trade reciprocity will eventually create open market conditions has stimulated a drive to develop a more efficient telecommunication supply environment on a world scale. The trend is towards the opening of equipment procurement to a greater number of manufacturers to stimulate the competitiveness of suppliers such as Siemens, Alcatel or Ericsson in Europe.[4] In the services market, new rivals have targeted the periphery of the Public Telecommunication Operators' (PTO) markets, e.g. value added services, and they have begun to challenge the core of their markets, i.e. the voice telephony market which still generates some ninety per cent of the PTOs' revenues. Competition in the international market, as well as in domestic markets, is regarded as the harbinger of greater flexibility and efficiency in the design and implementation of advanced telematics services.

These trends on the supply side of the market have been complemented by increasing heterogeneity on the demand side. The strategic goals of globally operating firms have become tightly meshed with the suppliers' interpretation of requirements for applications of voice, data, text and imaging services. Multinational business customers have become much more sophisticated in their knowledge of, and requirements for, all forms of communication services. Telematics services are also being developed for smaller firms and individual consumers. Together, they represent the market for all that is *potentially* available as a result of technical innovation.

3.3   The globalisation thesis: a new paradigm?

Insofar as the telematics industry is implicated in the logic of the 'globalisation' thesis, the antecedents can be located within the rise to prominence of the 'information society' and 'information economy' constructs. These have played an important role in the post-war years in encouraging a fascination with the information technology 'revolution'. For example, when Bell forecast the coming of the post-industrial society in 1959, he looked to information or knowledge as the organising framework around which other institutions would coalesce as well as to information technologies (Bell, 1973). The burgeoning of information services created a furore over the benefits of the information economy (de Sola Pool, 1990). The public switched telecommunication network (PSTN) provided one vehicle for the delivery of information and communication services, but by 1990 in the OECD countries, this component of the telematics network system was contributing an average of only 72 per cent of the total revenues of the PTOs. Their other business activities based upon leased circuits, data communication networks, text services such as electronic mail, image-based services, and mobile services accounted for the remaining revenues. By 1990 these 'new' services were growing at an annual rate of about 25 per cent.

In addition, the penetration of alternative modes of delivery for information and communication services was beginning to increase. In 1990 the number of television sets per 100 inhabitants in the OECD area stood at 55 as compared to the number of telephone main sets which had reached an average penetration of only 43 per 100 inhabitants. There were 19 video cassette recorders and 32 cable television subscribers per 100 inhabitants in the same year. The preoccupation with average penetration rates for telematics equipment and services within the OECD area has camouflaged the disparities within these countries and completely overlooked those between the wealthier countries of the Triad and the rest of the world (McKinsey & Company, 1993). For example, Figure 3.1 shows penetration rates for main telephone lines within several European countries and for selected developing countries.

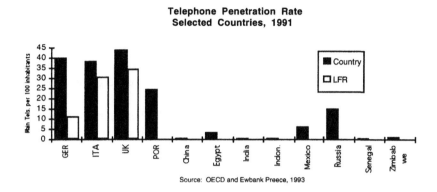

Source: OECD and Ewbank Preece, 1993

Figure 3.1. Telephone penetration rates, selected countries, 1991.

Much attention was focused in the 1970s and 1980s on the introduction of information technology policies, frequently with little regard to the factors that would mitigate against the fulfilment of many policy objectives. Furthermore, the public and private uses of information, and divergent interests in its production, were hardly considered. The priority was simply to stimulate the production and diffusion of hardware and software.

In the late 1980s, it was becoming clear, even to the most ardent advocates of the 'information economy' thesis, that neither information technologies themselves, nor the information and communication services they support, could be expected automatically to eliminate disparities in market power on the supply side of the industry. Nor could they be expected to resolve organisational problems. Disparities in the availability of advanced telematics network systems would also continue to be intractable and of concern as the expansion and deepening of world-wide markets for goods and services gathered a renewed impetus in the 1980s.

Another vision of development based upon the *globalisation* thesis has become prevalent in the 1990s. 'Globalisation' scenarios link the fortunes of globally operating firms to the availability and use of flexible telematics systems that connect suppliers and customers in local and distant markets (Ohmae, 1990). Theoretically, no corner of the world will be without access via pervasive telematics networks to the products of an interdependent social, cultural, economic and political order. The 'globalisation' of markets is also said to involve footloose corporations in a myriad of international strategies ranging from direct foreign investment to formal and informal strategic alliances. Ohmae argues, for example, that 'it does not matter who builds the factory or who owns the office building...what matters is that the global corporations...act as responsible citizens' (Ohmae, 1990). Hu, in contrast, suggests that the so-called global company is really a national company with some international operations and that such companies do not lose their international identity or differentiating characteristics (Hu, 1992). Regardless of the characteristics ascribed to 'globalising' companies, it is recognised that the role and grip of national (or regional) governance structures and their relationship to the strategies of such companies are undergoing substantial change.[5]

Closely associated with the 'globalisation' phenomenon is a 'new' conception of the firm as a *network corporation*.[6] This type of corporation is based upon 'inter-company alliances of technical, production, financial and marketing competencies across national boundaries' (Soete, 1991). The network corporation depends upon the public and private telematics infrastructure to achieve its goals. As these corporations undergo restructuring it has become increasingly evident that the trading advantages of firms and countries are shifting from the possession of 'natural' assets to the possession of 'created' assets.[7] These include intangible assets such as business culture, attitudes to wealth creation, education styles, etc., but they also include the strengths, weaknesses and 'interconnectedness' of the telematics network system.

Thus, as Dunning has argued:

> because the economic welfare of countries is ultimately the responsibility of the Governments of those countries, it may be argued that, in a very real sense, national administrations compete with each other to ensure that their macroeconomic and organisational strategies and policies are such as to provide their wealth creators with the maximum possible incentives to sustain and advance their competitiveness vis-à-vis their foreign rivals.
>
> (Dunning, 1992)

'Globalisation' requires the use of the telematics network system within countries to support the management and control of complex internal and external information flows within and between public governance structures and private corporations.

The capacity of the 'globalisation' scenario to give rise to the expected benefits in terms of wealth creation and distribution is based upon the rapid diffusion of a global telematics network system which supports all facets of the network corporation's information-related activities. It is assumed that the benefits of developments in the telematics network will become available, not only to the network corporations, but also to all their suppliers and customers as well as individual consumers, thus completing the cycle of production and consumption. The goals of the public and private sectors are interpreted mainly in terms of competitiveness strategies, efficiency gains, and the degree of closure or openness of markets.

In the strategic management literature, the social, cultural, political and economic implications of configuration of inter and intra-firm networks and their linkages with consumers are often homogenised into an unspecified process of institutional and technical change.[8] Outcomes are treated as the result of interacting, interdependent and balanced pressures among the strategies of network corporations, the trajectory of technical innovation, and the competitive advantages accruing from the use of electronic information networks. The requirements of the network corporation and the exigencies of 'globalisation' require that the design, structure and organisation of the telematics network system be revamped to reduce telecommunication costs for globally competing firms, increase flexibility in the management of information, and hasten the introduction of advanced services. Few writers consider the implications of 'oligopolisation' – the uneven distribution of market power on the supply side, or the potential for customer lock-in or lock-out which coincides with the restructuring of production and consumption. Nevertheless, it is here that equity considerations generally come to the fore.

In the European Community, the United States and Japan the social and economic implications of *disparities in access* to advanced electronic communication systems are gaining increasing visibility within the telematics policy and regulatory agenda. The evolution of telematics networks that can support advanced service applications requires technical performance characteristics far exceeding the capabilities of the public and private networks which are in place today. For example, stand-alone high performance test beds operate at gigabits per second. Today's telecommunication networks are only beginning to approach speeds in excess of 100 Mbit/s.

The development and implementation of advanced services could evolve slowly and incrementally through the gradual interlinking of isolated islands of test bed activity such that network access becomes available to the elite of the scientific and research communities.[9] Alternatively, advanced applications could provide a stimulus for a radical upgrading of the public telecommunication infrastructure. Switched broadband networks supporting powerful multimedia applications running at gigabit speeds could become accessible to businesses and consumers early in the next century.

The rate and timing of investment, and the diffusion and ubiquity of advanced high capacity telecommunication networks in Europe, the United States and Japan, will lie along a continuum between incremental and radical change. There are those who favour a predominately market-led process of change. In this case, demand for advanced applications must be clearly demonstrated before steps are taken to create the necessary infrastructure. There are also those who argue for the early introduction of high capacity, fibre-based, ubiquitous networks. Here, the assumption is that technology push will create opportunities for innovation and the growth of advanced telematics service markets.

The outcomes will reflect the ways in which corporate strategies and regulation are linked to public policy objectives. The accessibility of the 'information superhighways' of the future will reflect decisions with regard to efficiency and equity that are taken over the next decade or more. These decisions, in turn, will shape investment in the advanced telematics services infrastructure and determine its accessibility. Investment trajectories reflect public and private sector decisions which are deeply informed by judgements regarding efficiency and equity.

3.4   Telematics networks and institutional innovation

In the 1980s, policy innovations resulted in a major technical shift in telecommunication from analogue to digital switching and transmission. There was a quantum leap from limited computerised control of electronic switching to reliance upon intelligent software-based functions within, and peripheral to, the public telecommunication network. Alongside this technical shift, there was a policy shift which is increasingly being reflected in the marketplace. Competition was embraced as a superior means of organising the telecommunication market and it began to take precedence over the monopoly forms of organisation of the past.

The policy and regulatory role shifted from direct state responsibility for telecommunications and/or regulatory oversight of private monopolies, towards the goal of creating a liberalised and competitive market environment in which switched and dedicated telematics systems are mixed and matched, and distinctions between public and corporate networks are blurred. There have been some limited innovations in regulation and in the structure and organisation of governance institutions. In Europe, for example, new regulatory institutions such as the Office of Telecommunications in the United Kingdom and an increasing number of European policy groups are being created with the aim of ensuring that public policy goals are achieved as a plurality of networks and services, suppliers and customers, emerges.[10] However, the competitive era has made it far more difficult to reach consensus among all parties with an interest in the electronic communication environment on what the goals of policy should be, on the powers and modalities of decision making, and on the consequences of alternative policy prescriptions, regulations and enforcement mechanisms. It is no longer possible or sufficient simply to advocate that traditional public or universal service goals should be met. Inevitably questions arise as to what these terms mean, whether they should be abandoned or redefined, and if so by whom and with what consequences for competitiveness or consumer lifestyles.

In the private sector, companies are moving towards fully integrated regional structures and redesigning their core business practices.[11] As they integrate their information systems across national borders, they are relying upon intelligent telematics infrastructures. Companies like DuPont, Shell and Reuters are creating 'logical computing utilities' and building network environments with standardised user interfaces. They have argued that the public telecommunication network is not sufficiently standardised to support international services. Proprietary signalling systems are in use and many service applications are not portable across systems marketed by increasingly large numbers of vendors from both the computing and telecommunication industries. In Europe, for example, larger customers complain that it is not possible to make an Integrated Services Digital Network (ISDN) video call from Germany to the United Kingdom, that reliable leased circuits are often difficult to come by, and that coherent, transparent billing and secure network administration and management are difficult to achieve (Langhammer, 1993).

Research has also shown that macro-economic benefits are closely associated with the capacity to apply and integrate advanced telematics services within and between business organisations. For instance, one study on the potential economic impact of investment in advanced communication systems has estimated an improvement in the Italian gross national product of between 2.8 and 4.0 per cent by the year 2008. This result assumes that investment and the use of advanced communication networks are stimulated by greater competition within the Single European Market. Similar studies in the United States have shown even greater macro-economic gains.[12] Case studies in the automobile, electronics, financial services, aerospace and petro-chemical sectors have pointed to similar benefits for the corporate community (Mansell & Morgan, 1990). Nevertheless, telematics services will bring gains to the competitiveness of industry, *if and only if* the introduction of these services is combined with a wide range of organisational changes at the firm, sector and policy level.

The global telematics environment

The domestic telecommunication market and its national governance structures can no longer be the main focus of nationally or regionally based policy makers in the telecommunication field. The technical and policy shifts which have been described above have been influenced by, and have contributed to, major changes in the global telematics environment. Michael Porter has claimed that the telematics services *buyers*, rather than the *suppliers*, have all become enormously powerful. He has argued that the main barrier slowing the arrival of pervasive competition is the time needed for the monopolistic PTOs of old to learn how to compete. He has suggested that the removal of regulation would bring a competitive market to life much more quickly than the continuation of the vestiges of regulation from a bygone era (Porter, 1992). Thus, 'de-regulation' is advocated in order to achieve efficient supply and equity in the marketplace.

This outcome, however, is unlikely when the magnitude of *supplier* power in the market is considered. Global oligopolistic rivalry among 'supercarriers' characterises the new liberalised marketplace. This is far from a competitive marketplace in which no individual supplier or buyer can bias outcomes in the market. In the world market in the early 1990s, the traditional bilateral agreements between PTOs are still in place as shown in Figure 3.2. For example, BT can maintain its agreement to supply public telecommunication services with another operator such as AT&T.

Figure 3.2. The traditional bilateral agreements between PTOs in the world market in the early 1990s.

However, Figure 3.3 shows that these bilateral agreements are being challenged by ventures which bring the largest operators into each others' markets. The supercarriers are opening sales outlets in foreign markets and, where they are permitted in liberalised markets, they are investing in network facilities as well.

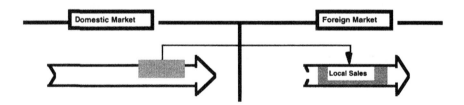

Figure 3.3. How bilateral agreements are being challenged by ventures which bring the largest operators into each others' markets.

BT can open sales offices, like Syncordia in Atlanta, to provide end-to-end global corporate telematics services, take a 20 per cent share in MCI – the second largest US long distance telecommunication carrier – and construct advanced facilities such as Project Cyclone in the United States. AT&T can maintain its historical bilateral relations with BT, and seek opportunities to open sales outlets and establish facilities in the UK.

The world market is beginning to look as complex as the diagram shown in Figure 3.4.

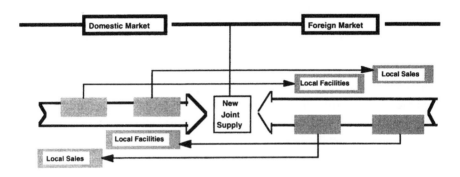

Figure 3.4. World market begins to become more complex. Note that the figure illustrates the fact that there is both competition and co-operation in the telematics marketplace.

These figures illustrate the fact that there is both competition and co-operation in the telematics marketplace. In international markets, reciprocity has not been worked out, but the 'globalisation' of markets means that the 'supercarriers' like BT, AT&T and a few other operators are concentrating on international markets for the expansion of their services to serve multinational customers.[13]

In the British market, for example, BT dwarfs its competitors and has retained substantial *buyer* power. In the domestic market in 1991, BT's network supported 25 million exchange connections, and it is from the domestic market that BT still generates some 98 per cent of its revenues. Mercury had only a little over 600,000 directly and indirectly connected customers (Office of Telecommunications, 1991). In the same year, there were 1.2 million cellular subscribers in Britain, and 260,000 cable telephony customers (Office of Telecommunications, 1991). In 1992, BT's turnover was £13.3 billion and its operating profit was £3.4 billion (British Telecom, 1992). In 1992, Mercury's turnover was £915 million, and its trading profit was only £155 million (Cable & Wireless, 1992).

In the global market, however, BT is one of a small number of 'supercarriers' which include NTT, DBP Telekom, France Telecom and AT&T. In 1991, BT was third if ranked by revenues among these top five public telecommunication operators. If ranked by pre-tax profits and by profits as a percentage of revenues, BT would be first.[14] BT's profits increased by 10.5 per cent over the previous year despite competitive threats. NTT's profits declined, as did AT&T's, but all these supercarriers have retained considerable *supplier* power.[15]

The strength of *buyer* power in the customer environment in shaping the technical and investment decisions of the suppliers is assumed to be increasing as business customers have become more vocal in calling for diversity and change in the telecommunication industry. These customers have become much more visible participants in industry fora and in standards setting activities. Nevertheless, research on the characteristics of 'user' participation within European standards fora shows a wide variety of justifications for participation and very little evidence of substantial *buyer* influence. For example, there is little, if any, user consensus on technical standards to meet their requirements and users face substantial difficulties in funding their participation in standards setting activities.[16] This is hardly indicative of substantial buyer power in the telematics market.

These developments are being played out in national and the regional markets such as the European Community. In Europe, the PTOs are facing pressures to be more responsive to large business customers. One central issue concerns the terms and conditions under which competitors and end users should access public telematics networks in a more competitive environment.[17] European Commission directives and national regulations and licence conditions will make it technically impossible for nationally based supercarriers to prohibit the interconnection of competing networks or to charge unduly high prices for access to their public networks. Nevertheless, the formal specification of policies and regulations provides little insight into the underlying processes of negotiation and bargaining among actors in the public and private sphere.

The public statements of the traditional public telecommunication operators are like those of any 'competitor' in a market. Despite the fact that they all claim to compete fairly, the dominant suppliers are aware of the market power that they wield. For example, it took Mannesmann Mobilfunk two years, despite intervention by the German government, to agree network access charges with the dominant mobile operator, Deutsche Bundespost Telekom (OECD, 1993). In the United Kingdom, disputes over the costs attributable to network access and use by competitors have been the subject of determinations by the regulator as to both the appropriate level of prices and the methodology used to calculate them.[18] In addition, there is evidence suggesting that regulatory authorities will need to intervene to limit dominant carriers from offering discount pricing schemes when they are challenged by competitors as abuses of market power.[19]

In Britain and the wider European Community, network operators and public policy makers are striking uneasy alliances. Public policy aims, on the one hand, to promote more efficient, globally operating, national champions and, on the other, to stimulate competition in domestic markets which some argue will merely serve to weaken the national champions. Some argue that BT, for example, should be unleashed from restrictions on its prices, and that BT and Mercury should be free to negotiate interconnection agreements, commercially with their competitors, without regulatory intervention. Such intervention may bias the selection of technologies or the timing of the take-off of new services such as personal communication networks. Others, in contrast, press their case for measures to restrain the dominant network operators from engaging in anti-competitive behaviour.

The distribution of equity and efficiency gains resulting from market liberalisation is decisively influenced by the regulations for pricing, standardisation and network access. The last of these is especially crucial because telematics networks are *systemic* technologies and co-operation agreements representing the rules of the market are essential. Network interoperability and access are often necessary preconditions for the diffusion of advanced telematics services.[20] Suppliers, customers and regulators recognise, for example, the need for co-operation on numbering plans, infrastructure capacity where this proves cost effective, and the technical information required to establish standards and to plan the roll out of new networks. Although, they have not reached a consensus upon the role of public policy or regulation in ensuring that co-operation actually occurs, regulation, imperfect as it is, continues to play a crucial role in monitoring, guiding and sometimes controlling, decisions by the players in the market. However, it is in this area that there are very few signs that regulatory innovation is keeping pace with changes in technologies and markets.

Innovation in governance institutions

The Commission of the European Communities observed a decade ago that changes in the structure and organisation of telecommunication markets would not imply modifications in the statutes or responsibilities of nationally based suppliers of public telecommunication networks. Nevertheless, it was argued at this time that in order to tap the full potential of technological innovations in telecommunications there would be a need for a new Community-wide legal and political framework. It was further observed that 'a legal framework does not imply, however, additional constraints and bureaucracy'. Change at the Community level would be 'counter-balanced by a reduction in regulations' (Commission of the European Communities, 1983). The intervening years have seen debate as to appropriate innovations in regulatory institutions and practices become increasingly controversial for the European Commission and the member states of the European Community, as well as for the wider international community.

What are the prospects for innovations in regulation? The continuing *supplier* power of the telematics network suppliers suggests that ensuring fair terms of network access for intermediate and end users requires public governance institutions to prevent them from jeopardising equity goals that, in the past, have been implicit in concepts of public services provided under monopoly conditions. The aim, in the 1960s through the mid-1980s, was to extend access to relatively homogeneous public telecommunication services as widely as possible. In the marketplace of the 1990s, there is no longer a consensus upon what comprises the 'public' network or on what the terms and conditions of access should be for different communities of users.

The United States has encouraged competition in telematics markets for longer than the European Community. The first signs of competitive entry in the American market were felt in the 1950s, when a small device called the Hush-a-Phone allowed a caller to shield sound from near-by listeners. Full terminal equipment competition took two more decades to establish. In public network service supply, AT&T was challenged in the late 1950s by private telecommunication users who won access to the radio spectrum to provide microwave services. Discount pricing strategies, proprietary standards, and reluctance to interconnect competing networks were the tools AT&T used to rebuff challenges to its market.

Today, after three 'computer inquiries', the divestiture of AT&T, and the introduction of open network architecture (ONA) arrangements,[21] the result has been a growing tendency to rely upon regulation by technical standards. For example, the dominant carriers in the United States must submit network architecture plans to the regulatory agency. They are required to 'unbundle' their services so that competitors can access their networks. Technical approaches to regulation have not prised open public networks, at least not in the way many customers and competitors would like. Services have not been sufficiently unbundled to eliminate barriers to new entry, especially in local or regional markets. Rivalry is still favouring the larger telecommunication users in terms of choice and the costs of services.[22] The American regulatory institutions are having difficulty coping with technical change in the telematics industry.

In the European Community, market liberalisation has come later and has moved comparatively more rapidly in some areas. However, liberalisation has created a growing need for co-operation and the need for imaginative regulatory innovation. But there are few signs of innovation in the way regulators are attempting to control the market power of dominant players such as BT. The 'level playing field', for example, is being sought in the United Kingdom, mainly through the use of technical standards and price regulation.

There is a need for more effective regulation to ensure that equitable access to networks is not overshadowed by the supercarriers' global aspirations. In the United States, the regulatory model has produced detailed procedures of administrative oversight and cost accounting methodologies for assessing whether tariffs are fair. This system of governance has built a vast edifice of information requirements and a bureaucracy of legal experts, economists and public interest advocates. As they grapple with the increasing plurality of networks which springs from market liberalisation, European policy makers appear to be moving down a very similar path. They run the risk of recreating the features of American public utility regulation which have been tried, and found wanting.

In both the United States and Europe, the public policy making institutions have found it difficult to create an environment which would promote debate to provide an answer to a crucial question: for whom should the public telematics infrastructure be designed? Public networks are increasingly designed to meet the stringent requirements of large customers and this has a high cost. The requirements of larger customers outstrip the average quality and capabilities of the public network. Discrepancies between the technical standards and pricing structures that promote the extension of telematics networks and services which meet the requirements of the majority of smaller customers and those needed to support advanced services for globally operating corporations will continue to diverge just as they have historically.[23]

The dominant public telecommunication operators have an incentive to invest heavily to meet the needs of the multinational firms who generate an increasingly significant proportion of their revenues. This is not a conspiracy or the result of collusion among supercarriers. It is a pragmatic response to the internationalisation of markets. The outcome of rivalry among the supercarriers:

> is going to make a difference to the consumer, [but] more important are the design principles (both in technical architecture and public policy) under which the winning entry or entries operate...Openness is either present or absent in every aspect of the network. A network is either open or closed with respect to who may have access to it, who determines its specific uses, who may supply content, who can provide the equipment used, how interfaces and standards are determined, and whether the technical details are public or private.
>
> (Kapor, 1993)

Radical innovation in regulatory institutions is unlikely to surface until efforts are made to reach consensus on the terms and conditions of network access. There are steps which could be taken to increase the probability that such initiatives will be taken. One innovation would be to unleash the 'supercarriers' to confront the full force of oligopolistic rivalry in international markets. This would require structural separation of the global and domestic operations of the 'supercarriers' from the provision of the public access network. Some of the 'supercarriers' are already undertaking internal studies to determine whether they should remain in the business of operating certain parts of the domestic infrastructure.[24]

As a result, network operators licensed to provide access to end user customers would face the same set of incentives to negotiate interconnection arrangements to complete the *systemic* feature of their networks, i.e. the need to both originate and terminate services. Their choices as to service portfolios, network configurations and the ubiquity of network access would become more transparently a function of the costs of network access and market characteristics than the opaque result of the differential impact of the market power. An alternative to structural separation is the use of accounting mechanisms which is currently being explored in the United Kingdom and elsewhere in the European Community. However, as the United States' experience has illustrated, the accompanying bureaucracy which proliferates under this approach and the extent to which methodologies are subject to dispute, suggests that this is a second best alternative.

As liberalisation and competition take hold, the 'supercarriers' will continue to pursue their goals in international markets and they will become increasingly reluctant to bear public service responsibilities. However, in the interests of both equity and efficiency in the market, there will be a need to ensure that a common public network continues to evolve. The regulatory problem is not one of specifying abstractly which network configurations, features or services *must* be accessible to the widest possible community of users. It is one of creating the institutional environment in which such issues can be meaningfully negotiated on an ongoing basis as technologies change and markets are restructured. Radical regulatory innovation would seek to create such an environment in different ways depending on the cultural, political and economic nuances of national or regional governance systems.

3.5   The determinants of regulatory innovation

There are tensions at the interface between the production and consumption of telematics services that shape the design of telematics networks and its implications for efficiency and equity goals. These are characterised differently according to the assumptions incorporated within alternative models of technical and institutional change. On the one hand, there is what we might refer to as an *idealist* model of technical and institutional change. Although the supplier–customer interface in the telematics industry is recognised as a site where the negotiation of technical and institutional alternatives takes place, from the *idealist* perspective, the contradictions and conflicts in this process are masked by a scenario of an increasingly interdependent global communication environment. On the other hand, there is an alternative model which we might designate as the *strategic* model. This model seeks to analyse the ways in which negotiation and bargaining power are instrumental in structuring the characteristics of the telematics network system.[25]

The *idealist* model is derived from theories which envisage the emergence of mature and fully articulated competitive markets. It is assumed that a large number of sellers are active in the market such that the impact of one seller on the market is negligible; buyers perceive that sellers produce a homogeneous product; and buyers have access to perfect knowledge, or at least sufficient knowledge, to enable them to make informed rational decisions (Clark, 1961). This type of competition is characterised by the absence of barriers to market entry and exit.

In contrast, the *strategic* model is rooted in theories of imperfect competition, monopolistic competition (competition among differentiated products), oligopolistic rivalry (competition among small numbers of suppliers), and monopoly.[26] Institutions are characterised by indeterminacy and unstable oligopoly. Multinational corporations employ short-run pricing strategies to achieve long-run entrenchment and monopoly power in national or regional markets. The structure of markets is interwoven with technical change and the determinants of changes in institutions are located within a broad array of social, cultural and political arrangements.

The prevailing 'globalisation' paradigm envisages trends in the development of the telematics network system in line with the assumptions of the *idealist* model. The notion that a trajectory of technical development will prove inherently superior and will come to be reflected in the technical composition of advanced communication systems is deeply rooted in this model.[27] Insofar as the process of technical innovation in telecommunication and computing technologies is left to the forces of the competitive market, the network will tend to embrace the collective interests of suppliers and users.

A more realistic account of the strategic and tactical manoeuvring of multinational firms and the determinants of policy and regulatory regimes is offered by the *strategic* model. In this model there is continuous rivalry among a relatively small number of dominant firms. Rivalry, monopolisation and institutional restructuring do not serve all market participants equally well. Rivalry among suppliers and customers creates the impetus for changes in public and private institutions of governance. The *strategic* model emphasises the ways in which new market distortions are created and become embedded in the design of technical artefacts such as the telematics network.

Telematics networks are assumed to be evolving in very different ways according to these alternative models. The *idealist* model (see Table 3.1) assumes that the combined forces of technical innovation and competition erode monopolistic control of the telematics system. The PTOs argue that the diffusion of advanced systems means that no single supplier will dominate the market sufficiently to discriminate unjustifiably among customers. There is a period of transition as the forces of effective competition take hold, but in many countries this has already occurred. In countries or regions where the diffusion of telematics services has been slower, competition provides the best incentive for stimulating a 'catch-up' or 'leapfrogging' of earlier phases of network development. The PTOs and other suppliers are fully answerable to all their customers and universal services are ultimately provided. The telematics network provides a technical solution to the need to ensure that comparative advantage is 'created' in a way that contributes to the competitiveness of nationally or regionally based firms.

Permeable Seamless Networks
Ubiquitous (Universal) Service Diffusion
Demand-led Telecommunication Industry
Open Systems, Common Interface Standards
Co-operative Partnerships, Transparent Network Access
Minimal Regulation to Achieve Efficiency and Equity

Table 3.1. The idealist model.

The *strategic* model (see Table 3.2) draws upon theories of institutional change to determine the modalities through which such power is executed. This model suggests that where competition does exist, it will display signs of superficial product differentiation, effective service competition only in certain submarkets, and the closure of telematics network systems to a potentially significant number of intermediate and end users.

The *idealist* model envisages an open telematics network system and competitive markets. The assumption is that a global permeable network will evolve as a result of its inherent superiority over other solutions. This model provides the grist for the rhetoric which is effective in persuading governments to promulgate policies in line with the *idealist* vision. Disparities in the accessibility of networks can be neglected since the long-term trend is for the benefits of competitive markets to outweigh any temporary social or economic costs.

Fragmented Networks
Reduced Ubiquity in Service Diffusion
Supply-led Industry, Multinational User Pressure
Weak Stimuli for Competition in Most Sub-Markets
Rivalry, Non-Transparent Network Access
Increasing Regulation

Table 3.2. The strategic model.

The *strategic* model of telematics network development forecasts increasing segmentation in the development of public networks. Network segmentation is a reflection of the way technical innovations in the telematics system are being institutionalised. It mirrors the relative market power of major network operators and equipment manufacturers. The dynamics of monopolisation and rivalry, and their expression through the technical design of the telematics network, provide a more realistic explanation for the 'globalisation' process which is underway. For Clark, 'monopolisation *refers not to monopoly as such but to the activities of firms (usually dominant ones) who are seeking to build up or maintain a position of market power.* Such activities include predatory and exclusionary tactics, for example selling at a loss and exclusive dealing' [emphasis added] (Clark, 1961). Technical innovations in telematics network systems are leading to new systemic biases in the way telematics services are produced and used. These systemic biases tend to favour the multinational firms and they are echoed in the complexity of the institutions which represent the telematics supplier, customer and policy communities.

Acknowledging the role of institutionalised market power in the technical 'selection' process is only a first step toward the unmasking of the *idealist* 'globalisation' thesis. The *strategic* model of institutional and technical change calls for the investigation of disparities in power and control through their articulation within institutions of public and private governance. The framing of the analytical issues which are embodied in controversies with regard to questions of equity and efficiency in the evolution of telematics networks often suffers from the propensity of research to seek evidence of the 'impact' of technical change or market liberalisation on the viability of public institutions of governance such as the formal apparatus of regulation. A more productive framing of the issues is one which seeks to analyse the way in which political and economic power is mediated by the processes of innovation in technologies and institutions – including markets, corporate entities and regulatory agencies. Within the *strategic* model, attention can be focused upon the ways in which relevant actors mobilise to forge an emerging consensus upon the appropriate understanding of equity and efficiency in the telematics marketplace. It can also 'bracket' this level of analysis of strategic conduct and focus upon the structural elements or rules and resources available to public and private institutions of governance, thus bringing to light the extent of the capacity for change in existing institutions and the likelihood that emergent institutions will reflect alternative market outcomes.[28]

3.6   Conclusion

Thus far the consensus formation process in the United Kingdom, and the European Community more generally, is stalled in the details of technical standards, highly charged debates on interpretations of the 'relevant' costs of service supply, and the impact of pricing strategies. Embedded in these debates are conflicting views of the appropriate balance between equity and efficiency considerations. A radical regulatory innovation would redirect regulatory activity to a minimum set of essential and manageable tasks. The resources of regulators would be targeted to promoting the development of telematics networks that are optimised to provide access to the majority, not an increasing minority, of users. One priority would be to monitor the extent to which gaps are appearing geographically and demographically as a result of uneven market development. Another would be to create fora which enable more effective and ongoing supplier and user participation in decisions on the need for public policy intervention to redress imbalances in network access. Such intervention would inevitably be highly political and would have far-reaching economic consequences. There would be a need, for example, to consider when, how and to what extent public financing is needed to strengthen incentives for investment in infrastructure and services or, alternatively, whether incentives can be created to speed up or alter the present trajectories of investment in telematics services which are guided mainly by market considerations.

The goal of regulatory innovation would be to institutionalise a means to establish a changing consensus upon the minimum set of telematics services that would meet any given public service requirements. This form of regulation would only be effective if it were linked directly to a regulatory institution with the power and resources to recommend and implement change.

National or European-wide regulatory institutions cannot seek to manage or replicate the decisions of network operators. In this the proponents of the *idealist* model are correct. This approach has overwhelmed the regulatory apparatus in the United States for both political and organisational reasons. For example, BT's chairman has declared:

> I believe that an increasingly interventionist regulatory approach is doomed to failure, if only because the complexity and sophistication of the market...will be such as to put it beyond the wit of the regulators to regulate. Modelling [the] industry will no longer be a practical possibility; and f you cannot model you cannot regulate; you can intervene only in the know‥dge that you have no means of assessing the consequences. Rational, respɔnsible, intervention is in fact impossible.[29]

Nevertheless, public intervention in the name of public service and equity considerations is not only possible, it is essential. As the historian, Lewis Mumford commented in 1934 (paraphrase of original):

> The problem of integrating the machine in society is not merely a matter...of making social institutions keep in step with the machine. The problem is also one of altering the nature and rhythm of machines to fit the actual needs of the community.
>
> (Mumford, 1934)

Technical innovations in telematics services are contributing to new complexities in the marketplace. The 'supercarriers' are moving beyond the wit of the regulator – as presently understood. But the nature of the machine, in this case the public telematics network, needs to be designed to fit the needs of the widest community of users. If the regulatory process and related institutions of public governance are to keep pace with technical innovation, they are likely to need to engage in institutional innovations that provide fora for active *consensus building* on the criteria and actions need to ensure access to the electronic communication environment.

Such institutional innovations hold the promise for more effective regulation to ensure that equity and efficiency goals are met in an increasingly complex marketplace. At one extreme, it might be concluded that simple access to a copper wire pair at a reasonable price is all that is required. At the other, access to fibre-based networks and gigabit speed information applications could be required on a universal basis. In between lies the reality of network and service investment decisions guided by the exigencies and pressures of a global marketplace and, increasingly, by economic efficiency considerations. This environment is the result of a consensus on the need for a growing role for the market as a stimulus to effective competition. There is a complementary need for innovation in the public institutions of governance to inform, and shape, innovation in the telematics technical system.

In summary, regulatory institutions have not been coping effectively with technical change. Access to the advanced telematics networks and services of the future may need to be at least as pervasive as voice telephony is today.

The 'supercarriers' are becoming less interested in public or universal service goals as they turn their strategies to the global marketplace. Structural changes in domestic markets are needed, but these changes would not result in a sufficiently radical reorientation of regulation. Regulatory innovation is also needed to ensure that consensus is reached upon the need for equity and efficiency in the provision of telematics services.

This chapter was originally a paper prepared for the PICT National Conference, Kennilworth, UK, May 1993, and was also presented at the European Association for Evolutionary Political Economy Conference, Barcelona, 28–30 October, 1993.

References

Bell, D. (1973). *The Coming of Post-Industrial Society: A Venture in Social Forecasting.* New York: Basic Books.

British Telecom (1992). *Directors' Report and Financial Statements 1992,* British Telecom: London, p. 5. In 1990–91, BT's return on capital reached 21.8 per cent, National Audit Office (1993) *The Office of Telecommunication: Licence Compliance and Consumer Protection,* Report by the Comptroller and Auditor General, London: HMSO, 12 March, p. 26. (Net assets method adjusted for dividend and current portion of long-term debt.)

Cable & Wireless (1992). *Report and Accounts 1992,* London, p. 50.

Clark, J. M. (1961). *Competition as a Dynamic Process,* New York: The Brookings Institution.

Commission of the European Communities (1983). COM (83) 329 final, Brussels, p. 10.

Dunning, J. H. (1992). The global economy, domestic governance, strategies and transnational corporations: interactions and policy implications. *Transnational Corporations,* **1** (3), p. 21.

Freeman, C. (1988). Introduction. In: G. Dosi, C. Freeman, R. Nelson, G. Silverberg and L. Soete (eds.), *Technical Change and Economic Theory.* London: Pinter, p. 2.

Hu, Y. S. (1992). Global or transnational corporations and national firms with international operations. *California Management Review,* **34** (2) pp. 107–27.

Hughes, T. P. (1987). The evolution of large technological systems, pp. 51–82. In: W. E. Bijker, T. P. Hughes & T. J. Pinch (ed.), *The Social Construction of Technological Systems: New Directions in the Sociology and History of Technology.* Cambridge MA: MIT Press, p. 1.

Kapor, M. (1993). Where is the digital highway really heading?   The case for a Jeffersonian information policy, *Wired,* July/August, p. 57.

Langhammer, H. (1993). Conference paper presented by H. Langhammer, Manager, Global Telecommunications Services, DuPont, Germany, at the 3rd Annual Networked Economy Conference, Paris, 10–11 March.

Mansell, R. & Morgan, K. (1990). Perspectives on advanced communications for Europe *PACE '90*, Vol. VII, Commission of the European Communities, Brussels.

McKinsey & Company (1993). WORLDTEL – *Establishing an Entity to Promote Telecommunications in the Developing World*. Pre-feasibility study prepared for the International Telecommunication Union, May.

Mumford, L. (1934). *Technics and Civilization*. London: Routledge & Kegan Paul, p. 367.

OECD (1993). *Review of Mobile/PSTN Interconnect Tariff Policy in OECD Member Countries*, by D. Laval and K. Hansen, Schema UK, draft, Paris, 15 March, p. 11

Office of Telecommunications (1991). *Annual Report 1991*, London, pp. 106–124.

Ohmae, K. (1990). *The Borderless World*, London: Collins.

Porter, M. (1992). On thinking about deregulation and competition. In: H. Sapolsky et al. (eds.) *The Telecommunications Revolution*, London: Routledge.

Soete, L. (1991). *Technology and Economy in a Changing World*, OECD Conference on Technology and the Global Economy, Montreal, 3–6 February, p. 52.

de Sola Pool, I. (1990). In: Noam, E. (ed.), *Technologies without Boundaries: On Telecommunications in a Global Age*, Cambridge MA, Harvard University Press.

Notes

1   For an analysis of the assumptions which typically characterise 'impact' oriented analysis in the information and communication technologies field, see R. Mansell (1994) 'Introductory Overview (pp. 1–16), in R. Mansell (ed.) *The Management of Information and Communication Technologies: Emerging Patterns of Control* London: ASLIB Publishers.

2   Capital investment in public telecommunications in US$ at 1990 constant prices and exchange rates: 1981–83 $67.7 billion; 1990 $89.5 billion. See OECD (1993) T*he Communications Outlook 1993*. OECD, Paris.

3   Investment associated with network modernisation is generally required to replace or augment the capabilities of existing plant and equipment. Data are supplied to OECD by PTOs and/or national governments. Accounting systems and regulatory incentives can result in variations in the proportion of investment designated as attributable to network modernisation.

4   In 1990/91 the top telecommunication equipment vendors ranked by telecommunication equipment sales were AT&T, Alcatel, Siemens, NEC, Northern Telecom, Ericsson, Bosch Telecom, Motorola, Fujitsu, GPT, Philips, Italtel, Ascom, Nokia and Matra.

NEC claimed to be spending 16.1 per cent of total sales in comparison with only 7.0 per cent for AT&T. See OECD (1993) *The Communications Outlook 1993*. OECD, Paris, p. 36.

5   See also P. Drucker (1989) *The New Realities*. London: Mandarin; and M. E. Porter (1990) *The Competitive Advantage of Nations*. New York: Free Press. For a comprehensive review of the literature in the area see P. Tang and R. Mansell (1993) *Telecommunication, Multinational Enterprises and Globalization: Implications for Future Network Development*. Report prepared for Rank Xerox Cambridge EuroPARC by Brighton Science Policy Research Unit, 10 February.

6   As Freeman has observed, this concept is not particularly new, see C. Freeman (1990) *Networks of Innovators: A Synthesis of Research Issues*, Workshop on Networks of Innovators, Montreal, 1–3 May.

7   See J. H. Dunning, (1992) 'The global economy, domestic governance, strategies and transnational corporations: interactions and policy implications.' *Transnational Corporations* 1 (3), pp. 7–45 and R. G. Lipsey (1991) *Economic Growth: Science and Technology and Institutional Change in a Global Economy*. Canadian Institute for Advanced Research, CIAR Publication No. 4, Toronto, 1991.

8   See R. Mansell (1995) Innovation in telecommunication: bridging the supplier-user interface, in M. Dodgson and R. Rothwell (eds.) *Handbook of Industrial Innovation*, Cheltenham, Edward Elgar Publishing, pp. 232–242.

9   See R. Mansell (1993) *High Performance Computing: Network and Institutional Scenarios*, Report prepared for the OECD Information, Computer and Communications Policy Division, Paris, August.

10   Such as the Direction de la Réglementation Générale (DRG) in France, the Danish National Telecom Agency and ECTRA, the European Committee for Telecommunication Regulation Authority. The European Commission has introduced directives to stimulate terminal equipment competition, to create more transparent procurement rules, and to open some, and possibly all services, to competition. See also Commission of the European Communities (1992) '1992 Review of the Situation in the Telecommunication Services Sector', IV/A/3/GL/cd; XIII/D/2/HU/mrd, 10 July 1992; 'Proposal for a Council Directive on the Mutual Recognition of Licences and Other National Authorizations for Telecommunications Services including the Establishment of a Single Community Telecommunications Licence and the Setting Up of a Community Telecommunications Committee', ONPCOM91-79bis, 3 March 1992.

11   See P. Tang and R. Mansell (1993) and reprinted as SPRU CICT Report No. 8. University of Sussex, Brighton.

12   Results presented by Teknibank, Milan, 19 March 1993 as part of a project on the 'Macro-economic Impact of Advanced Telecommunications in European Main Countries', RACE Project 2086, Workpackage 2-A1. Analysis is being undertaken for the Germany, French and British economies. This compares with the 3.8 to 6.4 per cent gains from 1992 to 2008 estimated for the US economy, see R. Cohen (1992) *The Impact of Broadband Communications on the US Economy and on Competitiveness*, Special Report, Economic Strategy Institute, Washington, DC.

13   For further details see R. Mansell (1993) 'Should local and long-distance operations be separated?' paper prepared for 'Competition and Choice in the Local Loop', IBC Conference, London 23-24 March.

14   In 1990/91 revenues were: US $ (millions), in NTT – $43.174; DBP Telekom – $25, 117; BT – $23,364; France Telecom – $21,116; AT&T – $20,410 (telecom services only). Data collated by OECD, telecommunication network operators – trading performance, 18 March 1993.

15   For a recent argument about the likely continuing market power which can be exercised by the long distance carriers in the United States market as a result of their investment

in high capacity fibre backbone networks, see P. Huber, M. Kellog and J. Thorne (1993) *The Geodesic Network III: 1993 Report on Competition in the Telephone Industry*. Unofficial 'Triennial Review' of the state of competition in the US industry, available from Little, Brown & Company, Washington, DC.

[16]   See, R. Hawkins (1993) 'Changing Expectations: Voluntary Standards and the Regulation of European Telecommunication', submitted to *Communications & Strategies*, March, SPRU Mimeo and R. Hawkins (1993) 'Standards for Technologies of Communication: Policy Implications of the Dialogue between Technical and Non-technical Factors'. Science Policy Research Unit, University of Sussex, Unpublished D.Phil. Dissertation.

[17]   For example, even after almost a decade of competition in the United Kingdom, BT still has about 97 per cent of local terminations and the most fully developed long distance network. The aim of policy is 'to obtain the best possible deal for the end user in terms of quality, choice and value for money...principally by promoting efficient competition..' See Office of Telecommunications (1993) 'Interconnection and Accounting Separation', Consultative Document, London, pp. 2–3.

[18]   See T. Rhodes (1993) 'Competitive Entry into Regulated Markets', Speech to Cranfield School of Management, Director of Competition Policy, Mercury Communications Ltd, 17 February. Rhodes estimates that revenues generated by interconnect charges from Mercury, the cellular companies and cable television operators are in excess of £400 million in revenues to BT.

[19]   For example, in June 1993, the UK Office of Telecommunication was considering complaints by Mercury and the cable television operators that BT has abused its dominant position by charging special offer prices that are below the cost incurred by BT. See, A. Adonis (1993) 'BT may face Oftel order to limit future special offers', *Financial Times*, 30 June.

[20]   Prices for interconnection and services must not so confuse, or exclude, the customer that the efficiency gains due to competition outweigh equitable access to public networks and new services. Various kinds of *agreements* regarding costs, transfer payments, and maintenance are essential.

[21]   For a review of the history of these see US Court of Appeals for the 9th Circuit, *State of California v. FCC*, No. 87-7230, 6 June 1990.

[22]   See F. Bar and M. Borrus (1992) 'The Future of Networking in the US.: Summary Report', Report prepared for the Commission of the European Communities, Berkeley Roundtable on the International Economy, University of California, Berkeley.

[23]   See A. Davies (1991) 'The Digital Divide: A Political Economy of the Restructuring of Telecommunications', University of Sussex, Unpublished D.Phil. Dissertation; R. Gabel (1969) 'The early competitive era in telephone communication, 1893-1920', *Law and Contemporary Problems*, Vol. 34, pp. 340–359; R. Mansell (1993) *The New Telecommunications: A Political Economy of Network Evolution*, London: Sage; and H. Trebing (1969) Common carrier regulation – the silent crisis', *Law and Contemporary Problems*, Vol. 34, pp. 299–329.

[24]   Personal communication, representative of continental European public telecommunication operator.

[25]   There are many sub-genres within each of these two categories. This analytical divide has been the preoccupation of much scholarly work and has been articulated in slightly different ways depending upon the analytical 'discipline'. The intention in this chapter is not to rehearse the determinants of this divide.

[26]   See, for example, J. M. Clark's discussion of alternatives to the static competitive market model (Clark, 1961) See also J. A. Schumpeter (1954) *A History of Economic Analysis,* New York: Oxford University Press (edited by E. B. Schumpeter). For a

discussion of perspectives on the role of entry and exit barriers under conditions of imperfect competition in telecommunication, see W. G. Shepherd (1984) ' "Contestability" vs. Competition.' *American Economic Review,*74 (September): 572-85.

27   This assumption contrasts sharply with David and Bunn's observation that 'where network technologies are involved, one cannot justifiably suppose that the system which has evolved is really superior to others which might have been developed further, but were not'. See P. A. David and J. A. Bunn (1988) 'The economics of gateway technologies and network evolution: Lessons from the electricity supply industry.' *Information Economics and Policy,* 3: p. 169.

28   See, A. Giddens (1979) *Central Problems in Social Theory*, Berkeley: University of California Press, and A. Giddens (1984) *The Constitution of Society*, London: Polity Press, for a discussion of the relationship between strategic and institutional levels of analysis.

29   I. Vallance, Chairman BT (1993) 'Competition and Regulation in the Global Telecommunications Industry', Speech to Cranfield School of Management, 13 January, pp. 10–11.

4

Media, communication, information and the 'revolution' of everyday life

Roger Silverstone

4.1   Introduction

The world of media, communication and information – increasingly in and through its technological and industrial convergence, a world of multimedia – is, we are told, poised on the cusp of yet another major and revolutionary advance. Digital compression, the capacity to transmit hundreds and even thousands of separate signals – of voice, image, text and data – down a cable or a twisted copper wire, is ready, like the shock troops of an invading army, to advance across the landscapes of our more or less cosy media lives. We are promised interactivity. We are promised an infinite choice of media products. We are promised universal reach and instantaneous connection. We are promised a world of ever increasing image production. Greater control, greater access, the possibility of near total immersion in an electronic culture. The hyper-real in real time.

We confront this possibility with mostly exaggerated hopes and fears. The alternative utopias and dystopias are familiar enough. So too are the circumstances of their creation. The utopias are the product of industrial, marketing and media efforts to create a self-fulfilling prophecy in which such changes are seen not only to be welcome but inevitable, natural and necessary. The dystopias are their mirror image. They embody the fears and anxieties of those who see technological change as a *deus ex machina*, a kind of napalm burning its way through the fabric of all that is good and genuine in our lives. Here technological change is seen as neither welcome, necessary nor, indeed, certain.

In trying to assess something of the realities in the relationship between technological and social change we need – and I shall argue as much in this chapter – to step back from the apocalyptic or millenial metaphors.

Above all it seems that we should confront the arguments which lead one to expect that rapid or even revolutionary change in the design of new technology will lead inevitably and inexorably to equivalent revolutions in the way we live, in the conduct of our everyday lives. Of course our lives both with or without technology change, sometimes change quite radically. There is no denying the consequences of the arrival of a brand new Sega Mega Drive on the life of a twelve or thirteen year old boy. At last he has the opportunity and justification to get out of the bowels of the family and he can now – despite his mother's anxiety about the possibility that he will be turned into some kind of brainless technoholic – retire to his bedroom with the full support of his peer group and the culture at large. But equally there is every reason to think that the extreme effects of such novelty will be relatively short-lived. And there is also every reason to think that if the Sega had not come along to provide the excuse for withdrawal, something else would have done (as Radio Luxembourg or some other semi-licit media-related activity might have done a generation earlier). His life is changing anyway – adolescence will be *his* first revolution.

Similarly there is no denying the consequences of the arrival in a household of the teleworking computer, bringing with it a shift of family culture and altering the relationship of the household to the outside world. But even this revolution is limited in its capacity to alter fundamental dimensions of family life – the household division of labour and the traditional role of the woman at home remain largely unaffected for example. And indeed we could argue that it is not the computer here so much as the work which is the catalyst. In this most radical case of technologically implicated social change in everyday life, it is clear that technology does not act alone, nor indeed is it even the most important factor.

It would, of course, be hard to doubt the importance of new media and information technologies both in the world of work and in our everyday and domestic lives. But we should note that the consequences of such innovation are uneven. Not everyone can take advantage of all that new technology has to offer. Those that can are not always pleased or comfortable with the results. This unevenness, both of takeup and of consequence, the recognition that the information 'revolution' is a stratified one, is not particularly novel. But it is extremely important. We have been warned about the emergence of the information rich and the information poor. We should recognize that this is not just a matter of international differences but of national and local ones.

This brings me to my final introductory point. New technologies arrive in an already technologically rich, complex but also a more or less accepted world. Our lives are lived through media images and media information. We take our capacity to pick up the phone and call a relative in another continent entirely for granted. The patterns of our everyday lives, structured through the times and spaces of work and leisure, have become technologically dependent, and that dependence is, for the most part, invisible – and it is conservative (Thrall, 1982). New machines, new products and services are now commonplace, offering supposedly new delights but also challenging the comfortable relationship with what we know and what we can, within our more or less limited resources, manage to use. Revolutions are evolutions in disguise. They are also hard won. And needs have to be created. They do not simply emerge fully formed from natural desires, innocent perceptions or even previous experiences.[1]

In this chapter I would like to address some of these questions and issues. I will draw on ongoing research, funded by the Economic and Social Research Council under its Programme on Information and Communication Technologies (ICTs).[2] This is documenting and analysing the social and cultural dynamics of the adoption and use of media and information technologies in contemporary households in the UK. It is concerned with the patterns of acceptance of, and resistance to, new technologies. It is concerned with the dynamic role that consumers and users play in defining their particular relationships to both old and new media. And it is concerned with the consequences of adoption and use: consequences for the conduct of family life, for the relationship between households and the wider world, and for demands for future hard and software.

We have studied nuclear families, teleworking households, lone-parent households and are currently working with the newly retired. Our methodology is principally qualitative. It involves intensive work, mostly through interview, with small numbers of households. Within those interviews we seek to understand the social and cultural context (both in biography or family history as well as through the patterns and rituals of daily life) in which media and information consumption takes place. We have sought to document something of the variety and complexity of people's lives with technologies, and to recognise that this variety and complexity is the product of the distinct cultures of households – distinct and changing across class and culture, and through time.

Our concern has been with the dynamics of a complex process, a process in which users and consumers are seen to be active, not just passive, participants. We recognise that media and information technologies are not just material or functional objects but have a powerful symbolic charge. We recognise, too, that this symbolic charge is itself the product of the activities of those who, together, design, market and use technologies. But that ultimately the meanings and significance of all our media and information products (both hardware and software) depend on the participation – with varying degrees of commitment and interest – of the consumer. And so we come to think of the relationship between the producers and consumers of ICTs as a profoundly political one. It is political in the widest sense of the term: that is as a struggle over meaning and use, a struggle for control. I am going on to suggest this struggle over meaning and use is a struggle not only for the 'success' of a given product or new technology, it is a struggle over how that product or technology will be incorporated into the everyday lives of those who adopt it.

4.2   Domestication

From these starting points we have begun to see the innovation process – especially as it relates to media and information technologies and services – as a process of domestication. Domestication is itself, in the terms which have just been identified, political. The politics of domestication is played out at the interface of commercial and industrial interest, technological potential, marketing strategies and consumer choice.[3] It is pursued by producers and regulators who wish to control both the environment and the trajectory of technological innovation. It is pursued by advertisers and market makers through their own rhetorics. And it is pursued by consumers who seek to manage and control their own electronic spaces and to make mass-produced objects and meanings meaningful, useful and intelligible to them.

This is a process of domestication because what is involved is quite literally a taming of the wild and a cultivation of the tame. In this process new technologies and services – unfamiliar, exciting but also threatening and perplexing – are brought (or not) under control for and by domestic users. They are bought, subscribed to, or rented; understood or misunderstood; used or rejected. But in their ownership and in their appropriation into the culture of family or household and into the routines of everyday life, they are at the same time cultivated. They become familiar, but they also develop and change. And these developments and changes, the product of the work consumers do in taking possession of new technologies and services, feed back into the innovation process, reinforcing it, diverting it, sometimes rejecting it more or less completely. This is why the innovation process is so difficult to predict and why its path is littered with the debris of failed or marginal media and communication technologies. Teletext. Video phones. Laser discs. Telephone broadcasting systems. It is also worth noting, of course, that in the dynamics of domestication, and in the mostly unequal politics over the meaning and influence of new technologies, it is not only the technologies which shift, for cultivation also affects the cultivator and his or her culture.

We have followed this far-from-finished work of domestication in a recent brief case study of the early days of Philips' CD-i in which, through interviewing producers, advertisers, trade journalists, retailers and early consumers, we were able to chart the complex, uncertain and often contradictory emergence of a technology whose initial (and possibly continuing) meaning in the marketplace and as a consumer product was unstable, inchoate, and vulnerable to competing claims and contrary definition. CD-i is not only a new product, but a new medium. Though how new, and how significant, is of course very much still the issue. What emerges from this research is the extraordinary and punishing uncertainty that accompanies such new developments, especially when they are claiming, at least in part, a revolutionary status. The result is an indeterminacy in the innovation process that can only be begun to be grasped in the interaction of all the players – but especially the consumers – as they negotiate a place for a new machine, a new service or a new medium in the already dense and demanding culture of their everyday lives (Silverstone and Haddon, 1993).

This case study reveals the limited capacity of even a company of the size and experience of Philips to command the market – even once they have established an agreed standard and are not constrained by national or international regulation. Success does not appear to be a matter of merely getting the technology right (however hard that might be and whatever that might mean) or even being first in the marketplace but of gaining control of its meaning relative to existing and competing technologies, services and products (Cawson, forthcoming). It is also a matter, often, of creating a need. This is a rhetorical activity in which many are involved, each with their own interests and agendas. New ICTs for the domestic market are subject to constant and often contested definition and redefinition in design, advertising, marketing, retail display and in the secondary discourses of specialist magazines and consumer guides. Even early adopters, those most enthusiastic about new technologies, once the urgent impulse to buy the latest product has been satisfied, confront their new machine with a mixture of excitement, impatience and uncertainty. They have committed themselves but they are concerned that they have made the right choice: is there enough software and is it going to be good enough? In a world of incompatible standards have they chosen the winner rather than the loser? The relationship between producer and consumer needs to extend beyond the initial marketing or after sales service. The consumer needs to feel that the producer will keep faith: will keep his or her interests at heart as the technological marketplace continues to change. In this under-determined space that remains, once the initial act of consumption has taken place, there are opportunities for creative consumption which can and do go both with and against the grain.

It is this cultural space that I want now to explore. To do so I will discuss some of the findings both of our work with teleworking households – whom one can presume to be, mostly at least, somewhere at the cutting edge of the information revolution as it affects the domestic sphere. And I will also discuss some of the findings of our work with lone parents – at the other extreme in many cases, and likely to be increasingly disadvantaged as media and information technologies themselves increasingly define the terms of our participation in contemporary society.

But what kind of cultural space am I talking about? It is the space which I have already referred to as the domestic sphere. By the domestic sphere I do not merely mean the home, the family or the household, though each of these offer different ways of characterising it; as respectively a cultural, a social and an economic entity. What I want to convey is an idea of just such a cultural, social and economic space within which we create and sustain our identities and values: a place called home, more or less clearly defined, but in constant tension with the pressures, both material and symbolic, which emerge from the public world: a set of social relationships which, despite its ideological and sociological vulnerability, we still think of as 'family': and a set of economic activities both inside and outside the home which in their coordination and motivation we see as the basis for the viability of the household. The domestic sphere is a space certainly, but it is important to see it also as a product and a set of relationships, constantly changing in response to circumstance and to the opportunities both offered and denied by a world of increasing commodification and, for many perhaps, also increasing uncertainty.

The domestic sphere – and the particular character of our own domesticity – is the product then, and must be understood within the various social, cultural and technological networks that lock a given household into the constantly shifting structures of everyday life. Our domesticity is mobile and uneven in quality, alternatively pervious or impervious to influence. It is vulnerable to changes in the technological environment of course, but it is also, and just as significantly, vulnerable to changes in demography or economic cycles. The increasing presence, throughout the twentieth century, of media and information technologies in our homes and households, and their increasing centrality in the patterns of communication and the overall culture of contemporary society have made it impossible to think of the domestic sphere (never mind the public sphere) without them. But the reverse is also true. No account of technological innovation can ignore the particularity of that domesticity and the processes by which it is sustained. As many have argued, our domestic lives are to a greater and greater extent defined by and through our consumption of the objects and meanings of contemporary capitalism (Bourdieu, 1984; Douglas and Isherwood, 1979; Miller, 1987). It follows that consumption can be considered not just the life-blood of our industrial system and our public sphere but also the life-blood of our domestic sphere. Indeed it is precisely in and through consumption that the two are forever intertwined.

We have tried, in the research, to define a way of thinking about the domestic sphere through an understanding of the dynamics and processes of consumption. It is an attempt to think through the complex inter-relationship between technological and social change in a way that avoids the dangers of claiming that either technology or social change by themselves determine any given outcome; and also a way of thinking that enables us to approach in a hopefully more convincing way than is often the case, the complexities of technological innovation in everyday life. It will also provide a wider context for the specific studies that follow of teleworking and lone parents and their use of media and information technologies.

4.3 Consumption

Consumption consists, we suggest, in three distinct but related practices. The first is *commodification* in which, as a result of the activities of industrial designers, public policy makers and regulators and market makers, specific claims for a function and for an identity of a new product or service is made – in this case a new machine, a new piece of software or a new television programme. Commodification also includes, involves and even requires the parallel work of imagination, in which consumers, prompted no doubt by the seductions of advertising and the blandishments of social and cultural competitiveness, engage in the eternally frustrated fantasy that the next commodity will indeed really satisfy.

The second is *appropriation* in which socially located individuals (individuals distinguished by class, age, gender, ethnicity, and as members of families or households) accept enough of the relevance of the publicly defined meaning of something to their own circumstances to buy and then incorporate the new object or product into their own domestic environment. This process of appropriation is an active and to a greater or lesser degree also a transcendent or transformative one because for an object or technology to be accepted it has to be made to fit into a pre-existing culture. It has to be found a space, literally, in the home. It has – if it has a function – to be fitted into a pattern of domestic time. It has, in short, to be invested with value. Such appropriation is complicated, of course, by the social dynamics and politics of families and households. There are conflicts over use and location; over ownership and control. There are anxieties to be dealt with: about the disruption a new product might introduce into the security of familiar routines and rituals, the challenges it might create to an individual's competence or skill, or the threats it offers to a household's moral values. And the pressures to accept or reject, as well as to modify, the meaning of a new object or technology are not generated only by the complex politics of domestic life, but come too from the conflicts between domestic and public values; from, for example, the competing claims of parents or peer groups.

The third component of consumption is one which reconnects the household into the public world of shared meanings and the claims and counterclaims of status and belonging. We call this *conversion* and it signals the importance of the need to legitimate one's participation in consumer culture in the display of competence, and ownership. Such conversion extends from showing off the new videophone to the neighbours to the endless gossip about the latest episode of a soap opera. It is also the case that through conversion that the spiral of consumption continues to turn, for in our converting activities (and not just through initial rejection) those involved in commodification (producers, regulators, advertisers and the rest) learn about consumption and may or may not alter their products and services to fit what they think they have learned.

These three dimensions of the process of consumption are also three moments in both the domestication of (in this case) new technologies and services, and of the construction of the domestic itself. Media and information technologies are central to both because they are themselves both objects to be consumed and the facilitators (through their status as media) of consumption. Through our involvement with them we learn both how to consume and what to consume. And through our involvement in consumption we learn to display who and what we are.[4]

Our understanding of the place and significance of information and communication technologies in the domestic sphere and the process of domestication which puts them there is in turn dependent on exploring some of the key social and cultural (as well as economic) dimensions of that domesticity. This begins with a concern with the obvious but crucial differences which differential access to economic resources creates. This is a matter not just of the level of disposable income or economic capital, it is also a matter of the allocative rules of family or household income: the pattern of its earning, its management and its control (Pahl, 1989).

However, families and households are much more than economic units. There is also a cultural – a moral – economy to be considered (Silverstone, Hirsch and Morley, 1992). And here we are concerned with the temporal and spatial dimensions of households; with gender and with the gendered division of labour. We are concerned with the domestic politics of households: with who controls access to what – who makes the decisions to purchase, who commands the skills of operation, who has entitlement to privileged access. We are concerned with the dynamics of family and household life in time and through time. This is a matter of the stage the family or household has reached in its life cycle; the presence or absence and age of the children as well its past history and future trajectory. And it is also a matter of charting the pattern of everyday life through a day or a week. And, finally but just as importantly, we are concerned with the household's place within the wider culture; with individuals' isolation from, or involvement with, others through formal or informal networks – both technologically facilitated and face to face.

Running through all these concerns is a focus on values; on priorities, on hopes, fears and anxieties, because it is through values and their expression in language and action that the more objective determinants of social life appear. A family or household's relation to time, for example, is a question not just of the way in which it succeeds or fails in synchronising the activities of its members throughout the day, but it is also a question of orientation: the particularities of its relationship to past, present and future; the particular salience of time itself in its own value system. How far, for example, it is important always to be amongst the first to purchase a new piece of equipment. How crucial is the capacity to 'save time' or 'shift time'?

Will members of a family or household seek out and value new technologies because they enable the recovery of the past (as Walkmen are often seen to be able do musically, or video cameras are seen to be able to do visually) or capture the future (as the computer was, and still is, believed to be able to do, when it is bought by parents in the hope that it will magically transform the economic prospects of their children)?

And we try to understand as much as we can of the dynamics of these things, how they change, what their causes are and what their consequences.

Let me illustrate some of these arguments, by reference to our work with teleworkers and lone parents.

4.4   Teleworking

The teleworkers in our study included both the employed and the self-employed, the professional and clerical, as well as both male and female workers. They included those working with sophisticated computer and telecom equipment and those with limited word-processing facilities and the plain old-fashioned telephone. We studied 22 teleworking households. As I have already indicated the aim of the study was to chart the similarities and differences within the teleworking experience with an especial interest in the consequences of its introduction for the fabric of domestic life, and above all for the changing relationship of home and work, free time and leisure time, and public and private space that one might expect it to signal (Haddon and Silverstone, 1992, 1993).

In our conclusions to this study we outlined four themes. The first concerned the issue of control. The second the issue of the technological culture of the household as a whole. The third the role of social and technical networks. And the fourth the question of flexibility. Together, and in turn, they make the point that media (within which I include both media and information technologies) are themselves mediated. They are mediated by the social, economic and political processes – both public and private – which contain, constrain and facilitate their use.

Control is central. It lies at the heart of the successful management of telework both from the point of view of the capacity of the central organisation to manage its dispersed workforce, and from the point of view of the teleworker him or herself to manage the work. But these control problems are not confined to, nor independent of, the wider politics of both organisation and household. The politics of the household defines a context in which teleworking is more or less successfully adopted. This household politics is a gendered politics. It relates above all to the differential – but remarkably intransigent – responsibilities that men and women have for their households. These differences are exaggerated, perhaps, in families with children. They also depend on the relative status of the work of the teleworker and partner and their material contribution to the income of the household. The male teleworker can bring the office home with very little significant effect on his overall contribution to the everyday life of the household. The fact that he is now at home most of the day (and even with his wife out at work) is not necessarily likely to produce much in the way of the 'new man'. The milk will remain on the doorstep until his wife comes in from the office. And his involvement with the microwave may extend no further than occasional inedible experiments (Silverstone and Morley, 1992).

Nevertheless it can be said that there is nothing more likely to shift these otherwise stubborn patterns of domestic power than the increased income of the previously dependent partner. And in so far as many forms of telework enable women both to extend their contribution to the household resource base (though at the same time often still maintaining primary responsibility for childcare and household tasks) as well as developing their skills, then it can be seen that the domestication of technologically facilitated work (telework) could make significant differences to the politics of the household into which it is introduced. We have some evidence from our study that this can and does happen.

The second conclusion relates to what we have called the technological culture of the household as a whole. Teleworking households, despite enormous variations in sophistication, all share a commitment to the functional use of information and communication technologies. Computers can be, and are, still used for children's games but they must also be used for work.

Telephones can be, and are, still used for conversation and gossip, but they also must become a central link between a professional and his or her clients, a clerical worker and his or her customers, or an employee and his or her manager. It is in this functional commitment that teleworking households are distinctive, and even if we have noted that the domestication of new technologies is never exclusively or unambiguously functional, in such households the claims of work are paramount. How these functional demands extend into the rest of the household, and how far the presence of 'money-making' machines influences the non-teleworkers in a teleworking household to become more involved in the use of technologies varies substantially. No household in our study has succeeded in totally isolating teleworking from the rest of what goes on at home. In this sense then teleworking is always to some extent a compromised activity. On the other hand some encourage its integration (by letting children use the computer, or using the computer for domestic tasks or leisure); some have a hard time keeping it apart (especially in the management of the telephone); in others, for example where there is only a single telephone line or extension for both work and social calls, there are new skills and new rules to be learned as family members find themselves involved, willy-nilly, in the new work culture of the household. And finally teleworking in many households, constrains both the teleworker and non-teleworker's participation in other dimensions of the household's electronically mediated culture – especially where the work machines both displace and disrupt access to television and video.

Teleworking households are, however, even at their least sophisticated, often leaders in the domestication of information and communication technologies. To some extent as a result they become informal (or sometimes formal) apostles for the new domestic arrangements. They become opinion leaders within a wide network of family and friends, as well as experts (or supposed experts) and providers of technical resources in neighbourhood or community. Teleworking then provides some possibilities for compensating for the inevitable isolation that it creates. There is always of course the chicken and egg issue in such cases. We will always find it difficult to distinguish the social isolates who choose teleworking from those whose teleworking produces a degree of social isolation.

The other great claim of the promoters of telework is that it extends flexibility. This flexibility is *de facto* a spatial one. We can, supposedly, choose whether to work at home or not. It is also a temporal one. We can choose when to work. Both of these flexibilities are however far from absolute and in many cases are chimerical. The decision to work from home is not always a voluntary one, nor is it, even in the absence of institutional constraints, an unequivocal one. Likewise, the capacity to define when work will be done is constrained, often determined, as much by the still intrusive demands of public time and the connections that still need to be made to others who are working 9 to 5, as by the more insidious demands of the domestic day and week. Once again the technology offers a potential, at best, which the realities and the pressures of everyday life can either realise or resist.

Teleworking provides an excellent case study for exploring the domestication of the information revolution and of the capacity of technology to transform everyday life, for it suggests that even at its strongest – in the overdetermination of technological change by changes in the organisation of work – technology-linked and defined changes are subject to significant variation in scale, scope and speed once they confront or enter domestic space. Teleworking households are already multimedia households but the relative importance of the media concerned is dependent on function rather than leisure. The commitment to high-tech culture in many such households can, and often does, squeeze out time available for leisure or entertainment. Priorities are set by the demands of work.

4.5   Lone parents

If teleworking is the strongest case against which we can measure the revolutionary capacities of new media and information technologies, the case of the single or lone parent must be the weakest. But it is not quite as simple as this. The exploration of the lone parent and her (principally it is her) relationships to media and information technologies provides an almost equally dramatic illustration of the inequalities of the media revolution, and of the implications of social and economic disadvantage for access to technology. While it is by no means the complete picture even within our own study (a number of the households were economically active and independent) it is the case that those who are struggling to maintain a semblance of home and hearth at the limits set by social security and family income supplements, are struggling with a world in which media and information technologies can be on the one hand seen as a consummate irrelevance and on the other as an absolutely vital link to the society and culture from which they would otherwise be almost entirely excluded.

The empirical work from which the following observations are drawn followed the same procedures as have been defined for the other parts of the study. Twenty lone parents were interviewed and their use of time described. We were concerned here, as elsewhere, to place their consumption and use of media and information technologies in a context of biography and family history, in a context of the patterns of everyday life, and in a context of future expectations and hopes. In no case did we interview the estranged partners.

Lone parenthood is a distinct and different, though still very varied, kind of domesticity. While it is often associated with economic disadvantage (both as a precondition and as a consequence) it is not necessarily such. Some members of the present royal family offer a case in point. In focusing on those amongst our sample who are struggling with economic hardship we do not want to suggest that lone parenthood is in some sense the fault of the individuals concerned or that the problems posed are unique to them. The loss of resources associated with the loss of a partner is only one example of a more general problem of disadvantage. Our purpose in pursuing it in this case is to explore the implications of that material disadvantage for social and cultural participation and for the role of media and information technologies in ameliorating or exacerbating that.

Lone parenthood almost always imposes additional strains on all the individuals involved. The demands of childcare, the inability to leave home, the anxieties associated with financial management, the sense of isolation and loneliness, are all elements in a familiar situation with which many lone parents have to deal. Of course this is not a simple or straightforward matter, and the equation is a complex one. Lone parenthood is sociologically extremely varied and disadvantage is both a complicated and relative notion. Lone parenthood can be, and is, experienced in different ways. While some lone parents are clearly overwhelmed and oppressed both by the weight of poverty and social isolation, others find in their release from what might have been an overwhelming and equally oppressive relationship new freedoms and a new sense of personal space.

However, in a real sense the study was indeed one of technological disadvantage. Lone parents, either unable to work because of the age of their children, or under– (or non-) supported by their estranged partners, are clearly economically extremely vulnerable. This weakness – this poverty – has obvious implications for both their ownership, and their use of, media and information technologies. Televisions are old, bought second hand or at the end of their technological career, having been passed through a network of family or friends. Telephones are never more than plain and old, and in some cases absent entirely. These technological disadvantages have direct and significant implications for the capacity of lone parents to participate in a public world increasingly defined and articulated through such technologies.

It is this theme which emerges as the dominant one in the research. And it is media and information technologies' capacity to provide links with the world beyond the front door which is crucial. Both the telephone and the television are the vital connections with that world, but in both cases use is restricted and the quality of the communication is compromised.

Those lone parents who have telephones, and who see it as a technology which is – sometimes quite literally – a life saver, are never without anxiety about the bills. They manage their calls with enormous care, but equally with constant frustration, since the costs of calling in the morning are perceived as prohibitive and in any event those they might want to call are at work, and by evening childcare responsibilities or the fear of calls waking the baby are equally disincentives. One lone parent in our study without a phone found that she could not participate in the more or less spontaneous activities in her local network simply because she was not contactable. In other cases it is the children who are restricted in their access to the phone and therefore to their own peer group culture. Equally the presence of even a modestly advanced technology does not guarantee that its user can take full advantage of its potential. One lone parent who did have an answerphone recorded a message which asked her callers to call back, since she felt unable to pay the cost of returning the calls herself. This is yet another example of the way in which the presence of the technology is not by itself enough to facilitate a change in social relations, but on the contrary an example of how economic and social constraints limit how a technology will be used.

Likewise with television: poor reception on old sets; limited ownership of videos; the constraints of space and time; cost; as well as the distinct quality of family or household culture make access to, and use of, television just as problematic. In one household television watching is rationed not for fear of its influence on the children but because of the cost of the electricity to power it. In another it is used as a low level light source for the late night or early morning feeding of the baby. In yet a third the mother feels that she need not be too concerned about the effects of violence on the screen since her children have seen so much real violence in their own lives – against her from her ex-boyfriend. Nevertheless for many, many lone parents the television is a companion, a source of information about the world to which they have otherwise little access, and a source of pleasure, and shareable pleasure amongst friends and acquaintances.

This pattern of media and information technology use – or under-use – has to be understood too in a wider social context: one in which, for example, mobility might be restricted both by the costs of public transport and the challenges of managing double strollers in supermarkets, shopping malls and public transport. It has to be understood in the context, often, of a wider anxiety about the dangers of being out and about in public space. It has to be understood, too, in a context of pressures from children who in their turn are pressured by their peer group and sometimes by their estranged father. The household politics of lone parenthood is both more simple and more complex than that of one in which two parents are present. For while the lone parent may have a much less compromised relationship to her children for much of the week, for many the weekends take the children into another household, a household which is often economically more secure and one in which the seductions of media and information culture and technology are much more in evidence. This is the source, often, of both conflict and anxiety for the primary carer.

My point in raising something of the experiences of this group here – a group which I am well aware is not likely to be in the forefront of any new multimedia revolution – is the reason for conducting this part of the study in the first place. It is to draw attention to the scale and implications of the inequalities of our so-called media revolution. Lone parents, and they are not unique, find as a result of social and economic circumstance that their full participation in a world of advancing media and information technologies is being denied. That exclusion is not insignificant. Far from being able to take advantage of the benefits of new media and information technology – and in most cases being unaware of what those advantages might be – they are progressively being denied access to those benefits. These are benefits that include full participation in contemporary media culture as well as the benefits derived from participation in an information culture which in many practical ways – for example access to public information databases, or the ability to work from home – would enhance the quality of their lives.

It is through this exclusion that such groups are being forced into a media and information under-class. They are forced to become increasingly marginal consumers of inadequate technologies, and as a result they run the risk of becoming, both relatively and absolutely, socially, culturally and politically isolated.

4.6   Conclusion

Let me draw some of the threads of my argument together. The main point I want to make is that an awareness of the dynamics and processes of everyday life is a precondition for understanding the present and the future of technological change. It is to say first of all that one cannot read off the trajectory of social and cultural change from an analysis of technological change. Technology is a social product, a product of the complex, uneven and uncertain politics of development and regulation (Mackenzie and Wacjman, 1985) and the consequences of its introduction are just as complex, uneven and uncertain. It is to say, secondly, that innovation itself is a historically and a sociologically situated process involving many different players with different and competing interests, but it is one above all that does not stop at the point of purchase. Consumers are active not just in making the decision to purchase and handing over their money for a new good or service. Their activity extends, particularly in their use of media and information technologies and services, into the ways in which these technologies and services become (or do not become) both meaningful and useful. And, as I have pointed out, those dynamics are neither predictable nor uncontradictory.

It is to say, thirdly, that there can be no such thing as a technologically led revolution of everyday life, if by revolution we mean a more or less uniform transformation of the way in which we conduct our activities in the daily round. It is precisely the fundamental differences and inequalities within everyday life, its rationalities and irrationalities, its utopian fantasies and its anxious fears, that define the particular, uneven and often stumbling path both of innovation and technologically led social change. And it is to say finally that if we were desirous of stimulating some such revolution we would need to take into account not just the social and cultural dimensions of the domestic and everyday lives of those in a position to take advantage of what new technologies might offer, but also the circumstances that deny a substantial sector of our population from even getting a whiff of the gunshot.

As for a technologically convergent or multimedia future, what these examples begin to show is that it is likely to be full of paradoxes. High-tech households may be low-tech when it comes to entertainment. And low-tech households who are high consumers of home-based entertainment will not be able to afford the latest technology or services. I acknowledge, of course, that the high-tech teleworker and the low-tech single parent are extremes, but it is often necessary to point to the extremes in order to illustrate what would otherwise be even more difficult to see in the more mundane realities of everyday life. The space between is of course where the particular future of multimedia will be won or lost. And the winning or losing will be determined as much if not more than by the activities of engineers, designers and advertisers, by the successes or failures of families and households – differentiated by class and culture – actively to engage in the domestication of media, communication and information technologies: to bring new machines and services into their homes and to make them their own. I hope I have illustrated something of what we need to take into account if we are better to understand this process.

References

Bourdieu, P. (1984). *Distinction: A Social Critique of the Judgement of Taste*, London, Routledge and Kegan Paul.

Cawson, A. (forthcoming). Interactive computer disc-based multimedia. In: A. Cawson, L. Haddon, & I. Miles, *The Shape of Things to Consume: Bringing Information Technology into the Home*.

Douglas, M. & Isherwood, B. (1979). *The World of Goods: Towards an Anthropology of Consumption*, Harmondsworth, Penguin.

Fanshaw, D. G. J. (1994). Home systems. In: K. Berg, & K. Borreby, (eds.) *HOIT (Home Oriented Informatics and Telematics) 94: Proceedings of an International Cross-disciplinary Conference*, Copenhagen, June 27th – July 1st, pp. 363–372.

Haddon, L & Silverstone, R. (1992). Information and communication technologies in the home: the case of teleworking, CICT/SPRU Working Paper 17, University of Sussex, October.

Haddon, L. & Silverstone, R. (1993). *Teleworking in the 1990s: A View from the Home*, SPRU CICT Report Series, 10, University of Sussex, August.

Mackenzie, D. & Wacjman, J. (1985). *The Social Shaping of Technology*, Milton Keynes, Open University Press.

Maslow, A. H. (1954). *Motivation and Personality*, New York, Harper and Row.

Miller, D. (1987). *Material Culture and Mass Consumption*, Oxford, Blackwell.

Pahl, J. (1989). *Money and Marriage*, London, Macmillan.

Silverstone, R. (1994). *Television and Everyday Life*, London, Routledge.

Silverstone, R. & Haddon, L. (1993). *Future compatible? Information and communication technologies in the home: a methodology and a case study.* A report prepared for the Commission of the European Communities Socio-Economic and technical Impact Assessments and Forecasts, RACE Project 2086, SPRU, Sussex.

Silverstone, R. & Haddon, L. (forthcoming), Design and the domestication of ICTs: households, families and technical change. In: R. Mansell & R. Silverstone (eds.) *Communication by Design: The Politics of Information and Communication Technologies*, Oxford, Oxford University Press.

Silverstone, R. & Morley, D. (1991). Families and their technologies: two ethnographic portraits. In: D. Putnam & C. Newton (eds.) *Household Choices*, London, Futures Publications, pp. 74–83.

Silverstone, R., Hirsch, E. & Morley, D. (1992). Information and communication technologies and the moral economy of the household. In: R. Silverstone & E. Hirsch. (1992). *Consuming Technologies: Media and Information in Domestic Spaces*, London, Routledge, pp. 15–31.

Thrall, C. A. (1982). The Conservative Use of Modern Household Technology, *Technology and Culture*, 23 (2), pp. 175–194.

Notes

1   This is a point about how difficult it is for users of technology to imagine, let alone conceptualise what they want from the 'next' technology. Abraham Maslow's (1954) hierarchy of needs is often cited as the starting point for an analysis of demand and of future consumption patterns. Such analyses (eg. , failing as they mostly do to consider that needs are socially constructed, rarely in turn succeed in getting beyond an elementary and inadequate understanding both of the complexity of need as a social phenomenon and, in its stimulation by the rhetorics of, among other things, advertising, as a political one (cf. Fanshaw, 1994).

2   The fieldwork for this research is currently being conducted by Leslie Haddon who has also provided a number of extremely helpful comments on earlier drafts of this paper.

3   We are beginning to conceptualise this relationship in terms of a 'design/domestication interface', in which the motivated activities of producers in a world of mass produced objects and artefacts confront the no less motivated activities of consumers who, with varying degrees of competence and freedom, work to convert those objects and artefacts into materially and symbolically meaningful resources in their everyday lives (see Silverstone and Haddon, forthcoming).

4   For a more developed and contextualised account of this model of the consumption process, see Silverstone (1994).

5

Driving into the future of communications?
Check the rear view mirror

William H. Dutton

The press, industry and government are approaching the 21st century with a renewed optimism about the future of communications. Despite controversy over the details, contemporary visions of information superhighways, multimedia networks and virtual communities have rekindled the imagination of journalists, leaders of business and industry and politicians alike. Unfortunately, most optimistic forecasts skate too quickly over the past, as if the industry had no memory. Earlier efforts to introduce video phones, video conferencing, interactive television and videotext services are instructive. These same services remain central to many present day scenarios for a multimedia future. However, past experience can be problematic as a guide to the future, particularly with respect to information and communication technologies, where industry has made major advances over the last several decades. While the lessons drawn from this history are open to debate, it seems unwise to venture full speed onto the new information highways without reflecting on earlier experience. It is one of the only empirically grounded perspectives we have on the future of communications.

5.1   Introduction

Visions of information superhighways, global networks and virtual communities, combined with concrete technological advances and huge 'multimedia' mergers, have rekindled interest in video phones, interactive services and all sorts of other new media. On occasion, proponents of new multimedia services will acknowledge the controversial history of earlier innovations, such as the Picturephone. However, very few draw lessons from this history to inform discussion of the future of communications.[1]

It has become a cliché within the industry that you should not fix your eyes on the rear view mirror if you are driving into the future. This is a legitimate caution, particularly in an area like communications in which technological advances, regulatory change and public policy shifts can fundamentally change the political and economic rationality of alternative courses of development.

Nevertheless, safe drivers check the rear view mirror to help them steer forward successfully. Past efforts to introduce video telephones, video conferencing systems, interactive cable television and videotext are a source of possible insights for developing and introducing new interactive services. Digital video, multimedia and virtual reality sound quite new, but they offer different means for providing many of the same services and are built on many of the same assumptions as technologies of earlier years. These early trials and offerings can provide at least two useful types of insight valuable to new media developments.

First, they suggest areas of continuity and discontinuity with the past. In many ways the offerings of today are not new. It is useful to isolate these genuinely new features, if we wish to draw appropriate analogies between the past and present. Second, they offer an empirical basis to the growing and often ungrounded debate among media and telecommunications pundits over the opportunities and problems shaping the future of telecommunications, which discussion of the information superhighway has brought into full swing.

This chapter looks back at illustrative episodes in the history of new media ventures to see 'What's really new?' and 'What lessons can be learned?'. In the next section, I will discuss several areas of continuity with the past because it is this continuity in part that suggests we have much to learn from past experience.

5.2   Continuities and discontinuities[2]

Discussion of 'information superhighways', 'global multimedia mergers' and the 'fibersphere' creates a sense of revolutionary change in the making (Gilder, 1992; Lucky, 1989). We might well be facing a dramatic qualitative as well as quantitative change in telecommunication infrastructures and services. However, there are fundamental areas of continuity in the visions and services central to these new ventures, while there has been a noticeable shift in the geographical scope and backgrounds of the key players.

A return to earlier visions

Despite revolutionary developments in communications technology over the last several decades, the dominant images of the future of telecommunications have returned to many themes of an earlier period. While submerged in the mid to late 1980s, optimistic 1960s scenarios of all kinds of electronic services reaching all households and businesses of the major industrial nations are once again likely to shape policy and practice. 'Information superhighways' are reminiscent of earlier proposals for public information utilities as well as the information highways of a 'wired nation'.

In the 1960s, the development of online interactive computer systems fostered proposals for a 'public information utility' (Sackman and Nie, 1970; Sackman and Boehm, 1972). These computer utilities had many features in common with the idea of an information superhighway. Technology has changed, i.e., personal computers replace dumb terminals and gigabyte networks replace dial-up access, but the underlying conception of public access to huge electronic stores of information is remarkably similar.

Also in the 1960s, advances in cable systems spawned discussion of 'interactive' cable television (Smith, 1970). This was illustrated particularly by the development of coaxial cable – literally defined as the 'information highway' of that time – and the idea of marrying this with interactive computer technology. Academics and journalists outlined the exciting prospect of people being able to compute, shop, vote, send electronic mail, get medical assistance, and access information, radio, television and films over coaxial cable. This convergence of services over a single medium, albeit using analog versus digital signals, generated many of the same futuristic visions as today. This early vision became popularized as the 'wired nation' in which all households and businesses would have access to an integrated array of all kinds of electronic information and communications services (Dutton, Blumler and Kraemer, 1987; Goldmark, 1972; Smith, 1970, 1972).

Grand visions of the future of interactive communications could not withstand the perceived market failure of interactive cable TV in the early 1980s, particularly with the growing sense that a number of commercial videotext services were also floundering. They were replaced by more technocratic images of the future.

One of these was the push for 'ISDN' or integrated services digital network. This concept never succeeded in capturing the imagination of a non-technical constituency and even became a focus of jokes within the technical community, as everyone came up with their own words for renaming this acronym, such as 'Incredible Services We Don't Need'. Yet many services centrepieced by the promoters of ISDN were strikingly similar to those currently promoted by the developers of multimedia. Promotional videos of

ISDN often portrayed business colleagues, far removed from each other, simultaneously editing a document while consulting over a video conferencing link.

Since the mid-1980s, the idea of a 'Broadband-Integrated Services Digital Network' (B-ISDN) had a brief period of ascendence related to dozens of fibre-to-the-home (FTTH) trials in the US and elsewhere (McGilly, Kawahata & Dutton, 1990). Most of these were limited to technical trials with less than 200 subscribers. Driven by a few telephone companies and manufacturers, over two-thirds of the FTTH trials focused on voice telephony services only, comparable to the services provided over twisted wire pairs. Another 19 per cent experimented with cable TV as well as telephone services. Only about 1 in 10 experimented with broadband telecommunication services (McGilly, Kawahata & Dutton, 1990).

In the 1960s, telecommunications was viewed and later regulated as a vehicle for social and political reform. One reason is that the concept of a wired city in the US was developed in the context of Lyndon Johnson's so-called Great Society. In the 1980s, communication came to be viewed and deregulated as a vehicle for international trade and economic development, during a period in which policy arguments were dominated by economists wedded to competition versus regulation as the most efficient means to control prices and service. Public service visions were muted in favour of more nuts and bolts technical trials. In the 1990s, at least in the US, there has been continuing interest in telecommunications as an industrial strategy, but also a renewed commitment to using telecommunications to again pursue various social goals and objectives under a new Democratic administration.

The pursuit of convergence

The term 'multimedia' is new and has become the choice of journalists writing about almost any new media development. This reflects the prominence of the multimedia personal computer as a defining technology of the mid-1990s, just as videotext was often used as a generic covering term for new media developments of the early 1980s, before its market failure. The multimedia personal computer has also caught attention because it seems to be the latest embodiment of the idea of 'convergence' – the integration of the once separate technologies and industries of print, broadcasting and telecommunications.

The eventual realisation of convergence along with the transformation from analog to digital systems might well enable many old services to be provided in ways that fundamentally change the way we use the media. The vision of Nicholas Negroponte and others at MIT's Media Lab, for example, entails a shift from mass to more personalised media services as more intelligence can be embedded in telecommunication networks (Brand, 1987). Nevertheless, the idea of convergence should be familiar to the telecommunications industry.

The wired nation of the 1960s was anchored in the idea that radio, television, telecommunications, electronic mail, videotext, and more would all be conveyed to the business and home over the same coaxial cable infrastructure. Digital technology was not essential to convergence, as it is sometimes suggested, but analog or digital, convergence is far more than a technical issue of multiplexing signals within a single conduit. It entails industrial as well as technological restructuring and therefore has been far more difficult to achieve than the technical issues alone would lead us to believe.

Familiar new services

Most of the actual applications said to be enabled by the new 'multimedia' are also familiar to those tracking field trials and experiments over the years. Specifically, technological advances, such as in compression, switching and storage media, are expected to facilitate the provision of video telephony and conferencing, interactive television, video-on-demand, video and audiotext services, electronic mail and conferencing as well as applications of virtual reality. These services are in addition to conventional telephone, facsimile, cable and broadcasting services, which should be available at higher levels of fidelity and resolution in a fully digital future.

Over the last two decades, the major applications promoted today, including video-on-demand, multimedia, home shopping and video communications, were piloted in one or more sites around the world. Table 5.1 provides a selected list of some of the trials and offerings that might inform current discussion of each type of service enabled by advances in information and communication technologies. Many of these are discussed below.

In 1994, for example, video-on-demand trials in the US and UK vied for recognition as the first in the world, when video-on-demand was a central feature of the Hi-OVIS (Highly Interactive-Optical Visual Information System) project in the early 1980s. Hi-OVIS was an interactive cable television experiment in Higashi-Ikoma, Japan. They offered a video-on-demand service for about five years, although it was called a 'video request service' and limited to three channels – what today is sometimes called 'near video-on-demand'. Nevertheless, it was sophisticated enough to utilise a robot in the cable studio that would retrieve video cassettes and insert them in the video tape monitors for play back to the home. A decade later, a trial of video-on-demand in the US depended on a human being fetching video cassettes for play back to only four homes included on the network.

As noted above, multimedia personal computers are new, but there have been earlier introductions of multimedia terminals, such as in France Telecom's Biarritz trial and there are ways in which the history of videotext services could inform discussion of multimedia services. Perhaps the best example of continuity of service offerings is the cycle of attention given to interactive television services.

Type of Service	Selected Trials, Prototypes & Offerings
Video telecommunication	AT&T's Picturephone AT&T's VideoPhone 2500 France Telecom's Biarritz Trial Confravision AT&T's Picturephone Meeting Service
Two-way, Interactive	Interactive cable TV experiments (NSF, Hi-OVIS) Warner's QUBE Interactive television network GTE's Main Street Screen phones
Video-on-demand	Hi-OVIS Fiber-to-the-home trials (e.g., Cerritos) Video rental stores
Electronic mail & conferencing	Videotext (Prestel, Times Mirror and others) Arpanet, Internet Public and private bulletin boards
Multimedia Personal Computer or Game Machine	Videotext (Prestel, Times Mirror and others) Columbus, Ulysses Games (e.g., Nintendo and others) Multimedia Kiosks (e.g., Info California)

Table 5.1. Early trials and offerings of new services and applications.

Interactivity: continuing efforts to awaken a passive audience

'Interactivity' has regained a great deal of currency. Interactive television, interactive cable – even 'interactive Teddy Bears' – are among the range of new services of the 1990s. Again, however, interactive services have a quite interesting history over the last several decades (Dutton, Blumler and Kraemer, 1987).

In the early 1970s, 'wired city' experiments were tied most directly to both governmental and corporate investments in 'interactive cable television' projects in the US and Japan. In 1973, the Japanese Ministry of Posts and Telecommunications initiated a local cable TV experiment in Tama New Town, which was followed later by the Ministry of International Trade and Industry's launch of the Hi-OVIS project.

In 1974, the US National Science Foundation (NSF) supported a series of experiments with interactive cable, which joined academic researchers with cable operators in Reading, Pennsylvania; Spartanburg, South Carolina; and Rockford, Illinois (Becker, 1987). As technical trials, they demonstrated that a variety of public and commercial services could be provided over two-way cable systems (Brownstein, 1978). But these same experiments also cast doubt over any widespread consumer interest in new information services, suggesting that interactive offerings were only marginally, if at all, more effective than conventional broadcasts – but significantly more costly (Becker, 1987; Elton 1980).

So even by the mid-1970s, when these early NSF experiments and trials were first operational, glamorous images of consumer response to interactive cable had already begun to fade. Nevertheless, in 1977, Warner-Amex, a subsidiary of Warner Communications, introduced QUBE, a 30-channel interactive cable television system, on a commercial basis (Davidge, 1987). It was launched in Columbus, Ohio because this city was a test market of a number of products. A primary business rationale behind QUBE was to use interactive cable for audience research. QUBE offered two main interactive capabilities: it permitted viewers to send an up-stream data signal for polling or ordering a pay television programme and it permitted the cable operator to continually sweep homes to monitor who was watching which channel.

This second feature of their interactive network was the most central to their trials of new programming ideas, eventually leading to the national launch of such programmes as Nickelodeon, a children's television programme, and MTV, a video music channel (Davidage, 1987). Its live and interactive programmes were able to regularly draw nearly a quarter of QUBE subscribers, but they were never profitable given the costs of the productions for a local audience (Davidage, 1987: 84–85). Warner-Amex pulled the plug on QUBE in 1984 in large part because of the losses which its parent company, Warner Communications, incurred with its Atari subsidiary, when video game sales fell well below forecasts.

Hi-OVIS was in operation from 1978 to 1986. During its initial phase, the trial tested technical aspects of the system, while after 1980, they turned their attention to the market for and commercial viability of the services provided over the system, including retransmissions of television signals, character and still picture information services, video request services, and two-way interactive voice and video services. The trial was terminated in March, 1986, failing in the sense that the system was not diffused to other communities as a commercial venture.

As early as the 1970s, requiems were written for the 'wired city' and interactive television. Yet even in the mid-1990s, the future of interactive TV remains uncertain and the vision continues to motivate new service offerings. New 'interactive' television projects generally piggy-back on existing broadcasts of game shows and sporting events as opposed to being produced from scratch as interactive productions. The California-based Interactive Network Inc. uses a hybrid communication system. This combines broadcast television, FM radio and telephone systems to allow viewers to, say, play along with game shows from their homes, using a hand-held terminal that can receive the simulcast radio signals. A different system, marketed in the UK by Interactive Network Ltd, uses on-screen graphics, the vertical blanking interval rather than FM radio and provides four low-cost handsets so that members of the household can compete with one another as well as the larger audience as they view TV game shows. These systems dramatically lower the costs of interactive entertainment, by piggy-backing on existing broadcasts, and therefore raise new possibilities for establishing an audience over time.

Discontinuities

One discontinuity has been a shift in the geographical orientation of new media from local to more national and global networks. In the 1960s, the wired city was built on a foundation of local as well as interactive cable TV, in which the local orientation of systems was as significant as the notion of interactivity. In Britain, for example, this period was marked by experiments in community cable TV rather than interactive cable. This local orientation was in part driven by the early history of cable systems, which began as local 'community antenna systems' (CATV), as well as the belief that cable technology was inherently local since the attenuation of signals downstream limited the area covered by early CATV systems. In the US, it was also supported by a tradition in broadcasting that favoured, but failed to foster, localism. In fact, the arrival of satellite-linked cable systems in the late 1970s was the major impetus to the wider diffusion of cable systems in the US.

Many advocates of superhighways for the 21st century seem more focused on national information infrastructures, but with clear ambitions for extending them to a more global scale. This was driven by a variety of factors including the greater value of any network that could provide similar levels of service around the world, such as was the case with Internet as well as ordinary telephone networks. There are some exceptions to this global orientation, such as the emergence of local electronic bulletin board systems like Santa Monica, California's Public Electronic Network and, in the UK, Manchester's HOST system, where a local orientation is a central feature of the services. Another exception is the emergence of successful initiatives to launch 'neighbourhood television', such as in New England, USA (Dutton, Guthrie, O'Connell and Wyer, 1991). Yet these remain exceptional, despite the possibility that localism remains one of the few strategic advantages of wired over wireless systems, such as direct satellite broadcasting.

Another discontinuity is found in the centrality of the 'techies'. They represent a new set of players – technically adept networkers within the Internet community – who have risen to take a leadership role in debates over the future of communications. David Ronfeldt of the Rand Corporation refers to the experts in computer networking as 'cybercrats'. Clearly, the cybercrats influenced thinking within the Clinton–Gore administration and leaders within the computing industry, such as Bill Gates of Microsoft, have become key visionaries, reaching outside the computer industry per se. While leaders within the computing world were important to visions of a public information utility in the 1960s, and some like James Martin have remained key to discussions of the future of telecommunications, they seem to have been less central than leaders of the cable and telecommunications industry until recently.

Undoubtedly, the rise of players from an industry not previously well connected to entertainment and information services to the public at large is one factor undermining lessons from past experience. In the 1970s, cable enthusiasts included many investors and journalists unfamiliar with the broadcasting industry and therefore less sceptical than they might have been about the promise of local and interactive television. In the 1980s, most telephone company executives considering the provision of video-on-demand via fibre to the home were not closely involved with cable and broadcasting services. Likewise, many of the computer techies of the 1990s were not even alive when their predecessors advocated the construction of a public information utility and are also distanced from cable and broadcasting services.

5.3   Reflections

Some recurring issues cut across this history of telecommunication trials and commercial offerings. They are only a subset of any list that might be culled from this history.

The importance of visions

Al Gore and Bill Clinton captured the attention of politicians and journalists in the US and elsewhere in the early 1990s with their evolving concept of an 'information superhighway'. Public officials are now being asked to knock down all sorts of barriers between cable, telephone and broadcasting that might constrain the construction of a modern information infrastructure. Like the 'wired cities' concept, the idea of an information superhighway has gained a great deal of legitimacy in debate within industry and policy circles. If the past is any guide, we can expect this vision to play an important role in shaping public policy, whether or not it results in the concrete developments that its advocates propose. The 'information superhighway', 'multimedia' and 'wired cities' are often dismissed as rhetoric. As Professor Eli Noam of Columbia University put it: *"Words, words, words."* But words do matter.

A journalist, Ralph Lee Smith, popularised notions of a wired city in ways that helped convince key people at the US Federal Communications Commission (FCC) that the long-term social and economic benefits made it worth the known risks to the broadcast industry to knock down regulatory barriers to the development of cable and create regulation aimed at achieving the technological infrastructure of the wired city. Based on these visions of a wired nation, local and interactive cable TV experiments were undertaken in a number of nations in the 1970s. These visions led several companies to construct interactive systems on a commercial basis, such as QUBE. The axing of QUBE in 1984 reflected a general sense that local and interactive cable systems were not commercially viable at that time. Nevertheless, the cable TV industry moved into a more central role in broadcasting, at least in the US and Canada, if not in Britain, France and Germany.

A BBC *Horizon* programme, entitled 'Now the Chips are Down', provided a compelling view of the challenges confronting the British economy and provided a vision of Britain seizing opportunities to create new industries and compete internationally in areas such as software development where the UK might enjoy a competitive advantage. This programme and its vision played a significant role in convincing key ministers and civil servants in Britain to develop policies aimed at addressing the industrial implications of the microelectronics revolution in information and communication technologies. In fact, the 'chip' might have been as powerful a symbol in Britain during the early 1980s as the 'superhighway' has become in the US a decade later.

In the case of FTTH trials in the US, the lack of any compelling vision of the future of communications mattered greatly. Promoters of FTTH promised little beyond the targeting of video-on-demand as a source of revenue for constructing new telecommunication infrastructures. In this case, the lack of a compelling social and economic vision left the telephone companies with little support within the FCC and Congress, who saw no reason to jeopardise the cable television industry to create a video juke box. It was only when new telecommunication infrastructures became tied more closely to national economic competition, in part by way of the information highway metaphor, that the telephone companies gained more support among regulators and politicians.

The idea of a wired city captured the imagination of regulators and reconfigured communication policy in the United States. We might therefore expect contemporary discussion of multimedia superhighways to influence developments, if not always in the ways their promoters and originators expected or hoped.

Predictions of the unpredictable

Those who have tracked the history of innovations in information and communication technology learn to distrust nearly any forecast (Elton, 1991). Forecasters have had a remarkably poor track-record in anticipating the public's response to communication and information technologies. On the one hand, exciting forecasts of major markets for interactive cable television, the videophone, and videotext services were not fulfilled. On the other hand, dreary forecasts of a limited future for the facsimile machine, wireless telephony and video cassette recorders proved to be wildly off the mark as well.

Video telecommunications is a case in point. The idea of a telephone that transmits and receives images on a screen is at least as old as television. Bell Labs began experiments with video telephony in the 1950s, leading to the display of a prototype at the 1964 World's Fair in New York City. A number of major telephone equipment manufacturers designed video phones in the 1960s, including Nippon Electric Company, Stromberg-Carlson and the British Post Office (Dickson and Bowers, 1974).

AT&T developed the Picturephone for the commercial market in the late 1960s, forecasting a market of up to 1 percent of all domestic and 3 percent of all business phones by 1980 (Martin, 1977). It was to become a business status symbol. The Picturephone was even equipped with a signal that would indicate if the person called did or did not have a video phone, hoping to elicit the kind of social pressure exerted around the answering machine in the 1990s: '*You don't have an answering machine?*' Picturephone never reached this stage. Faced with an exceedingly limited response from business, AT&T withdrew the Picturephone in 1973 after investing from $130–500 million in its development (Dickson and Bowers, 1974).

In 1979, France Telecom, the government-owned telecommunications monopoly chose Biarritz, a resort and tourist centre in the south-west of

France, as the site for an experimental fibre optic network providing voice, video and data services. The government's objectives were to develop the technical know-how for building and installing fibre optic systems, and also to showcase French technology. France Telecom hoped also to explore the market for broadband services. The first 50 subscribers were connected in 1984, and all 1,500 residences covered by the project were connected by the summer of 1986.

The Biarritz system provided distributed services, including 15 cable TV channels and 12 stereo sound channels, and switched services, including video telephony. Subscribers were provided with a multiservice integrated (multimedia) terminal with a video monitor, camera, keyboard and telephone handset. The terminal could be used as a video telephone to transmit still or full-motion images. Subscribers could consult on-line image and data banks and access any of the thousands of videotext services provided over the Teletel system (better known as Minitel). Subscribers were charged a monthly tariff for cable service and both a monthly fee and a usage-sensitive rate for switched services.

France Telecom found that 'only a minority of connected households in Biarritz used their terminal as a videophone or picturephone, and only after a fairly long period of adaptation' (France Telecom, Fibre Trail Network: June, 1986, p. 15; Gérin & Tavernost, 1987). Later, in 1992, AT&T reintroduced a videophone, calling its product the VideoPhone 2500. Other companies, including Mitsubishi, Sony and BT, launched similar products in the 1990s. As before, the public's response to these video telephone services (in the short term at least) has been far below the expectations of its developers.

A. Michael Noll, a professor of communications and a former enthusiast of video services, who conducted market research on the video phone and video conferencing within AT&T, has taken such responses as solid evidence that the public simply does not need or want video telecommunications (Noll, 1992). Many others continue to regard video telephony as inevitable, once the cost and design are right. However, it is difficult to make any definitive judgement about the future of video telecommunications on the basis of such trials and offerings as Picturephone and Biarritz. Not only are both the technology and market constantly changing, but there are also multiple explanations for why each product has failed within the marketplace, from the absence of trigger services, through human factors' design issues and the lack of a critical mass, to concerns over privacy and cost (Table 5.2).

Optimists can identify changes, such as providing video communications within a window on a personal computer, that improve the prospects for a service that once failed. Sceptics of the new media can find much evidence from past failures to argue that history will simply be repeated. However, failure itself is a matter of some controversy.

For example, QUBE is often labelled a failure because local and interactive TV never became profitable and was dropped. However, local and interactive services drew a sizeable audience, QUBE provided a test market for new programming (e.g., yielding Nickelodeon and Music Television) and won Warner-Amex a number of major urban cable franchises. A business decision to withdraw from a market is likely to be based on a variety of rationales beyond the success or failure of a new service in the 'marketplace', such as the decision to drop QUBE, which was based in part on losses in the video game business by another Warner subsidiary.

If the existence of uncertainty is acknowledged, then industry and government can take a long-term perspective. Policies would aim at stimulating more field trials, encouraging more experimentation, accepting more failures, and supporting continued research and development rather than targeting sure winners.

Capturing the public's interest

When I first demonstrated digital video to my class at the University of Southern California I was astonished by their response. I had just shown them over 30 seconds of motion video with text and sound – all stored on a 3.5 inch diskette! All they had to say was: 'Television is better'. Many trials of new services experience the same reaction. Enthusiasm for some breakthroughs in video over telephone wires, multimedia and interactivity are basically technological versus market advances.

The personal computer was in some respects a technological breakthrough in microelectronics. However, its success beyond the hobbyist market was based on its provision of real trigger services, such as word processing and spreadsheets, which individuals would purchase a personal computer in order to use. Many of the new media have yet to offer this so-called trigger service or infamous 'killer ap' that will create a demand for the technology.

The hype that surrounds most new media ventures creates expectations of improved services that often do not square with the reality. Interactive cable was one case in point where great expectations were dashed by actual systems, which were generally limited to simple audience response systems permitting the polling of individuals from their homes. While interactive cable TV was judged to be a marginal success for some types of programming, these systems cost cable operators nearly three times the expense of installing a conventional cable network. Likewise, video-on-demand is based on the proven market for Hollywood movies. Television viewing and video rental stores support that claim. But the public is unlikely to be satisfied with lower quality video, even if available on demand and if they can beat the price at the video rental store.

Lessons:	Trigger Service	Design: Image v. Reality	Critical Mass	Media Habits	Privacy	Cost
POTS						√√
Video phone		√	√√	√	√	√√
Video conferencing	√	√√	√√	√	√	√√
Interactive TV		√		√√	√	√√
Video on demand		√			√	√√
Electronic mail & conferencing		√	√		√	√
Multimedia	√√	√		√		√√

Table 5.2. Reactions to field trials and commercial offerings of new services. Key: √ = a problem highlighted by field trials and experments.

In the early 1990s, the multimedia personal computer remained more of a technological than market breakthrough. It is conceivable that the multimedia personal computer could provide the facility for accessing all of the new services, from video telephony to personal computing, at least in business. A multitude of applications have been promoted for this technology in business (e.g., training), education (e.g., hypertext archiving and searching) and entertainment (e.g., games). But none of these offers the clear trigger service for the public at large, comparable to word processing or spreadsheets for the personal computer.

The most enthusiastic promoters of multimedia see the public interfacing with huge electronic libraries and video juke boxes through a mulltimedia window in which they control what and when they watch. In many respects, this scenario makes problematic assumptions about the public's interest in information, which I discuss below, and in exerting greater control over content. As experiments with interactive TV suggest, it is not clear that individuals wish to actively become involved in the control of video, particularly as a medium for their entertainment.

The desperation surrounding the search for a trigger service is evident in the claim that prurient interest will propel the multimedia market. Pornography is often suggested as the trigger for multimedia with quite incredible figures about the proportion of CD-ROMs for example that are devoted to pornographic material. 'High tech peep shows' are claimed to be the new 'killer application' (John Tierney, New York Times, Jan 9, 1993). Others argue that the impact of this market has already been felt (Greenberger, 1992: 142). Experience with other media underscores this point. Adult films were among the most popular pay-per-view movies on QUBE (Davidge, 1987), but they were not popular enough to generate a profit for QUBE or a market for interactive cable TV.

One interesting potential for multimedia lies in the use of kiosks in the delivery of electronic services, particularly in the public sector. The Department of Social Services in Tulare County, California has developed a kiosk system, which uses a multilingual, video and audio touch-screen connected to an expert system. Welfare clients step up to a kiosk at a district office, choose which language they wish to use, and are walked through a welfare application. The project was aimed at reducing costs by using the capabilities of an expert system to minimize errors in determining eligibility and calculating payments.

In late October 1991, California's Department of Motor Vehicles launched a nine-month pilot project called 'Info California' (Dutton et al., 1991). Fifteen information kiosks were initially placed in Sacramento and San Diego to pilot this experiment, permitting citizens to conduct a variety of transactions, such as registering an out-of-state vehicle. The system, developed by IBM and North Communications, was modelled after an automated teller machine. Based on early experience, the project has been extended and most recently drawn on by the State of California as a means to get more information to the victims of the 1993 earthquake in Los Angeles.

The interesting prospect surrounding electronic public services is that they provide an opportunity for the public to avoid things they don't like to do, such as waiting in queues or calling from office to office to locate relevant service providers. However, it is not the technology of the multimedia kiosk that will lead individuals to use the systems, but real improvements in service delivery.

Overcoming existing media habits

Many innovations in information and communication technology, such as flat screen displays and portable telephones, simply make it easier to do what users are already in the habit of doing – working at a computer or talking on the phone. But many trials of new media have bumped up against the existing media habits of the general public. As Hazel Kahan (1984), who worked with the QUBE system, put it: you should never underestimate the difficulty of getting someone to do something they have never done before, such as talk to their TVs, particularly if it's something they don't like to do. In the case of interactive television, most people watch television quite passively, sometimes treating the TV as the modern equivalent of the fire place. Habits change slowly.

In US and Japanese trials of interactive cable, providers could constantly monitor channel selections. One thing they learned was that even an activity as limited as channel selection took years to change from a habit of watching one channel all evening to more frequently switching from one channel to another. For better or worse, we take it for granted in the 1990s, particularly in multichannel environments like the US, that many people often graze through programmes, watching TV as often or more than they watch individual programmes. But this pattern took over a decade to develop and was not an immediate impact of remote control devices.

Of course, developers of new services often challenge existing communication habits even when they believe they are building on them. For example, developers of video telephony sought to emulate face-to-face communications. Instead, they created a quite different medium. Even early studies of the Picturephone found that video phones distort normal face-to-face communications as well as normal telephone use (Dickson and Bowers, 1974). Rather than fitting well within existing media habits, either face-to-face or over the telephone, video phone users experienced a very new mode of communications calling for new rules, a new etiquette and a change in communication habits.

Another example is the Picturephone. This videophone moved the image of the other person well within the conventional social distance that Americans are used to maintaining and created an abnormal level of eye contact between the users. Americans were not accustomed to being within three feet of those with whom they are speaking. Nor are they used to someone looking directly at them for a sustained period of time, even if the cameras fail to provide a sense of direct eye contact. It is uncomfortable.

Likewise, the developers of interactive television believe that they are building on an activity people already like to do – watching television. Or, are they introducing the mass audience to something they do not do and do not like to do – 'talking to their TVs' (Kahan, 1984)? Likewise, the developers of the UK's Interactive Network, which allows viewers to play along with game shows, believe that they are complementing the existing habits of viewers watching game shows who shout out answers and try to outwit the contestants.

If video telecommunications is provided within a window on a personal computer, is this innovation supporting and extending what computer users already do and like to do or introducing a quite different activity, interpersonal communications? Only field trials and experience will answer these questions.

Communication versus information

Any survey of literature on multimedia encyclopedias and other huge stores of information illustrate the degree to which the industry remains convinced that there is a widespread interest in getting access to information per se. Likewise, early visions of the public information utility were based on the assumption that the public is interested in information. In fact, many assume that the public is composed largely of avid information seekers.

However, this assumption might well be a misleading guide to the development of services. Experiments with electronic services have reinforced an observation made by many involved in the early market trials of videotext services, which is that the public might be more interested in specialized services and in communication than in information per se (Hooper, 1985, p. 190). Videotext trials in the US and the French Minitel system underscored the centrality of interpersonal and group communication to electronic networks.

For example, Times Mirror's commercial offering of its Gateway videotext service found a growing interest in electronic mail among its subscribers. But Times Mirror was a publisher interested in the future of the newspaper business. Realising that it would be quite some time before videotext competed with the newspaper, Times Mirror saw no reason to continue with Gateway. The logic seemed to be that if there was a market for electronic communications, then let the telephone companies provide it.

This point is striking from research on electronic bulletin boards, such as the Santa Monica PEN system, as well as from usage of Internet, the success of which has been a major driving force behind the promotion of an information superhighway. In fact, arguments about the rapid growth and saturation of Internet capacity is central to proposals for the next generation of infrastructures to support this service. Arpanet, which later became Internet, was developed to support remote access to computing services, permitting students and researchers at one university to use computing facilities at other universities. The actual use of Arpanet did not support remote computing. The network evolved instead to become primarily a medium for interpersonal communications – 'e-mail'. Today, individuals use Internet facilities primarily to send electronic mail and manuscripts to their colleagues at local and distant locations. Communications is clearly the trigger service for these computer networks.

All of the most successful computer-based information services for the public, such as SeniorNet and CompuServe, have made electronic mail and conferencing a central aspect of their operations (Arlen, 1991). The popularity of electronic bulletin boards in the US is again anchored in the value of communication, not accessing information.

Given the potential value of communication versus information services, it becomes quickly apparent that one of the most central problems facing the new media is getting to a point at which there is a critical mass of users. The value of any telecommunications network increases in a non-linear fashion as more people are connected to the network. France Telecom's experiment with video telephony in Biarritz quickly discovered that a small number of video telephones in a local community failed to incorporate a critical mass (Gérin and Tavernost, 1987). Thoughts of experimenting with video telephony with five sites in Cerritos, California quickly bumped up against the same realisation. In this case, early hopes for a market trial quickly were converted to a technical trial.

All of the trials and experiments with the video phone and other new interpersonal communication technologies are limited by the lack of a critical mass of users. This is not a design problem but one of how to subsidize users until a critical mass of users exists, at which point the need for a subsidy would diminish.

Today, however, we are presented with unbelievable statistics on the 10 percent per month growth of Internet that suggest electronic mail and conferencing is diffusing to a rapidly expanding base of users. It might well have moved beyond a point of critical mass and become significantly more valuable to new users. Nevertheless, there are problems in accessing these claims. The actual use of electronic mail and conferencing systems is often substantially different from any formal measures of registrations, official users, or account sign-ups. Also, Internet usage is subsidized to the point that many users often realise no cost for their use. Also, despite progress, the user interface on most electronic mail networks is difficult and non-intuitive for most users. Finally, some existing systems that have moved outside the university setting and into the public at large are already experiencing difficulties with their regulation, with respect to privacy, speech and access. All of these problems raise cautions and suggest the need for more systematic and disinterested research on actual usage patterns over time.

Reality costs

The Clinton–Gore campaign staff posted a simple message on their wall to remind everyone that they should focus on the economy. In the main offices of a major US aerospace firm, which is developing computer simulations for training applications, reminds its staff that: 'Reality costs'. Simulations can be closer and closer to reality, but as they move closer to reality, they will cost more. In a narrow sense, this is a lesson learned by a history of trials with new media, which are often based on the assumption that users want to more closely approach face-to-face human communication.

For instance, a number of experts laid the failure of video phones on their cost, which in the case of Picturephone was about ten times the cost of an ordinary telephone call (Martin, 1977). Price remains substantial. AT&T's VideoPhone 2500 was introduced at $1,500, 100 times the cost of an ordinary telephone. Even if the use of a VideoPhone 2500 costs no more than an ordinary call over the telephone network, the equipment costs remain substantial for residential customers.

The issue of cost was one major factor leading AT&T to move away from video telephone services for individuals in the 1970s to the use of its Picturephone technology in supporting video teleconferencing for executives. Its major cost justification was as a telecommunications substitute for travel to executive meetings. However, trials of AT&T's Picturephone Meeting Service (PMS), which continued into the early 1980s, made a transition from Picturephones to full motion, broadcast quality video conferencing systems, which AT&T provided on a trial basis well below actual cost. PMS as well as other publicly accessible video conferencing facilities, such as Confravision in the UK, met with similar problems of building a viable customer base of repeat users. Individuals would use these rooms, often expressing quite positive opinions about the experience, but then not return on any regular basis.

Again, there are numerous explanations for this failure to build a video conferencing market in the 1980s. Very few executives feel like they travel too much and few wish to substitute a video conference for travel unless it is to an unpleasant site. One of the only successful public applications of video conferencing in the US is between the courts and prisons and between police stations and district attorney offices, making it possible for victims of a crime to talk with the district attorney's office without travelling to the office (Dutton et al., 1991).

Generally, business executives and managers don't perceive that visual information is critical to most meetings nor that video communications is critical to most of their business conducted over a distance. They also face critical mass problems as well as the difficulties entailed in travel to a video conferencing facility. While PMS facilities were located in a number of major cities in the US, is it not an exaggeration to note that travel within metropolitan areas such as Los Angeles and New York City is sometimes more difficult than long distance air travel!

Issues of convenience and critical mass might be overcome by permanently installed, private video conferencing facilities within the key offices of major corporations. The trade literature frequently claims that privately installed rooms are now quite commonplace. However, there are few systematic, non-proprietary studies of the actual utilization and effectiveness of these privately installed facilities.

Taking account of social concerns

Trials have also highlighted the potential significance of enduring social concerns, such as privacy, equity of access and freedom of expression. The Picturephone and other video telephones, for example, were perceived to be an intrusive technology that invaded the privacy of the user (Dickson and Bowers, 1974, p. 102). The most common concern raised by those with whom I discuss video communications is being on camera in their homes. Almost uniformly, individuals draw analogies to when and where they use their telephones, such as when they step out of the shower, to raise concerns over being seen. Here again, design changes such as smaller screens and locating phones in offices and in the windows of computer screens might address this issue in part. But these solutions, such as linking video communications to a computer screen, raise other problems, such as making telecommunications less versatile, portable and convenient (Dutton, 1992).

Hi-OVIS was arguably the most innovative of the interactive cable television trials, particularly in offering two-way video communications. A video camera installed on the TV set of the Hi-OVIS households permitted live video from the home to be transmitted to the cable head-end and then broadcast to the other Hi-OVIS households (Kawahata, 1987). Households were broadcast live on local cable television. Families literally cleaned their homes and dressed up for television. Critics argued that this kind of participation clashed with cultural traditions in Japan that discouraged individuals from attracting such attention to themselves. But in any culture, the design and use of the system highlighted the intrusive potential of video communications in the household.

5.4   Conclusion: lessons learned

Checking the rear view mirror might well cause some enthusiasts to drive right off the information superhighway. They might conclude that this history does not demonstrate a proven mass market for 'multimedia' or interactive video communications per se. But it would be a mistake to forecast failure simply by extrapolating from the past. In the same way that it does not demonstrate a proven market, neither does this history provide solid ground for the opponents of new media ventures. Any 'failure' is a matter of debate, open to alternative interpretations.

Nevertheless, understanding the history of new communication media provides some valuable lessons that suggest ways forward. The following points seem most critical from this overview:

1. New media have histories. There are continuities and discontinuities with the past, but most developments are evolutionary rather than revolutionary in the way information and communication technologies are designed and taken up over time.

2. A knowledge of the history of new media developments shows that visions like the wired city or the information superhighway can be influential in shaping industrial strategies and public policy, even if not always in the ways intended by the visionaries. Words make a difference, particularly when, as in the case of the information highway, they help organise and focus an otherwise fragmented industrial and policy community around a more common goal.

3. Uncertainty surrounds any forecast of the future of information and communication technologies. The key decision makers in the US (in contrast to Japan) predicted the fax machine to fail and it did fail to diffuse widely for decades before literally taking off to become an almost ubiquitous medium within the space of a few years. Predictions abound in the communications field, but they remain quite problematic and contentious.

4. For the most part, the public is uninterested in technological breakthroughs, such as digital video, but in services that are markedly better than existing services. Media habits buttress existing services. So many patterns of information and communication behaviour are habitual rather than simply instrumental, such as reading a newspaper or watching television, that even real improvements in a service will take years if not decades to find widespread acceptance. New technologies demand that we change the way we do things – requiring behavioural change that will inevitably lag behind advances in equipment.

5. Trials and commercial offerings demonstrate that the public at large is more interested in communication than information per se and this recognition directs attention to the necessity of creating a critical mass of users if new media are to succeed. Public subsidy of Internet may have solved the

critical mass problem for electronic mail, but it has still taken decades to be overcome.

6. The actual and perceived cost of services can be critical to the success of new media. While there are multiple explanations for the failure of any new service, cost provides one major explanation for the failure of many. Also cross-national differences in the diffusion of some media, such as electronic bulletin boards in the US as compared with the UK, suggest that costs – real or perceived – might play a more influential role than often recognised.

7. Issues of privacy, freedom of expression, equity of access and other social concerns are critical to the take-up and long-term viability of information and communication services. Privacy concerns have been a factor in video communications and such new services as call-line identification. Free expression is raising problems for electronic communities. Public responses to new media offerings truly affect the 'bottomline' (Silverstone, 1991) and are ignored at real cost to the industry.

References

Arlen, G. (1991). SeniorNet services: toward a new electronic environment for seniors, *Forum Report*, No. 15. Queenstown, Maryland: The Aspen Institute.

Becker, L. B. (1987). A decade of research on interactive cable. In: W. Dutton, J. Blumler & K. Kraemer (eds.) *Wired Cities: Shaping the Future of Communications*. Boston: G. K. Hall.

Brand, S. (1987). *The Media Lab*, New York: Penguin Books.

Davidge, C. (1987). America's talk-back television experiment: QUBE. In: W. Dutton, J. Blumler & K. Kraemer (eds.) *Wired Cities: Shaping the Future of Communications*. Boston: G. K. Hall.

Dickson, E. M. & R. Bowers. (1974). *The VideoTelephone*, New York: Praeger.

Dutton, W. H. (1992). The social impact of emerging telephone services, *Telecommunications Policy*, **16**, No. 5 (July 1992), pp. 377–387.

Dutton, W. H., Blumler, J. G. & Kraemer, K. L. (eds.) (1987). *Wired Cities: Shaping the Future of Communications*. Boston: G. K. Hall.

Dutton, W. H., Kendall, G., O'Connell, J. & Wyer, J. (1991). *State and Local Government Innovations in Electronic Services*. Report for the U.S. Office of Technology Assessment, December 12, 1991.

Elton, M. C. J. (1980). Educational and other two-way cable television services in the United States. In: E. Wilte (ed.), *Human Aspects of Telecommunication*, pp. 142–55. Berlin: Springer Verlag.

Elton, M. C. J. (1991). *Integrated broadband networks: assessing the demand for new services*. Unpublished paper presented at the Berkeley Roundtable on the Industrial Economy, New York: Columbia University.

Elton, M. C. J. (1992). The US Debate on Integrated Broadband Networks, *Media, Culture and Society*, **14**, pp. 369–395.

Elton, M. C. J. & Carey, J. (1984). Teletext for public information: laboratory and field studies. In: J. Johnston (ed.), *Evaluating the New Information Technologies*, San Francisco, CA: Jossey-Bass.

Gérin, F. & de Tavernost, N. (1987). Biarritz and the future of videocommunications. In: W. H. Dutton, J. Blumler & K. Kraemer (eds.) *Wired Cities: Shaping the Future of Communications*. Boston: G.K. Hall, pp. 237–254.

Gilder, G. (1992). Into the Fibersphere, *Forbes* ASAP, pp. 111–122.

Goldmark, P. C. (1972). Communication and the community. In: *Communication, A Scientific American Book*, San Francisco: W.H. Freeman.

Greenberger, M. (1985). *Electronic Publishing Plus*, White Plains, NY: Knowledge Industries Publications.

Greenberger, M. (ed.) (1992). *Multimedia in Review: Technologies for the 21st Century*. Santa Monica, California: The Voyager Company and Council for Technology and the Individual.

Hooper, R. (1985). Lessons from overseas: the British experience. In: M. Greenberger (ed.) *Electronic Publishing Plus*, White Plains, NY: Knowledge Industry Publications.

Kahan, H. (1984). *How Americans React to Communications Technology: Technological Craps*. Paper presented at the Wired Cities forum, Annenberg Schools of Communications, Washington DC.

Kawahata, M. (1987). Hi-OVIS. In: W. H. Dutton, J. Blumler & K. Kraemer (eds.) *Wired Cities: Shaping the Future of Communications*. Boston: G. K. Hall.

Lucky, R. W. (1989). *Silicon Dreams*. New York, NY: St. Martin's Press.

McGilly, K., Kawahata, M., & Dutton, W. H. (1990). *Lessons from the Fibre-to-the-Home Trails*. Los Angeles, CA: Annenberg School for Communication, Un. of Southern California.

Martin, J. (1977). *The Future of Telecommunications*. New York: Prentice-Hall.

Noll, A. M. (1985). Videotex: Anatomy of a Failure, *Information and Management*, **9**, pp. 99–109.

Noll, A. M. (1992). Anatomy of a failure: picturephone revisited, *Telecommunications Policy*, **16**, No. 4, (May/June), pp. 307–316.

Rogers, E. M. (1986). *Communication Technology.* New York: The Free Press.

Sackman, H. & Boehm, B. (1972). *Planning Community Information Utilities.* Montvale, NJ: AFIPS Press.

Sackman, H. & Nie, N. (1970). *The Information Utility and Social Choice.* Montvale, NJ: AFIPS Press.

Silverstone, R. (1991). *Beneath the Bottomline*, PICT Policy Research Paper, No. 17, Brunel University: The Programme on Information and Communication Technologies.

Smith, R. L. (1970). The Wired Nation, *The Nation*, May 18.

Smith, R. L. (1972). *The Wired Nation: Cable TV: The Electronic Communications Highway*, New York: Harper and Row.

Notes

1   There are a number of exceptions, including some overviews of field trials and experiments that provide a far more detailed review and assessment than I can provide in this chapter (e.g., Dutton, Blumler & Kraemer, 1987; Elton, 1991; Elton & Carey, 1984; Greenberger, 1985, 1992; Noll, 1985, 1992; and Rogers, 1986).

2   This section draws from my work on wired cities, see Dutton, Blumler & Kraemer (1987, pp. 1–26).

6

Designing organisations using telematic technologies: risks and benefits

Noel Sheehy

6.1 Introduction

Organisations are created and maintained through the manner in which people choose to communicate. Communication is not derived from organisational activity but provides the psychological glue that makes social organisation possible. For example, organisations that are regarded as having hierarchical structures are sustained as such by the manner in which their members regulate their communication. Less hierarchical organisations are created and maintained through different communications protocols. Some organisations are more conspicuously consultative or democratic and indicate this through their communications customs, while others are less so and adopt more command-and-control dialogues. Organisational work comprises more than time and effort spent in the performance of product-related tasks. It encompasses the talk surrounding those activities. Much of this organisational talk occurs informally. It can appear to be frivolous and irrelevant to the primary tasks and goals of the organisation. In fact it provides the social basis of organisational activity and for most members it carries important messages about what it feels like to be a member of an organisation.

Communications technologies can have a profound impact on the structure and function of organisational activities because they can influence the communications processes that sustain their existence. New communications technologies afford significant opportunities for enhancing organisational communication, for example by facilitating the design of communications networks, but they also carry risks that can affect an organisation's ability to repond appropriately to changing environmental demands.

6.2   The time spent communicating

How much time do people spend communicating during the course of a working day? How is 'communicating time' separated from other activities? These and related questions touch on important aspects of the analysis and measurement of the impact of telematics on organisational communication.

One of the first and largest studies of how people spend their work time was conducted at the Case Institute of Technology during the late 1950s. The 1,500 industrial chemists sampled were found to spend about 50 percent of their working day in communications tasks and about 25 percent of their time on technical (i.e. non-communications) tasks. Technical engineers spent about 56 percent of their time communicating and their supervisors spent about 87 percent of their time (Hinrichs, 1964). We have known for some considerable time that managers, in a variety of industrial settings, spend between 75 percent and 85 percent of their time communicating – principally in conversation or discussion with employees or clients (Stewart, 1967; Burns, 1954; Graham et al., 1967).

It is often thought that some types of tasks, and some groups of workers, spend relatively little time communicating. The overwhelming finding to emerge from communications audits is that the principal focus of activity for professionals, administrators, clerks, technicians and secretaries is communicating with co-workers and with clients and that rates of communication are rarely affected by physical aspects of the work context, such as office size. For many people most of the working day is spent communicating in one way or another and up to two thirds of that time may involve conversational exchanges (Klemmer and Snyder, 1972).

6.3   Quality vs. quantity of communication

Early attempts to explore the socio-economic effects of telecommunications largely ignored psychological dimensions in the management and organisation of dialogue. For instance, during the 1970s Reid's (1971) Telecommunications Impact Model attempted to establish the extent to which an organisation's face-to-face communications could be transferred to the telephone. The model is in four parts and takes a combination of factors into account:

1   The amount of communication in an organisation.

2   The types of meeting that occur (problem solving, information seeking, etc.).

3   Social and economic calculations of the extent to which different types and quantity of dialogue could be effected via different telecommunications devices.

4   Opportunities for relocating parts of an organisation's tasks and personnel and an assessment of the economic and social implications.

Socio-economic models such as those of Reid (1971) are based on economic assumptions including:

1   Telecommunications can be regarded as a substitute for travel.

2   The effectiveness of communications can be operationalised in measures of task efficiency.

Such models tend to regard communication as a *product* of organisational activities rather than the *basis* for those activities and do not address the psychological dimensions of telecommunications. While information can be regarded as a resource and a commodity it has a number of social attributes which distinguish it from other economic entities. First, it is intrinsically diffuse. Second, it reproduces through use; it is not consumed in the way other commodities can be. In this sense 'consumers' of information are agents for its reproduction and expansion. Third, information can only be shared, it cannot be transacted: someone who supplies or communicates information is not automatically dispossessed of it. This greatly complicates commerce: it introduces a range of psychological and social processes into economic transactions where communication processes form the organisational basis for the buying and selling of communications.

Users of telematic systems have concerns which over-ride arguments about the technical excellence or economy of telematic systems. Three studies have illustrated this:

Case 1: Bell Telephones - 1

Bell Telephones asked 3,000 employees to indicate which of a range of media could provide acceptable substitutes for face-to-face dialogue. Only 2% would accept sound-only systems and 85% insisted that they needed systems requiring both sound and vision .

Case 2: Bell Telephones - 2

In a transport survey 6,000 Canadians on inter-city journeys (road, rail and air) were invited to indicate which of a number of telecommunications systems would have provided an acceptable substitute for their current journey. Only 20% indicated that the telephone could have provided an acceptable substitute – and of course none of them had elected to use that medium as a substitute for their journey!

Case 3: British Telecom

British Telecom has supported an extensive programme of research to evaluate user acceptability of a wide range of communication technology applications. For the vast majority of users the critical decision relates to the choice between face-to-face dialogue and telecommunications-mediated interaction. Differences between various types of telecommunications media are of secondary importance (Christie and Holloway, 1975).

6.4   Computer-mediated dialogue

Computer-mediated messaging systems impose particular requirements on users and have been shown to have the following characteristics:

1 Participants engage in less overt agreement and more opinion giving than comparable face-to-face groups (Hiltz and Turoff, 1987).

2 Computer-mediated group discussion is less likely to produce polarisation or shifts to extremes on a risk-caution dimension than in face-to-face interaction (Hiltz and Turoff, 1987).

3 North American findings suggest a greater incidence of swearing, insults, name calling and hostile comments than occur in comparable face-to-face exchanges (Kiesler, Siegel and McGuire, 1984). British findings suggest the contrary (Wilbur, Rubin and Lee, 1986).

The discrepancy between the North American and British findings on the incidence of acrimonious exchanges requires further investigation to determine whether it is attributable to cultural differences or to differences in the tasks and objectives of those in the two samples.

While computer-mediated dialogues are characterised by high levels of task-related interaction one cannot conclude that computer-mediated dialogues are entirely task-governed. A significant part of the working day is spent communicating and it is hardly surprising then that in one Fortune 500 company 40 percent of all message traffic was found to be ostensibly 'frivolous' and unrelated to work (Sproull and Kiesler, 1986). That estimate is low, relative to the earliest studies of time spent communicating. Nevertheless it reinforces the point that the creation and maintenance of social contacts is crucial to effective co-ordination and task accomplishment. Knowing who one's co-workers are extends beyond a definition based on competence-on-task. Just as telephone users have invented conventions for overcoming the limitations of that technology so regular users of e-mail have invented a catalogue of simple icons to overcome some of the limitations imposed by text-based messaging systems. The following are examples of iconic representations of facial expressions (sometimes called 'emoticons') and can be more easily understood by rotating the book clockwise:

:-)   Used to inflect a sarcastic or joking statement
;-)   Used just make a flirtatious or sarcastic remark.
:-(User did not like the last statement or is upset or depressed.
:-/   Used to indicate skepticism
:-D   Used to indicate laughter

6.5   Abnormal communication

People have to create new ways of conversing in order to overcome functional limitations imposed by the technologies they use for that purpose. A relatively neglected aspect of this kind of skill development has to do with the detection and repair of 'trouble'. An organisation's members will develop ways of detecting and dealing with the troubles and difficulties of others. Co-workers who are hassled, angry, worried or in other ways stressed will send signals – many of them non-verbal – that others can recognise. Most of this recognition can be accomplished as a matter of routine where people share a work environment and can see and be seen. People who become seriously stressed in their work can often convey this to co-workers in the manner in which they conduct themselves in conversation.

If we are sufficiently familiar with a colleague we may even be able to detect this in their 'telephone voice'. In this regard point-to-point desk-top video-conferencing will pose new challenges for users who will develop subtle skills for presenting and reading a 'video face'. They will do this because face-to-face conversations conventionally involve synchronising eye-contact, voice characteristics and inter-personal distance. For example, confidential conversations are managed through a subtle combination of close physical proximity, appropriately managed eye-contact and quiet speaking (Argyle, 1989; Argyle and Dean, 1965). Current point-to-point desk-top videoconferencing applications support face-to-face communication while eliminating physical co-presence and introducing subtle transmission time delays. Until either broadband channels or improved coding algorithms are a reality, users will need to develop new conventions for having different kinds of conversations under these circumstances.

It seems likely that people will develop skills for signalling trouble even for conversation mediated by conventional computer-based technologies. Computer-mediated dialogue is unlikely to eliminate the expression of stress through dialogue but people may learn to use the technology in new ways in order to signal their troubles. A small number of studies have explored how people can become 'addicted' to computer-based conferencing systems and the following indicators have been identified (Bezilla and Kleiner, 1980; Shotton, 1982):

• Logging unnecessarily many times in a day
• Excessive irritation when the system is inaccessible
• Preference for composing thoughts on line
• Preference towards developing concepts on line
• Preference towards conducting relationships on line
• Logging on 'just one more time' before stopping work.

These indicators or 'symptoms' are not unique to computer-based systems. Exactly the same kinds of behaviour can be detected in face-to-face dialogue where one of the co-workers is stressed: unnecessary conversations with the same person several times a day; excessive irritation when a colleague is temporarily unavailable; preference for composing thoughts 'as they come' in conversation and so on.

The development of good management practice, effective organisations and the fostering of a healthy social climate for workers are founded on the acquisition and application of skills for detecting and avoiding impending trouble. Many 'troubles' can be detected and repaired through conversation. Computer-mediated dialogue removes most visual and acoustic cues for detecting impending difficulties but the technology has its own operating characteristics which are likely to capture aspects of a user's broader intentions and needs. In other words, users may learn to convey both propositional content (*what* they say) *and* illocutionary force (*how* they say it) in their interactions with other system users (Searle, 1969). We do not yet know what these operating characteristics are for different telematic devices, nor are we yet in a position to describe features which can be used reliably to allow managers and other system users to identify and resolve impending task- and personnel-related difficulties.

6.6   Summary

The most important psychological feature of voice-only telecommunication devices is that they remove in different ways and in varying degrees important social cues that are present in face-to-face interaction. Fewer social cues are associated with experiences of increased psychological distance, diminished social spontaneity and engagement, a greater focus on task completion and diminished rates of compromise. Table 6.1 summarises the principal characteristics of face-to-face interaction and interaction among workers whose activities and tasks are organised over computer networks.

6.7   Describing organisational communication

While most organisational members engage in high rates of communication across a range of physical contexts the type of communication varies according to functions and roles. For instance, managers are likely to spend a good deal of their time requesting, advising, consulting, ordering, etc. Junior secretaries are likely to spend more time requesting, stating and answering, etc. Some of these types of communication, such as asking and receiving information, can easily be conducted via telecommunications links. Others, such as advising, persuading and consulting, which may require a high degree of interaction, can be more difficult.

It is commonly recognised that communications media have different bandwidth characteristics and that the relationship between a communications medium and its messages are complex. Messages that are intended to influence, persuade or advise are often more effectively communicated on a face-to-face basis. Messages which report, command or transfer information can often be successfully communicated through restricted communications channels. In other words, organisational communication can be described in terms of its 'human bandwidth' requirements. Some forms of communication are preferred when completing complex organisational tasks and require broad bandwidth – for instance, through face-to-face dialogues. The 'broad bandwidth' of face-to-face communication can be described in terms of the large number of complex messages that need to be shared and critiqued. Other kinds of communication service are better suited to supporting simpler tasks and require narrow bandwidth – such as short memoranda. The 'narrow bandwidth' of these kinds of communications can be described in terms of a small number of messages and their relatively simpler functions.

Characteristics of Computer-Communication Channels

	Face-to-face	Mediated
Message flow	One-to-few	One-to-many
Source knowledge	Source has knowledge of 'audience'	Source less likely to have knowledge of 'audience'
Segmentation of messages	High	High
Degree of interactivity	High	Medium\high
Feedback (Quantity)	High	Medium\low
Feedback (Speed)	Fast, parallel	Slow, sequential
Ability to preserve messages	Low	High
Socio-emotional content	High	Low
Focus on task	Variable	High
Non-verbal band	High	Low (usually)
Control of communication	Potential for equal control is high	Potential for equal control is more limited
Privacy	Variable	Variable

Table 6.1. Characteristics of interpersonal and text-based computer-mediated dialogue.

Different kinds of organisational communication can be described using a classification system based on the concept of a communication act. A communication act is a combination of social behaviour (verbal and non-verbal) that can be said to represent the intention within a communication offered by a person (Searle, 1969). In other words it is possible to survey the communications that create and maintain an organisation and to classify them as different kinds of communication act. The potential in such an approach can be illustrated by comparing the kinds of communications that predominate in organisations, or parts of organisations, that are 'person-oriented' and those that are 'task-oriented' (Jewell and Siegall, 1990). Person-oriented organisations attend both to task objectives and workers' needs and tend to achieve their task objectives by attending to the requirements of those responsible for those tasks. Task-oriented organisations place a premium on task objectives and regard workers' needs as secondary or even incidental. Person-oriented organisations concern themselves with dialogues where one interactant is attempting to understand or change the 'psychological state' of another. For example, persuading, evaluating and apologising are concerned with the perspectives, beliefs or attitudes of others. Asking, referring or giving can be thought of as more task-oriented forms of communication. Table 6.2 groups 18 communicative acts into those that are principally person-oriented and those that are task-oriented. The classification is not hard-and-fast – a single communicative act can be used for different purposes, but the dichotomy is useful as a conceptualisation tool.

Task-oriented	Person-oriented
Say	Heed
Declare	Believe
Survey	Forecast
Notify	Evaluate
Explore	Discuss
Suggest	Desire
Charge	Urge
Refer	End
Decide	Supply

Table 6.2. Task- and person-oriented communication acts.

The dichotomy described in Table 6.2 is reminiscent of that used to classify organisations by structure (Buchanan and Huczynski, 1985). This is not coincidental. Hierarchical organisations, or parts of organisations, tend to adopt task-oriented modes of communication. They are hierarchical because members adopt communications roles and responsibilities that create a sense of social hierarchy.   More horizontal organisations, or parts of organisations, tend to adopt more participative, person-oriented modes of communication. Thus, the communications taxonomy can be used to elaborate structural classification systems of organisations.

Telecommunications bandwidth correlates with information complexity. Communication acts which are person-oriented require broad bandwidth – in human and technical terms – whereas task-oriented acts can often be successfully transmitted through narrower bandwidths. Table 6.3 summarises some of the important inter-relationships between human communication bandwidth and the bandwidth of the technology that is available to support it.

Narrow bandwidth places a considerable burden of effort on the user to engage in person-oriented communication. Users are required to develop new skills and make special efforts to ensure their complex messages are accurately encoded and properly understood by the recipient. Broad bandwidth places a lesser burden on the user. On the other hand task-oriented communication can usually be supported comparatively easily within both narrow and broad bandwidths, which implies that broad bandwidth may be unnecessary for some task-oriented dialogues.

		Bandwidth	
		Narrow	Broad
User Effort	Person C_acts	High	Low
	Task C_acts	Low	Low
Value added	Person C_acts	Low	High
	Task C_acts	High	Low
Organisational structure	Vertical	High use	Low use
	Horizontal	Low use	High use
IT as change catalyst		Low	High

Table 6.3. Inter-relationship between communication acts (C_acts) and bandwidth

Telecommunications can add value to users' messages: the medium can interact with and enhance the message, thereby increasing its cost effectiveness. Narrow bandwidth can actually increase task productivity by removing extraneous cues and information. Broad bandwidths may prove less productive and carry little or no added value. By contrast, broad bandwidth adds considerable value to person-oriented communication whereas narrow bandwidth is likely to be less effective and may act as an impediment.

Vertical organisational structures are more likely to engage in task-oriented communication and their tasks can be serviced by narrow band communications technologies whereas horizontal structures are likely to prefer broad bandwidths.

Finally, narrow bandwidth is unlikely to act as a catalyst for change because users cannot easily encode the complex person-oriented communication that is necessary for interactants to review and re-organise their communicative structures and procedures. In other words they cannot easily use this bandwidth to talk about their work. Stated crudely, narrow communications bandwidth technology, such as telex, affords few opportunities for interrupting what another is saying, whereas broad bandwidth technologies accommodate interruption opportunities closer to those experienced in face-to-face inter-personal dialogue. A side effect of the use of narrow bandwidth may be to reduce opportunities for organisational change. This may not be a difficulty when an organisation decides to minimise change opportunities. Broad bandwidth can more easily accommodate such dialogues and thereby act as a catalyst for evolution and development. It can do this by allowing organisational members more opportunities for unplanned talk about how they are doing things and how they might be done differently.

6.8   The 'workstation'

In a variety of ways telecommunications technologies can give impressions of how organised groups of people do their work which conflict with what we know about organisational communication. Effective organisations spend a great deal of time talking about the work they are doing. Organisational communication is as much concerned with talking about work as it is with doing it. Unfortunately theory and practice in relation to uses of telematics have adopted the concept of workstation as a reference model for the design and development of computer-based work technology. The concept of the workstation rests on several assumptions about the practice and context of work which do not accord with the evidence we have on how organisations function.

The term 'workstation' implies that work is conducted at fixed locations by individual workers using their own machines. These individuals are usually imagined to work within conventional office contexts. There are two arguments which challenge the validity of these assumptions. First, some routine tasks, such as data entry, can be accomplished within the confined physical setting of a desk and workstation but the majority of an organisation's personnel are expected to be more versatile and flexible than this. They are normally required to perform multiple tasks of varying complexity. There are comparatively few organisations whose staff perform just one task in a single physical location. Moreover, even data handling tasks, when they go wrong, are repaired through intensive use of communications networks (Brodbeck et al., 1993). Second, the overwhelming body of evidence to emerge from studies of organisational communication indicates that the majority of staff in most organisations spend the greater proportion of their working day communicating with others. It is essential that they do this because the communication network creates, maintains and manages the organisation of work – it *is* the organisation of work.

The evidence that the assumptions embodied in the notion of the 'workstation' are wrong is largely ignored but it is useful to refer to some of it here:

1 In many offices in most organisations desks can be found unoccupied for long periods of time while workers converse with one another in other settings.

2 In most organisations workers switch between functions supported by the technology on their desks (workstation and phone) and those available elsewhere (fax, telex, photocopying, printing, etc.).

3 In both large and small organisations it is not unusual to find idle machines consuming power for long periods of time.

4 In many offices there is a simple functional machine-to-task mapping. One machine hosts a word processor, another accounts, another reservations and so on. By contrast the workstation operators are normally expected to perform multiple tasks.

That the assumptions underlying the workstation concept do not apply to most kinds of work in most organisations has not until now been regarded as a cause for serious concern. Superficially the workstation concept seems ideally suited to the development of new, distributed organisational structures and consonant with the idea that teleworking or computer-supported co-operative work (CSCW) could be undertaken by solitary or paired workers, separated by geographical and/or temporal boundaries. Work, at an organisational level, means more than this. Our commitment to the workstation as a conceptual and technological reference model ignores the life of workers outside the confines of the physical workstation and task procedures specified in the software therein.

Of course, increasing the communications opportunities within the 'workstation' can lead to a gradual expansion in the range of activities users can perform there. For example, it can focus and support informal communication that might otherwise have taken place away from the office desk – in corridors and canteens. In other words, organisational talk about the work can be encouraged to migrate to individual desk areas.

There are risks in allowing this to proceed in an unplanned or haphazard fashion. An organisation's members may lose creative opportunities if they are required to squeeze 'broad bandwidth conversations' into narrow bandwidth technology. For example, well established broad band, horizontal organisational structures may be inadvertently replaced by more narrow band hierarchies. Possibly the biggest challenge for telematics lies not in determining whether interface ergonomics can be generalised to the many different physical contexts in which workers may be located, but rather in providing support for workers who will increasingly rely on those technologies for quality maintenance of the organisation of their work.

6.9   Designing organisational communication

Why might managers want to design their organisations in ways which would focus formal and informal communication on desk-based activities? Some managers do not like the idea of informal networks and consider them intrinsically counter-productive. For some, the design and comprehensive monitoring of communications networks is valid in itself, notwithstanding the ethical questions such practices raise (Marx and Sherizen, 1989). Aside from Machiavellian motives, management objectives are often broadly in sympathy with the wish to create effective organisations through efficient communication architecture and protocol. Telematics affords new opportunities for managers to realise these objectives.

Organisations are more than conglomerates of people. They have structures and their members use their communications skills to create and manage those structures in order to support organisational objectives. Within an organisation the number of interactions between pairs of individuals can be described as: $N(N-1)/2$, where N is the number of individuals in the organisation. Some combinations occur with greater frequency than others. This is how communications networks are made and defined. The idea of communications networks is not new – notions of sociometry and sociograms appeared over 50 years ago (Moreno, 1934). Important practical implications of this approach relate to the requirements placed on organisational managers to attend to issues concerned with defining team memberships and with communication climate.

There is a subtle and important connection between the architecture of networks linking people and the organisations that these links can create. Computer networks, for example, are not haphazard but have formal structures which are designed to allow links to function reliably. They can also influence the conduct of business depending on the linkages. Star topology, for example, requires central control and is commonly considered desirable for occasions where users mainly plan to interact with a central station. Ring topology requires distributed control and message routing procedures. In bus topology there is distributed control but message routing procedures are very simple since all junctions check every message and intercept those that concern that access station.

Classical information theory can be applied to the study of these communication networks and provides management indicators concerning:

Traffic: The extent to which group members communicate.

Closure: The extent to which the group is accessible to 'outsiders' and to 'outside' ideas.

Convergence: The extent to which groups members are on an equal footing with respect to the generation and reception of messages.

The choice of topology carries implications beyond technical considerations. It has implications for the conduct of business and for users' sense of participation or engagement in collective work. Figure 6.1 depicts three simple configurations and describes some of the psychological characteristics commonly associated with each.

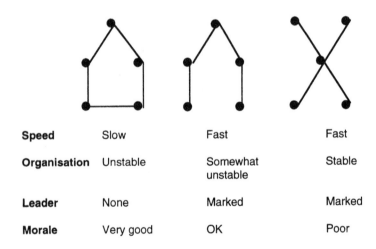

Speed	Slow	Fast	Fast
Organisation	Unstable	Somewhat unstable	Stable
Leader	None	Marked	Marked
Morale	Very good	OK	Poor

Figure 6.1. Characteristics of three communication networks.

Different kinds of network also have implications for organisational decison making processes and outcomes (Butler, 1991). Even very large, multi-department organisations can be described in terms of a relatively limited number of network configurations. The circular topology with bi-directional links between adjacent pairs is associated with high levels of morale and a sense of distributed leadership. The inverted U topology is associated with hierarchy, strong leadership and a sense of isolation and lower morale by those at the periphery. The star configuration is associated with perceptions of central control and leadership and a high sense of isolation and low morale among those located at the periphery.

Management teams are increasingly concerned to promote competitiveness through teleworking initiatives that can support high levels of team effectiveness on a low-cost, high flexibility base (Chapman et al., 1994). The attraction may be strongest for management teams that regard organisational talk as frivolous and perceive opportunities to design out informal networks and 'gossip chains'.

Increasingly there are commercial pressures to de-centralisation and a growing recognition that organisations can successfully conduct their business by providing a distributed work-force with reliable, effective telecommunications tools. There are also legitimate commercial concerns regarding the management and administration of such organisations. Telecommunications technologies for supporting teleworking and CSCW also provide managers with new opportunities for designing and managing organisational networks of choice. There are, however, risks in encouraging managers to create bespoke organisational structures by editing network connections between individuals. The management of organisational structures has always been concerned with these issues. However, to the extent that an organisation's staff share a physical work environment they have opportunities to communicate and work in ways which were not envisaged by managers. There are opportunities in traditional organisations for people to talk to whoever they wish, to share space with colleagues from different departments and to create and use informal communication networks to achieve personal and task objectives.

6.10 Conclusion

Telecommunications and allied technologies can be used to facilitate organisational tasks, particularly with reference to the following criteria:

• synchronising communications among members
• maintaining conversational and task coherence among members
• detecting and repairing communication and task failures
• maintaining shared focus among a work team
• achieving task objectives.

The extent to which technologies can meet these criteria for organisations can usefully be described using the idea of a communication act. Communications acts can be used to classify organisations, or parts of organisations, and to describe telecommunications technologies that can best support them. Some technologies can accommodate larger and more varied communications structures and it is possible to describe the communications bandwidth of the various technologies using a communications taxonomy as a metric.

The choice of network topology is based on three considerations: technical limitations, commercial costs and the structure of communication within the extant organisation. The tendency may be for organisations to implement teleworking and CSCW networks which reflect extant communication patterns, or a preferred sub-set of those patterns. In so doing, the technology may introduce additional barriers to changes in organisational dialogue. Implied practices may inadvertently become set in technological concrete and the creative potential in the social organisation of work may be diminished.

References

Argyle, M. (1989). *The Social Psychology of Work*. Harmondsworth: Penguin.

Argyle, M. & Dean, J. (1965). Eye contact, distance and affiliation. *Sociometry*, **28**, pp. 289–364.

Bezilla, R. & Keliner, A. (1980). Electronic network addiction. Paper presented at the National Computer Conference, Arnheim, California.

Broadbeck, F. C., Zapf, D., Prumper, J., & Frese, M. (1993). Error handling in office work with computers: A field study. *Journal of Occupational Psychology*, **66**, pp. 303–317.

Buchanan, D. A. & Huczynski, A.A. (1985). *Organizational Behaviour*. London: Prentice Hall.

Burns, T. (1954). The directions of activity and communication in a departmental executive group. *Human Relations*, **7**, pp. 73–97.

Butler, R. (1991). *Designing Organizations: A Decision-Making Perspective*. London: Routledge.

Chapman, A. J., Sheehy, N. P., Heywood, S., Dooley, B., & Collins, S. C. (1994). The organizational implications of teleworking. In: C. L. Cooper and I. T. Robertson (Eds.), *International Review of Industrial and Organizational Psychology*. Chichester: Wiley.

Christie, B. & Holloway, S. (1975). Factors affecting the use of telecommunications by management. *Journal of Occupational Psychology*, **48**, pp. 3–9.

Graham, W. R., Wagner, C. B., Gloege, W. P. & Zavala, A. (1967). Exploration of oral/informal technical communications. Report AIR-F-46-8/67-FR. Washington: American Institutes for Research.

Hiltz, S. R. & Turoff, M. (1978). *The Network Nation.* Massachusetts: Addison-Wesley.

Hinrichs, J. R. (1964). Communications activity of industrial research personnel. *Personnel Psychology,* **17**, pp. 193–204.

Jewell, L. N. & Siegall, M. (1990). *Contemporary Industrial/Organizational Psychology.* New York: West.

Kiesler, S., Siegel, J., & McGuire, T. W. (1984). Social psychological aspects of computer-mediated communication. *American Psychologist,* **39**, pp. 1123–1134.

Klemmer, E. T., & Snyder, F. W. (1972). Measurement of time spent communicating. *Journal of Communication,* **22**, pp. 142–158.

Marx, G. T., & Sherizen, S. (1989). Monitoring on the job. In: T. Forester (Ed.), *Computers in the Human Context.* Oxford: Blackwell.

Moreno, J. L. (1934). *Who Shall Survive? A New Approach to the Problem of Human Inter-relations.* Washington, DC.: Nervous and Mental Diseases Publishing.

Reid, A. (1971). What telecommunication implies. *New Society,* **18**, pp. 1284–1286.

Searle, J. R. (1969). *Speech Acts.* Cambridge University Press.

Shotton, M. A. (1982). *Computer Addiction?* London: Taylor and Francis.

Sproull, L. & Kiesler, S. (1986). Reducing social context cues: Electronic mail in organizational communication. *Management Science,* **11**, pp. 1492–1512.

Stewart, R. (1967). How managers spend their time. *Management Today,* June, pp. 92–160.

Wilbur, S., Rubin, T., & Lee, S. (1986). A study of group interaction over a computer-based message system. In: M. D. Harrison and A. F. Monk (Eds), *People and Computers: Designing for Usability.* Cambridge University Press.

Part 3   Applications

7

Studies of multimedia-supported collaboration

John C. Tang & Ellen A. Isaacs

7.1 The promise and perplexity of multimedia-supported collaboration

The growing need to support technical and social activity that occurs across geographical distances has not been fully satisfied by the current technologies of phones, faxes, electronic mail, and video conference rooms. Video conferencing systems have been promoted as a technology to support remote collaboration at least since AT&T unveiled the Picturephone in the mid-1960s (Falk, 1973), but so far this vision has not been fully realized.

However, recent technology and infrastructure developments are lowering some of the barriers that have prevented the widespread adoption and use of multimedia to support remote collaboration (Gale, 1992). The emergence of digital audio and video technology allows voice and images to be computationally manipulated and transmitted over the existing computer networks. Improved compression algorithms running on faster hardware will soon provide acceptable audio-video quality at viable network bandwidth rates. And the emergence of *information superhighways* promises to deliver large amounts of bandwidth to the home, office, and anywhere there is customer demand. The availability of affordable computer workstations, proliferation of digital networks, emergence of compression algorithm and network protocol standards, and marketing hype are all converging to bring multimedia capabilities to personal desktops.

Research prototypes that provide what is often referred to as desktop conferencing (audio, video, and computational connections between computer desktops) have been demonstrated using analog (Root, 1988; Buxton & Moran, 1990; Bly et al., 1993) and digital (Watabe et al., 1990; Masaki et al., 1991) video technology. For example, Olson and Bly (1991) reported on the experiences of a distributed research group using a network of audio, video, and computer connections to explore ways of overcoming their separation in location and time. These prototypes have demonstrated the technical feasibility of desktop conferencing, experimented with some of its features, and provided a glimpse of how people might use it.

However, the increased costs (e.g., upgrading networks, buying media-equipped workstations) and uncertainty over the benefits of collaborative multimedia have been significant barriers to its widespread adoption and use to date. While videophone products have recently reappeared in the marketplace, the lack of commercial success of Picturephone since it was introduced 30 years ago indicates that there is much yet to be learned about the deployment and use of collaborative multimedia technologies (Francik et al., 1991).

Furthermore, research to date on the effects of various communication media on collaborative activity has not provided convincing evidence of the intuitively presumed value of video (Williams, 1977). Ochsman and Chapanis (1974) examined problem-solving tasks in various communication modes including typewriting, voice only, voice and video, and unrestricted (working side-by-side) communication. They concluded that relative to communication modes using an audio channel: "...there is no evidence in this study that the addition of a video channel has any significant effects on communication times or on communication behavior." (Ochsman & Chapanis, 1974, p. 618). Conrath et al. (1977) explored using telecommunication systems to support remote medical diagnosis. They compared four different systems: hands-free telephone (audio only), audio plus black and white still frame video images, audio plus full-motion black and white video, and audio plus color full-motion video. They concluded: "We found no significant differences in diagnostic accuracy...time taken for the diagnostic consultations, and the effectiveness of patient management across the four communication modes." (Conrath et al., 1977, p. 12). However, when they surveyed the patients' attitudes about the four systems, they found that the patients preferred the more sensory rich (full-motion video, color) modes. Gale (1990) compared computer-mediated collaboration on experimental tasks under three conditions: sharing data only (via a shared electronic whiteboard), sharing data and audio, and sharing data, audio, and video. He concluded: "The results showed no significant differences in the quality of the output, or the time taken to complete the tasks, under [the] three conditions" (Gale, 1990, p. 175). However, Gale did find that collaborators' perceptions of productivity increased as communication bandwidth increased and suggested that higher bandwidth media enabled the groups to perform more social activities.

Some research has begun to identify uses of video in support of remote collaboration. Smith et al. (1989) compared computer-mediated problem-solving activity in audio only, audio and video, and face-to-face settings. They found that the presence of the video channel encouraged more discussion about the task rather than the mechanics of the computer tool being used for the task. Fish et al. (1993) equipped mentor-student pairs of researchers with a desktop conferencing prototype and studied their informal communication over several weeks. They found that the participants used the prototypes quite frequently for relatively short interactions, similar to how they used the telephone. They also reported an interesting novel use of the system; some participants occasionally created a "virtual shared office" where two people kept a connection open for long periods of time.

In light of the unconvincing evidence to date on the value of video, it is important to point out that most of the studies have used artificial groups (subjects randomly assigned to work together) working on short, contrived tasks (problems unrelated to their actual work). We hypothesized that evidence for the value of video would be most visible in actual work activity of real working groups. In fact, while some of the previous research did not find that adding video affected their measures of the resulting product (quality of decisions, medical diagnosis, completion time, etc.), they did make observations on how video affected the process of interacting together (perceptions of productivity, task focus, degree of interactivity, etc.). If the main contribution of video is on the work processes, perhaps there would be no measurable effect on the work products on such short, artificial tasks.

We set out to study real examples of synchronous, distributed, small group collaboration to understand how multimedia technology, and video in particular, could be designed to support that activity. The research pursued an iterative cycle of studying existing work activity, developing prototype systems to support that activity, and studying how people use those prototypes in their work (Tang, 1991b). In this chapter, we first describe two background studies that examine existing remote collaboration work practice – a survey of users' perceptions of an existing video conference room system and a study of a geographically divided work group in various collaboration settings. Then we describe the development of a prototype desktop conferencing system that embodied some of the design implications identified by the background studies. In a third study, we used that prototype to observe a distributed team under three conditions: using their existing collaboration tools, adding the desktop conferencing prototype, and subtracting the video capability from the prototype. We conclude by discussing evidence from the three studies that helps explain why users like video and suggest ways in which video would be most effectively integrated into existing environments to support remote collaboration.

7.2   Survey of video conference room users

The first background study surveyed users' perceptions of an existing video conference room system. The survey was conducted within Sun Microsystems, Inc., which at the time used commercially available video conference room systems (PictureTel Corporation model CT3100 operating at 112 kb/s bandwidth). These systems connected conference rooms among sites in Mountain View, California; Billerica, Massachusetts; Colorado Springs, Colorado; and Research Triangle Park, North Carolina. In addition to the audio-video link, they could also send high quality video still images on a separate video display.

A survey was sent via electronic mail to users of the video conference room system. The survey asked for usage information and for the users' perceptions of the system. A total of 76 users responded to the survey, with representatives from all four sites and a variety of types of meetings (e.g., staff meetings, presentations, design meetings).

Survey results

Users were asked to indicate the best aspects of video conferencing. Respondents could check more than one item from a list of choices as well as add their own items. Most respondents (89%) liked having regular visual contact with remote collaborators. Many also indicated that it saved travel (70%) and time (51%), although this survey measured only the users' perceptions of saved time and travel, not whether those savings actually occurred. A field study of video conference users in a geographically distributed company (Mosier & Tammaro, in press) also found that video conference rooms were heavily used and explored some of the trade-offs that users considered when choosing video conferencing rather than face-to-face meetings.

Users were also asked to indicate the worst aspects of their video conferencing experience. The percentage of respondents who checked each aspect is shown in Figure 7.1. The most frequently indicated problem (72%) was difficulty in scheduling an available room. Poor audio quality (poor microphone pickup, moving the microphones into range of the speaker, echo, etc.) was indicated by 55% of the respondents, 53% mentioned not being able to see overheads and other materials used in presentations, and 52% complained about the time delay (latency) in transmitting audio and video through video conferencing. Between Mountain View, CA and Billerica, MA, the system exhibited about a 0.57 second delay between capturing voice and video on one end and producing them on the other end. Poor video quality was relatively less troubling; only 28% mentioned it as a problem.

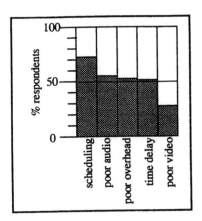

Figure 7.1. Worst aspects of video conferencing. Percentage of respondents who indicated the following as the worst aspects of their video conferencing experience: difficulty in scheduling the room, poor audio quality, difficulty seeing and interacting with overhead slides, time delay (latency) in audio-video transmission, and poor video quality.

Some sample comments from the survey illustrate these observations:

We need more video rooms! They are overbooked.

Audio quality is the real problem. Both audio quality and delay.

Difficulty in being able to make a comment – can't see a verbal opening coming because of the delays and image and audio quality.

Can't provide direct feedback on written material (e.g., by pointing and/or annotating slides and drawings presented remotely).

Respondents were also asked to rank order a list of additional capabilities (to which they could add their own) they would like to have in video conferencing. Figure 7.2 shows the five most frequently requested features with each item's average rank labelled on the bar chart (rank 1 is most urgently desired). The need for a shared drawing surface stood out as the most commonly requested feature; 68% of the respondents mentioned it as a desired feature, and its average rank order was 1.76. Respondents also indicated that they wanted a larger video screen (34%) and the ability to connect multiple sites together at the same time (30%). Only 18% wanted to incorporate computer applications, but its low average rank (1.75) suggests that those who wanted it considered it a highly desirable feature. Those users suggested incorporating software such as word processing, spreadsheet, and shared whiteboard applications. More comments from the survey:

> A shared drawing surface could be really useful. It should be a single device, so that you draw on the device and see your marks and the other person's marks on that same device.

> Networked [computer workstation] in each conference room would be nice, especially one that could project onscreen at the local site and at the remote sites... [Larger video screen] so I can really tell who's talking and get a fix on facial/body talk better...

A similar survey of users of video conferencing systems (Masaki et al., 1991) identified some of the same features as requirements for improving video conferencing. They found that users wanted a virtual common space (including a shared drawing space), integration of teleconference and computational tools, and multiple site conferencing capability.

Design implications from surveying video conferencing users

The survey did show that video conferencing users broadly appreciated the capabilities of video conferencing. Users' comments indicated that collaboration between remote sites would not be as effective or even possible without video conferencing. The survey responses indicated that multimedia tools to support collaboration should: be readily available for use; provide a shared workspace; and provide high quality, interactive audio among sites.

Note that the aspect of the system that users found most troublesome (scheduling difficulty) is a problem of use, not a technical problem per se. The technical benefits (and problems) of multimedia-supported collaboration tools will not be discovered if users cannot readily access them. Respondents' desire for a shared workspace reinforces research results identifying the important role of shared workspaces in remote collaboration (Olson & Bly, 1991; Tang, 1991a; Bly 1988). The responses also clearly indicated the need to improve the audio channel, both in sound quality and transmission delay. By contrast, users were not as disturbed about the image quality of the video channel. This pattern is consistent with results reported in the literature on the greater importance of audio relative to video in supporting remote collaboration (Gale, 1990; Ochsman & Chapanis, 1974).

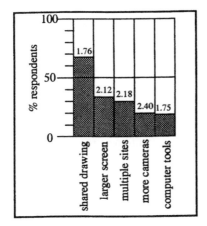

Figure 7.2. Desired features for video conferencing. Percentage of respondents who indicated the following as the features they would like to add to video conferencing: a shared drawing surface, larger video screen, connections among multiple sites at a time, more camera views, and access to computer tools while in a conference. The average rank of how urgently each feature was desired is also labelled (rank 1 being most urgently desired).

7.3   Study of collaboration in various settings

After completing the video conferencing survey, we studied a work group composed of four members from two different sites: three in Billerica, near Boston, and one (the second author of this chapter) in Mountain View, in the San Francisco Bay Area. Their discussions centered around graphical user interfaces for on-line help systems. The group conducted weekly video conference room meetings, supplemented by occasional phone conferences. At one point in the project, the Mountain View participant visited Billerica for a week of face-to-face meetings. Although some participants knew each other from previous work contacts, this was the first time they worked together extensively as a project team.

Over two months, meetings in each of the collaboration settings were videotaped and analyzed to identify characteristics of their collaboration that varied among the settings. The collected data consisted of eight video conferences, five face-to-face meetings, and one phone conference, amounting to over 15 hours of data.

Findings from the study of collaboration settings

From reviewing the videotapes, we found that the team experienced certain problems while using the video conference rooms that did not arise in face-to-face meetings:

• problematic audio collisions,
• difficulty in directing the attention of remote participants, and
• diminished interaction.

During their video conferences, there were many instances of audio collisions when participants on both sides started talking simultaneously and then had difficulty negotiating who should take the next turn. Although such collisions naturally occur in face-to-face and phone conversations, they were more problematic in video conferencing. In face-to-face conversation, turn transitions are largely negotiated verbally (aided by gestures) through precise timing (sometimes involving overlapping talk) and systematic, implicit organization (Sacks et al., 1974). The 0.57 second one-way delay in transmitting audio between video conference rooms markedly disrupted these mechanisms for mediating turn-taking. As a result, participants sometimes relied on gestural cues (e.g., extending a hand toward the camera conveying "you go first"), which, if seen, were usually successful.

The participants also had occasional difficulty directing a remote collaborator's attention to the video display so that these gestures would be seen. We observed several examples of "just missed" glances between remote collaborators when one participant looked up from her notes to glance at her remote collaborator, but after not getting a reciprocal glance within the usual wait time, looked back down at her notes just before the remote collaborator looked up at his video display to glance at her. These missed glances could largely be explained by delayed reactions caused by the transmission delays. However, just missed glances have also been observed in audio-video links that do not have any perceivable delay (Smith et al., 1989; Heath & Luff, 1991). Current research suggests that lack of peripheral vision and division of attention between video windows and the shared workspace disrupt the coordination of mutual glances.

Difficulties in negotiating turn-taking and directing participants' attention in video conferencing apparently combined to reduce the amount of interaction between the remote parties compared to face-to-face meetings. Video conferences tended to consist of a sequence of individual monologues rather than interactive conversations. We observed less frequent changes of speaker, longer turns, and less back-channelling in video conferencing than in face-to-face meetings. This reduced level of interaction appeared to affect the content of video conferences by suppressing complex, subtle, or difficult-to-manage interactions. Compared with face-to-face meetings, participants seemed inhibited from expressing their opinions and, in particular, avoided working through conflict and disagreement. Video conferences also exhibited a marked lack of humor (in part because humor relies on precise timing).

Design implications from studying collaboration settings

Comparing collaboration in video conferencing with face-to-face and phone conferencing settings underscored the need to provide responsive (minimally delayed) audio in technology to support interaction. The work group we studied was so frustrated by the audio delays in video conferencing that they turned off the audio provided by the video conferencing system and placed a phone call (using speakerphones) for their audio channel. Although this arrangement eliminated the audio delay, the audio now arrived before the accompanying video (i.e., audio and video were no longer synchronized), the audio quality was poorer, and speakerphone audio was only half-duplex (only one party's sound was transmitted at a time). Nonetheless, the collaborators strongly preferred this arrangement to the frustrations they experienced with the delayed audio. Their meetings conducted under this arrangement appeared to exhibit more frequent changes in speaker turns, more back-channelling, and more humor than those using the normal video conference configuration. A related study (Isaacs & Tang, 1994) explores some of these issues by comparing interactions among phone, desktop video conferencing, and face-to-face meetings.

This experience indicates that users prefer audio with minimal delay even at the expense of disrupting synchrony with the video. This observation again confirms research findings of the greater importance of audio relative to video (Gale 1990; Ochsman & Chapanis, 1974), and is also consistent with users' perceptions from the survey that audio quality and responsiveness are more important than video quality. This finding suggests that, given the limited bandwidth and performance currently available for desktop conferencing, more attention should be devoted to providing responsive, interactive audio. More research on the trade-offs and limits of degrading other parameters of desktop conferencing (e.g., video quality, video refresh rate, audio quality, audio silence suppression) is needed.

While our studies confirm the greater importance of audio relative to video, they also provide evidence for the value of video in supporting remote collaboration. Through the video channel, gestures were used to demonstrate actions (e.g., enact how a user would interact with an interface) and the participants' attitudes (e.g., vigorous head nodding indicating strong agreement). Especially under the delayed audio conditions of video conferencing, video was valuable in helping mediate interaction (e.g., using gestures to take a turn of talk) (Krauss et al., 1977).

7.4   Developing a desktop conferencing prototype

The observations gained from these two studies helped guide the design of our research prototypes for new multimedia technology to support collaboration. An initial phase of this research was to design and implement a prototype desktop conferencing system that provided real-time audio and video links and a shared drawing program among participants at up to three sites. The desktop conferencing prototype was built on a prototype hardware card that enabled real-time video capture, compression, and display on a workstation desktop. This prototype card, in conjunction with the workstation's built-in audio capability, enabled digital audio-video links among workstations on a computer network (Pearl, 1992).

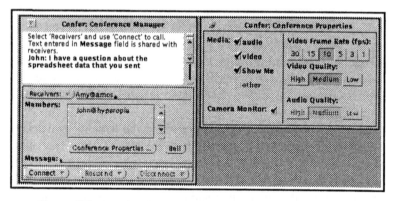

Figure 7.3. User interface for managing conference connections. John places a call to Amy to request a conference using the default conference properties of audio, ten frames per second video, and the Show Me shared drawing tool.

Figure 7.3 shows the user interface for establishing and managing desktop conferences. Initiating a conference was modeled after placing a telephone call. A user selected from a list of receivers to request a conference with them. An identical copy of the interface appeared on the receivers' screens, announced by three beeps. Each receiver could decide to join or decline the conference. A shared message area allowed users to send text messages among each other to negotiate joining or refusing a conference.

Once all receivers joined the conference, the collaborative tools selected in the conference manager were invoked. Figure 7.4 shows a screen image of the tools requested by the default settings in the desktop conferencing prototype. For a two-way conference, each user's screen displayed: a video window of the remote collaborator, a preview window of the video signal being sent to the remote collaborator, and a shared markup and drawing program (called Show Me) for drawing, typing, pointing, and erasing over shared bitmap images.

Show Me allowed users to create shared freehand graphics and to grab bitmap images from their screen and share them with the others. By default, Show Me was started automatically as part of a desktop conference, although users could choose not to invoke it.

The two studies of existing collaboration activity helped shape the design of the desktop conferencing prototype. The survey identified users' need for a shared drawing space, prompting a significant investment in the development of the Show Me shared drawing tool. The design of Show Me drew upon previous shared drawing research (Tang & Minneman, 1991; Minneman & Bly, 1991) to provide a drawing surface that remote collaborators could share in much the same way that face-to-face collaborators use a whiteboard.

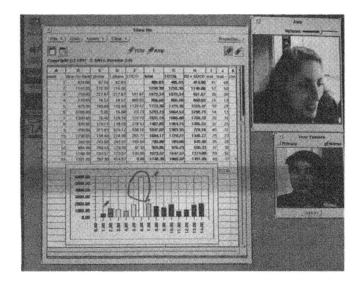

Figure 7.4. Screenshot of a desktop conference. A typical two-person desktop conference consists of the Show Me shared drawing tool (showing an image of a spreadsheet), a video window of the remote user (Amy), and preview video window of the outgoing video signal.

The study of collaboration settings identified the problem of audio delay and underscored the importance of the audio channel in mediating interaction.

The one-way audio delay in the desktop conferencing prototype was minimized to be in the range of 0.22–0.44 seconds (depending on computational and networking constraints). Since the audio and video data streams were being sent through a computer network that was shared with other users, spurts of heavy network traffic affected the prototype's performance. When network loading prevented video frames from being delivered at the requested video rate, the video image would occasionally freeze until an updated frame was received. More severe network loading caused cutouts in the audio signal. One characteristic of handling the audio and video data streams separately is that the timely delivery of video would degrade before the delivery of audio was disrupted. This behavior reflected the study's finding that immediate and responsive audio was more important than preserving audio-video synchrony.

7.5   Study of desktop conferencing use

We used the desktop conferencing prototype (DCP) to study the collaborative work activity of a distributed team in three different conditions:

1 *Pre*-DCP: using conventional collaboration tools (phone, e-mail, video conference rooms, etc.) as they currently were doing.

2 *Full*-DCP: adding the desktop conferencing prototype (audio, video, Show Me).

3 DCP *minus video*: removing the video channel from the desktop conferencing prototype (audio and Show Me only).

By measuring the team's use of these communication media and analyzing actual work activity across the three conditions, we sought to learn how desktop conferencing, and the video channel in particular, would be used in remote collaboration.

Background

The team we studied consisted initially of four members distributed across three locations. One member was located in Billerica, MA, another worked in a building in Mountain View, CA, and the remaining two members worked in offices near each other in a different building in Mountain View (over 500 yards away from the other building). The team worked together developing automated software testing tools. They were previously all located together in neighboring cubicle offices at the Billerica site but, for reasons not related to their work on this project, were relocated to these distributed sites a few months before the beginning of the study. During the second week of the study, a fifth team member was added at the Billerica site in a cubicle facing that of the other Billerica team member.

Although the team had no formal hierarchy, there were differences in their job responsibilities. The project leader (PL) was located alone in one Mountain View building. The two members located in the other Mountain View building were software developers (SD1 and SD2) who wrote most of the computer code. The customer representative (CR1) in Billerica communicated the customers' needs, requirements, and experiences to the rest of the team. The newly added member in Billerica (CR2) had a job similar to CR1.

Altogether, we studied the team's work activity for 14 weeks. After three weeks in the pre-DCP condition, the desktop conferencing prototype was installed into each team member's workstation. This installation involved inserting a prototype hardware card into their existing workstation, adding a second display screen, outfitting each office with a camera and speakers, and adding software to their system. The second display screen was added to display the output of the prototype hardware card. Because CR1 had limited desk space, he substituted this display screen for his usual display. Due to equipment limitations, we were unable to equip the added member of the team (CR2) with a prototype, but he often joined CR1 in desktop conferences or used CR1's workstation when he was not in the office. The team was studied in the full-DCP condition for seven weeks in an attempt to go beyond the initial novelty effect of introducing a technology to a more routine pattern of use. For the DCP minus video condition, the hardware card and second display screen were removed; the speakers and camera (camera's microphone was used for audio input) were left in their offices. The team was studied in the DCP minus video condition for four weeks.

Although the effects of the ordering of the conditions might be of interest, we arranged to study only one group and could not control for or explore order effects in an empirical study of this scope. We chose the order of the three conditions (pre-DCP, full-DCP, DCP minus video) to explore the transitions between conditions that we thought would be most interesting. We sought to see the effects of introducing a desktop conferencing system to a working group in the transition from pre-DCP to full-DCP, and we hoped to isolate the role of video in desktop conferencing in the transition from full-DCP to DCP minus video.

When operating at 30 video frames per second (fps), a desktop conference (audio, video, Show Me) consumed approximately 1.6 Mbit/s of network bandwidth. The bandwidth demand came mostly from the video stream and could be reduced almost directly in proportion to the requested video frame rate. At 10 fps, desktop conferences could use the existing local area networks without overly disrupting other network traffic. However, dedicated network bandwidth was needed for robust connections between the Billerica and Mountain View sites. A 0.5 Mbit/s link was leased that provided enough bandwidth to support conferencing at 5 fps. Because of this limitation, the default video frame rate was set to 5 fps for all desktop conferences among the team, although any user could change this rate before starting a conference. This video frame rate was noticeably less lively than the 30 fps used in full-motion video, and we wanted to learn if this video rate was usable.

Observation methodologies

A combination of observation methods were used to obtain information from different perspectives for this study.

- Phone calls received from other team members were automatically logged (number of calls, average duration) by the corporate internal phone system.

- Electronic mail messages sent to the other team members and to the team's distribution list were collected by the participants.

- Desktop conferences made using the prototype were automatically logged (start and stop time, who was being conferenced, conference parameters, etc.) by software built into the prototype.

- Face-to-face meetings among team members at the Mountain View site were logged by the team members.

These data provided an opportunity to observe many differences in the use of these communication media across the three conditions.

In addition to the quantitative data collected, we videotaped selected samples of collaborative activity in each of the three conditions. All videotapes were recorded from a stationary camcorder mounted on a tripod without any camera operator present at the meeting. Videotapes of the desktop conferences were captured by a camcorder aimed at the computer display screen of one of the participants. After each videotape was made, the participants were always given the option of erasing the videotape if they were uncomfortable with preserving a record of that interaction (which they requested in one instance).

The videotape data captured 19 interactions including examples of: all team video conference room meetings, all team face-to-face meetings, two-person face-to-face meetings, three-way phone conferences, two-way desktop conferences, three-way desktop conferences (involving all five team members), four-way desktop conferences, and two-way Show Me conferences (with phone audio). These tapes were analyzed by a multi-disciplinary group that included the designers of the prototype, a psychologist, and user interface designers. The group studied the tapes in the tradition of interaction analysis (Tatar, 1989) to understand how the team accomplished their collaborative work and compared similar types of activity across different instances collected on videotape.

Furthermore, we interviewed each team member individually to gather their perceptions about their work activities at various stages during the three conditions of the study at the following times: at the beginning of the study, to understand their existing work activity; before the installation of the desktop conferencing prototype, to survey their expectations of how they would use the prototype; mid-way through the use of desktop conferencing prototype, to see how they were responding to it; just prior to removing the video capability, to survey their expectations of how that would affect their use of the tools; at the end of the study, to review their perceptions of the experience.

Limitations of the data

It is important to note the context and limitations of these data to appropriately understand and apply the results from this study. Since this team previously had been co-located, they were in some respects not representative of distributed groups in general. On the other hand, they also knew how they had interacted when co-located and could evaluate how well the prototype tools fulfilled those interactional needs. Since video is believed to be especially useful in supporting social activities (Gale, 1990), the team's existing social relationships provided an opportunity to see if video effectively supported those relations.

Although we intended to collect data that would provide a clean comparison among the three conditions, several factors combined to complicate the data collection and the analyses that can be drawn from the data. In general, the quantitative data were relatively sparse and had large variances, making it less likely that we could demonstrate statistically significant differences. Several factors contributed to the variance in the data.

Company holidays shortened weeks 1 and 5 by one day. Training classes or travel caused one or more team members to be away from the office for an entire week during weeks 3, 4, 7, 8, and 11 of the study. These absences not only affected the data, but also caused some adjustments in the duration of the three conditions. A total of 15 other individual days of absence (e.g., illness, day off) occurred during the study. During the third week of the full-DCP condition (week 6), both CR1 and CR2 from Billerica traveled to Mountain

View to meet with the team and others there. Besides affecting the data collected for that week, the visit had an effect on the progress and nature of the team's subsequent work.

Also, several uncertainties were discovered in the phone, e-mail, and face-to-face meeting logging. Problems with the automatic phone logging of the Billerica team members resulted in lost data. Consequently, our analyses are based only on the data of calls received by Mountain View team members. Because CR2 was a new employee to the company, we excluded his e-mail data throughout the study. After the study started, PL realized that he was logging e-mail from only one of two sources from where he sends mail, resulting in some lost e-mail data from him. In addition, we allowed the participants to delete any e-mail messages that they did not want us to see before making their e-mail logs available to us. Although this added some uncertainty to the e-mail data collected, we felt that it was a worthwhile trade-off to accommodate their participation in the study.

Because we were relying on the team members to report their face-to-face meetings, some meetings were probably recorded inaccurately or not at all. These meeting logs also had some inherent uncertainty since individuals reported the same meeting differently (different start and stop times, different participants). We reminded them throughout the study to log their meetings to counteract any tendency to overlook their self-logging over time.

While all of these factors frustrated our attempt to get clean, quantitative data to compare among the three conditions, they were accommodated to preserve the team's actual working activity with minimal disruption from the study. The quantitative data were used to identify trends and raise issues that we could examine through the other qualitative data that we had collected. Even though these variations limit some of the claims we can make based on the quantitative data, we accept them as a characteristic of studying actual work activity, rather than studying behavior in an isolated, laboratory setting.

7.6   Analyzing the use of desktop conferencing

The quantitative and qualitative data were analyzed for any patterns or changes across the three conditions. We conducted statistical tests on the quantitative data to identify significant differences across the conditions. We used the videotape and interview data to discover changes across the conditions and to help explain patterns that were observed in the quantitative data. These analyses revealed that desktop conferencing:

• did not increase overall interactive communication,
• was used more heavily when video was available,

• reduced the use of e-mail messages,
• was perceived by the team members to replace some face-to-face and video conference room meetings,
• was perceived by the team members to reduce the use of the telephone,
• was a novel collaboration setting, and
• afforded some awareness of where people were looking (gaze awareness).

No increase in overall interactive communication usage

The data show no evidence that introducing desktop conferencing systematically changed the total amount of interactive communication (face-to-face meetings, phone calls, desktop conferences) among the team. A measure of usage for each medium of interactive communication was calculated by multiplying the duration of each interaction by the number of people involved. Figure 7.5 graphs the combined measures of usage for the interactive communication media per week. The most visible feature of this graph is the spike in week 6. This was the week when the team members from Billerica traveled to Mountain View to meet face-to-face together with the team. Because week 6 was not a typical week, data from week 6 is excluded from all subsequent quantitative analyses.

Besides the spike in week 6, there is no other visible pattern in the combined usage of interactive media throughout the three conditions. An analysis of variance showed no significant differences in the total measure of usage across the three conditions. This lack of an effect is itself a finding, suggesting that the additional desktop conferencing capability did not cause the team to spend more time in interactive communication. Instead, the introduction of desktop conferences apparently reduced the use of other forms of communication. A closer look at the data provides some insights into the usage relationships among the communication media.

Video encouraged more desktop conferencing

The data clearly show that the presence of the video capability correlated with more use of the desktop conferencing prototype. Figure 7.6 plots each of the communication media for the 14 weeks of the study (excluding the atypical week 6). For e-mail, the number of messages was counted as a measure of usage. A statistically significant decrease in the usage of the desktop conferencing prototype was observed during the DCP minus video condition when the video capability was taken away. This result indicates that the video capability was the determining factor in the team's decision to use the desktop conferencing prototype. Why did the users like using video so much?

Interviews with the team indicated that they strongly liked the video because they could see each others' reactions, monitor if they were being understood, and engage in more social, personal contact through video. Besides using desktop conferencing for technical discussions, they also reported using it for informal chatting. Some team members expressed that having the video markedly improved the communication among the team.

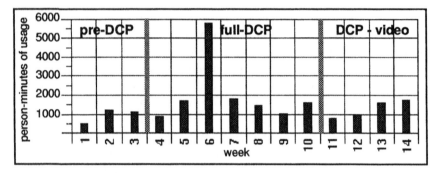

Figure 7.5. Total measure of usage for all forms of interactive communication. Total number of person-minutes of face-to-face meetings, phone calls, and desktop conferences combined per week. Note that weeks 1 and 5 only had four working days due to company holidays and the team met together at one site in week 6.

Turning to the videotape data of their use of the desktop conferencing prototype, we could see specific evidence of their use of video that would contribute to these positive perceptions. Video played a crucial role in facilitating their interaction. For example, it clearly helped remote collaborators interpret long audio pauses. We observed many pauses in desktop conferences, lasting up to 15 seconds, but the participants did not mark them as problematic. The video channel provided visual cues that explained the purpose of the pause (e.g., looking elsewhere on the computer screen or in the office, looking up at the ceiling while considering how to respond, preparing an image to send in Show Me). Without the video channel, these pauses would have been mystifying, as evidenced in video records of phone calls where participants frequently asked for feedback (e.g., "Right?", "OK?").

Other visual cues that facilitated their interaction included leaning into the camera when users could not hear what a remote collaborator said (usually prompting a repetition of the utterance) and hand gestures that indicated taking or yielding a turn of talk. Facial and body gestures often communicated whether a person was understanding what was being said, prompting the speaker to either continue explaining or move on to the next topic. The video channel conveyed many of the gestures people use to mediate their speech (Kendon, 1986).

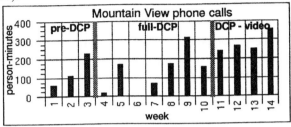

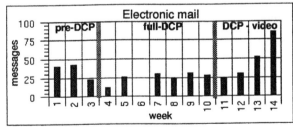

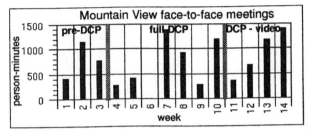

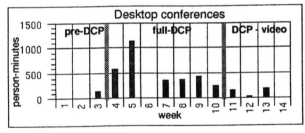

Figure 7.6. Usage of communication media. Weekly measures of usage of phone calls received by the Mountain View team members, face-to-face meetings held by the Mountain View team members, desktop conferences of the whole team, and electronic mail of the whole team across the three conditions. Phone calls, face-to-face meetings, and desktop conferences are measured in person-minutes. Electronic mail is measured in number of messages. Note that week 6 is eliminated since the team was all together at one site. Because it took two days to install the desktop conferencing prototype, some usage was recorded before the entire team was equipped for the full-DCP condition.

We also observed several examples of turn completions in desktop conferencing when one person would complete a sentence or turn of talk for a remote collaborator. Completions are a demonstration of mutual understanding that require tight interaction and coordination among the participants (Wilkes-Gibbs, 1986). The prototype demonstrated that it can support accomplishing turn completions between remote participants. Completions were notably absent when using the video conference rooms, largely due to the more than half-second audio delay.

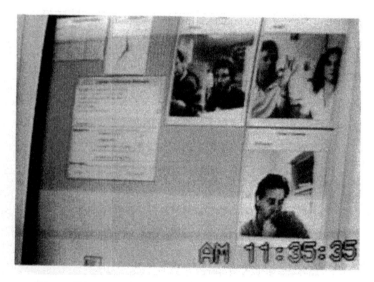

Figure 7.7. Gestural communication via the video channel. SD1 (in upper right video window) answers his own question "What does that benefit [this project]?" with a gesture indicating "zero".

The video channel was also used to visually convey information. Shrugs were often demonstrated through the video channel without any accompanying talk indicating indifference or "I don't know". Gestures and facial expression were sometimes used to subtly express disagreement. In a three-way conference involving all five team members, shown in Figure 7.7, SD1 rhetorically asks "What does that benefit [this project]?" and emphatically answers the question by synchronizing a gesture indicating "zero" without saying anything else. Occasionally, objects were held in front of the camera to show them to the others. Team members sometimes noticed activities happening in the background through the video channel. For example, they could often see people walking by at the Billerica site (which had open cubicle offices) and would wave and engage them in conversations.

The team seemed to use gestures naturally in desktop conferences much as they would in face-to-face interaction. Some of the users' gestures were not transmitted through the video channel because they were not within the camera's field of view, indicating that in some ways the desktop conferencing prototype elicited an illusion of face-to-face interaction beyond what it could actually support. At other times, the team members were aware that they were deliberately using the video channel to convey gestures. In one example, PL noticed someone he knew in Billerica looking in on a desktop conference he was having with CR1. PL waved his hand, but it was not within the camera's field of view. He quickly repositioned his wave within camera view, which finally elicited a response. The data contain evidence that users' activity both built on the familiar face-to-face experience and also accommodated the restricted capabilities of desktop conferencing.

As mentioned earlier, because of network bandwidth limitations between Billerica and Mountain View, the default video frame rate for desktop conferences was set to 5 fps. Although this rate is dramatically less than the 30 fps used in television video, the users found the lower frame rate to be usable for desktop conferencing purposes. There was only one instance (out of 72) where the users chose to increase the video frame rate (to 10 fps). When asked in the interviews about the slow frame rate, they commented that it was noticeably slow but tolerable. They did comment on a related problem of having the video image occasionally freeze when the network traffic or computational load was heavy. Under severe loading conditions, images were frozen for several seconds before a new image was received. Users found this to be annoying, although it was sometimes amusing if the frozen image captured a humorous pose of one of the collaborators.

In the interviews just prior to removing the video, all team members anticipated they would hardly use the prototype once the video capability was removed. The prototype's audio quality was considerably worse than the telephone, due to the perceptible delay and echo. While the poor audio quality is another reason that the use of the prototype decreased in the DCP minus video condition, it actually provides more evidence of how much the participants valued the video capability. Despite the prototype's poor audio capability, they still used it when video was available, and reported positive perceptions of using it. However, once the video capability was removed, they were not interested in using the prototype relative to the superior audio provided by the phone.

Although the Show Me shared drawing tool might have motivated continued use of the prototype after removing the video, it was not enough to counteract the lack of video and the poor audio quality. We did not collect statistics on the actual use of Show Me, but we got the impression that the team did not use Show Me heavily, even during the full-DCP condition.

Comments from the interviews indicated that the team found Show Me very satisfying and helpful when they did use it. However, the artifact that the team worked on most often was a large document in a word processor, and Show Me was not optimally designed to work through many pages of a document. The awkwardness of using Show Me for multi-page editing may largely explain the relatively light use of Show Me during the study.

Furthermore, it was less convenient to use Show Me in the DCP minus video condition. Show Me was integrated into their collaboration setting in the full-DCP condition, since it was started automatically with a desktop conference. In the DCP minus video condition, the team used the phone for interactive communication and Show Me would have been an additional tool to start on their computer workstations. Some participants commented that they did not think of starting Show Me while talking on the phone, even though they could think of situations when that might have been helpful.

Desktop conferencing reduced the use of e-mail messages

We did not expect the availability of desktop conferencing, an interactive communication medium, to have any effect on the use of e-mail, which is asynchronous. However, the e-mail statistics in Figure 7.6 and Table 7.1 show a statistically significant drop in the average number of e-mail messages per day in the full-DCP condition compared to the pre-DCP or DCP minus video conditions.

	total # msgs.	avg. msgs. / day	s.d.	avg. init./ day	avg. reply / day
pre-DCP	120	7.6	5.7	3.4	4.1
full-DCP	155	5.2	3.0	3.0	2.2
DCP - video	185	9.7	7.5	4.5	5.2

Table 7.1. Overall e-mail statistics across conditions. Total number of e-mail messages, average number of messages per day, standard deviation of the average, and average initiated and reply messages per day across the pre-DCP, full-DCP, and DCP minus video conditions.

Why would the availability of desktop conferencing affect the use of e-mail? One explanation offered in the interviews is that they would sometimes choose to respond to an e-mail message by desktop conferencing instead of replying with e-mail. One member said that he sometimes started composing a reply e-mail message, but then realized that he could respond with a desktop conference instead and discarded the unfinished e-mail reply. Some team members also commented that they disliked using e-mail when handling certain topics because they often exchanged many messages before resolving an issue. Issues that might require several cycles of e-mail messages could be easily and quickly resolved in an interactive group desktop conference.

We tested these explanations by reviewing the e-mail data to count the number of "reply" e-mail messages (containing the system generated "Re:" in the subject field) compared to the number of "initiated" messages (those not in reply to a previous message) across the three conditions, shown in Table 7.1. The data show that the proportion of reply messages was lower in the full-DCP condition than the other two conditions, but this pattern was not statistically significant.

Some team members also mentioned that the team rarely used e-mail among themselves when they were located together in Billerica (except when trying to avoid personal contact with someone). After moving to the three different sites, they began using e-mail heavily, especially since the three-hour time difference between Billerica and Mountain View made it difficult to contact remote team members by phone. Comments from the interviews indicated that they did not prefer using e-mail (except to send computer files), but resorted to using it because the other modes of communication were not effective, given the distribution of the team in time and space. The reduction in e-mail usage during the full-DCP condition could indicate that desktop conferencing restored some of the interactions they had when they were located at the same site, thereby reducing their reliance on e-mail.

These factors alone would not explain why using the phone was not perceived as offering the same benefits as desktop conferencing for reducing e-mail use. Phone calls, like desktop conferences, afford interactive rather than asynchronous communication, but they do not allow visual contact with the remote party. Perhaps the novelty effect of introducing a new technology (desktop conferencing) attracted the team to use it in ways that they did not use an existing technology (the telephone). However, the data show that the use of desktop conferencing did settle down after the first two weeks of the full-DCP condition, but the diminished use of e-mail stayed relatively constant throughout the full-DCP condition. There is no evidence in the data that the team, having learned the value of substituting interactive communication for e-mail, began using the phone to substitute for e-mail after the video capability was removed from the prototype. These observations reinforce the role of video in determining the use of communication media.

Perceived reduction of face-to-face and video conference room meetings

The Mountain View participants reported that they believed they were having fewer face-to-face meetings during the full-DCP condition, and that the meetings they had tended to be longer. We found no statistically significant patterns in the quantitative data to support their perceptions, although we did find some interesting anecdotal indications.

As Table 7.2 shows, the team averaged slightly fewer face-to-face meetings per day during the full-DCP condition than the pre-DCP and DCP minus video conditions. Similarly, the average duration of face-to-face meetings was slightly longer in the full-DCP condition compared with the pre-DCP and DCP minus video conditions. However, these data exhibited high variability and neither of these differences were statistically significant.

	mtgs / day	avg. length (mins.)	s.d.
pre-DCP	1.86	32.8	27.5
full-DCP	1.28	43.9	49.6
DCP - video	1.60	39.2	44.2

Table 7.2. Face-to-face meeting statistics across conditions. Average number of face-to-face meetings per day, average duration of meetings, and standard deviation of the average duration (indicating variance) across the pre-DCP, full-DCP, and DCP minus video conditions.

We found at least one occasion when we know a desktop conference substituted for a face-to-face meeting. In a desktop conference that we had videotaped for our study, the participants discussed a sensitive personnel issue. They asked us to erase our videotape of the conference so that there would be no record of the interaction. They said they normally would have had that discussion face-to-face, but were apparently comfortable enough with desktop conferencing that they were willing to use it for a sensitive discussion. The team members also indicated that they thought it was worth the effort of walking to a common meeting site for longer meetings with more than two people. These two observations indicate that the participants believed they were more likely to use desktop conferences than face-to-face meetings for short interactions, even though the statistics do not support this perception. However, since the face-to-face meeting data are based on self reports, and since the participants tended to round the meeting durations to the nearest quarter-hour, it would be interesting to investigate this perception with more precise data.

The data do show that desktop conferencing eliminated this team's use of the video conference rooms. In the pre-DCP condition, the team had just started using a weekly one-hour time slot in the video conference rooms to have all-team meetings. In the full-DCP condition, the team never used that time slot, but they resumed using it two weeks into the DCP minus video condition. Even though the prototype was not designed to support a five-way connection, they conducted all-team desktop meetings several times by having three-way conferences in which pairs of people shared a camera at two sites (see Figure 7.7). Although the team did not frequently meet all together via desktop conferencing, the sub-team desktop conferences apparently obviated the need for all-team video conference meetings.

While full desktop conferencing eliminated the use of video conference rooms for this five-person team, it should be noted that video conferencing between meeting rooms is different than conferencing between personal desktops. Video conference rooms allow planned meetings between moderate-sized groups (perhaps five or more on each side) in an environment that is relatively free from interruptions (e.g., telephone calls, e-mail arrival, impromptu visitors). Desktop conferencing on the other hand allows spontaneous interactions between individuals or small groups where each person has access to the resources of their own workstation and office. Although desktop conferencing eliminated the use of video conference rooms for this team of five people, we do not believe that desktop conferencing should generally be considered to replace video conference rooms.

Desktop conferencing was used to increase the frequency of visual contact between Billerica and Mountain View. Of the 72 desktop conferences logged, 28 (39%) involved team members from both sites. Thus in the six typical weeks in the full-DCP condition, there were 28 cross-site desktop conferences, while in the seven weeks of the pre-DCP and DCP minus video conditions combined there were only seven video conference room meetings where collaborators at both sites could see each other.

Although the team used desktop conferencing to gain visual access to remote team members, the majority of the desktop conferences (61%) were among the Mountain View team members. These team members could have walked to each other's buildings to meet face-to-face, but they elected to use the desktop conferencing prototype instead. Despite the degraded experience of desktop conferencing, it was used to avoid the six minute walk between buildings. On the other hand, SD1 commented that he thought it would be "decadent" to have a desktop conference between him and SD2, whose office was about 30 feet down the hall in the same building. There was only one short desktop conference recorded between SD1 and SD2 toward the end of the full-DCP condition. Thus, the data indicate a use of desktop conferencing among collaborators who are separated by thousands of miles as well as several hundred yards, but not as close as a few tens of feet.

There are several likely explanations for the relatively higher frequency of desktop conferences among the Mountain View members contrasted with cross-site desktop conferences between Mountain View and Billerica. There were more team members in Mountain View (three) compared to Billerica (two), and each Mountain View member had a DCP workstation in their own office while the two Billerica members shared one DCP workstation in CR1's cubicle. Furthermore, because of the three-hour time difference between the sites, there were effectively only three to five hours (depending on their availability during the two lunch hours) during the typical work day when members at both sites might be available for a cross-site conference, compared with seven to eight hours that were typically available among the Mountain View members.

	total # calls	avg. # / day	avg. length (secs.)
pre-DCP	26	1.9	461.5
full-DCP	78	2.7	348.2
DCP - video	58	2.9	453.3

Table 7.3. Phone call statistics across conditions. Total number of calls, average number of calls per day, and average duration of calls across the pre-DCP, full-DCP, and DCP minus video conditions.

Perceived reduction in the use of phone calls

In the interviews before installing the desktop conferencing prototype, some team members expected they would use a desktop conference for anything they currently did over the phone. In the interviews after they had used the prototype for a couple of weeks, all team members reported less phone use when they had the prototype. In contrast to their perceived reduction in phone call use, the measure of phone call usage (shown in Figure 7.6) did not show any significant differences across the three conditions. The phone call statistics in Table 7.3 show a slight increase in the average number of phone calls per day over the three conditions. The average duration of phone calls was shorter in the full-DCP condition compared to the pre-DCP and DCP minus video conditions, suggesting that desktop conferences may have replaced longer phone calls but they still used the phone for shorter calls. However, there was wide variation in the relatively sparse data, and these patterns were not found to be statistically significant.

Interviews with the participants provided some reasons why participants continued to use the phone rather than desktop conferencing for short calls. The prototype was not optimized for quick performance; starting a desktop conference could take about a half-minute. For quick calls (e.g., "Ready to go to lunch?", checking if someone is in the office before visiting), the users did not want to incur the overhead of starting a desktop conference since using the phone would be much quicker. Sometimes the participants would call to check if someone was in the office before going through the trouble of starting a desktop conference. Audio quality was also relatively poor compared to the phone due to the delay and echo. As mentioned earlier, desktop conferencing to someone nearby was also perceived to be less appropriate in some situations than calling or just walking down the hall.

Desktop conferencing is a novel collaboration setting

From the analysis of the videotapes, it is clear that desktop conferencing is a distinctly different collaboration setting than meeting face-to-face or talking on the phone. In desktop conferences, all members are located in their own offices where each person has access to his or her own resources and distractions (e.g., phone calls, e-mail arrivals, visitors). By contrast, face-to-face meetings are usually held in conference rooms (where everyone is isolated from their resources) or in one person's office (where only that person can access her books, phone calls, etc.). Consequently, in face-to-face meetings, it is generally considered poor etiquette to take long phone calls or spend much time reading e-mail while other people are waiting for attention. In the desktop conferences we analyzed, there were several examples of people reading e-mail and taking phone calls during a desktop conference. They seemed to treat desktop conferencing as a medium for focused interaction (like a phone call or meeting), but also one that tolerated significant amounts of attention to personal distractions. This kind of interaction is similar to the ebb and flow of group and individual activity that occurs when sharing an office or working in a computer-augmented meeting room (Stefik et al., 1988).

There are several reasons why desktop conferencing afforded this type of collaborative activity. Because all participants are located in their own offices, if one member attends to a personal distraction, every other member can easily attend to their own personal work while waiting for the conference to refocus. Also, desktop conferencing affords many cues (largely through audio and video) that enable a remote collaborator to make sense of what is happening when one person temporarily stops participating. By contrast, in a phone conversation it is often difficult to interpret long pauses. In addition, some users commented that since they did not have true eye contact with the remote collaborator, they felt that they were slightly detached from them, which allowed attending to personal work.

Although the users of the desktop conferencing prototype found themselves in a novel collaboration setting, they interacted in a very routine and seemingly familiar manner. They smoothly migrated from group interaction to individual work in a way that could not occur in any other medium, yet they did so in a natural way without marking the activity as novel. We believe that the desktop conferencing prototype, largely through the video channel, provided enough cues for participants to interpret the transitions between group interaction and individual work and accommodate a new style of interaction.

Although they were able to adopt a new style of working in desktop conferences, interview comments indicated that they did not necessarily like it. Several team members found it annoying when someone stopped to take a long phone call or continued doing private work while desktop conferencing. Although the video channel helped them detect such distractions, it still required a delicate social negotiation to try to manage them directly. Just as participants in face-to-face conversation are often reluctant to direct their partner's action (e.g., "Excuse me, you need to wipe off some food smudged on your face"), so desktop conference participants did not feel free to tell their partners to stop doing other work or to reposition their head to be in camera view. It is notable that many of the rules of politeness that govern face-to-face interaction also appear to be in force in desktop conferencing.

The group interaction that occurred in desktop conferencing was notably more like the exchanges seen in face-to-face meetings than in the commercial video conference rooms. In the videotaped desktop conferences, we saw instances when remote collaborators were able to interrupt each other, accomplish turn completions, and time jokes in their conversation. Such interactions were markedly absent in videotapes of their meetings held in the video conference rooms. This improved interaction was probably enabled by reducing the audio delay in the prototype. During the study, the one-way audio delay was measured to vary between 0.22 and 0.44 seconds (depending on processing and networking loads). Surprisingly, this slight improvement over the 0.57 second delay in the video conference rooms was apparently enough to noticeably affect the level of interaction they could accomplish. Still, the desktop conferencing's shorter audio delays were not ideal; while the participants were able to effectively compensate for them, comments in the interviews indicated that the delays were noticeable and sometimes bothersome.

Gaze awareness in desktop conferencing

To provide a sense of eye contact in desktop conferencing, the lens of the camera was positioned as close as possible to where the video window of the remote collaborator appeared on the screen. However, all the team members remarked that their inability to establish direct eye contact through the prototype felt strange. Rather than introducing half-silvered mirror devices that effectively provide eye contact (Buxton & Moran, 1990), we wanted to see if users could interact comfortably without true eye contact. Ishii and

Kobayashi (1992) raised a distinction between eye contact (seeing eye-to-eye) and gaze awareness (being aware of where others are looking). While eye contact is the expected form of interaction in face-to-face meetings, providing each collaborator with a confident sense of gaze awareness may be sufficient to enable effective and comfortable interaction.

We found considerable evidence in the videotapes of desktop conferences that the collaborators had a strong sense of gaze awareness and were able to make use of that information. Figure 7.8 shows a sequence of video images that show one example of the use of gaze awareness. In a desktop conference between CR1 and PL, CR1 visually expresses continued disagreement with PL by avoiding "looking at" PL. PL notices that CR1 is avoiding looking at him, so he gazes and speaks to CR1 in ways that invite CR1 to look up at him. After over 40 seconds of gaze avoidance, PL moves on to another topic, at which point CR1 immediately resumes looking up at him. The timing of the interaction strongly suggests that CR1 deliberately used gaze avoidance to express disagreement.

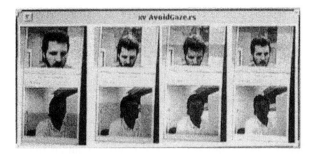

Figure 7.8. Demonstrating gaze awareness by avoiding "eye contact". This sequence of images show CR1 (top) and PL (bottom) in a desktop conference. At left, CR1 and PL are "looking at" each other. In the middle two frames, CR1 visually expresses continued disagreement by avoiding "eye contact" with PL for over 40 seconds. After PL moves on to another topic, CR1 resumes "eye contact" with him.

In the interviews, we asked whether the team members could tell when collaborators in a desktop conference were looking at them. After two weeks of use, some members were occasionally uncertain, but by the end of the study everyone said that they could. We believe that if everyone's equipment is configured to provide near eye contact, users can quickly gain a sense of gaze awareness and use that to convey cues in their interactions. Of course establishing actual eye contact would be ideal in desktop conferencing, but there may be situations when the trade-offs currently needed to accomplish that (e.g., added footprint and volume occupied by half-silvered mirror devices) are not merited.

Design implications from the study of desktop conferencing

This study indicates that, for a working team that is already familiar with each other, desktop conferencing is a useful medium for distributed collaboration. In contrast to studies that did not find a strong effect of a video channel, we found that video was the determining factor in how much desktop conferencing was used. The video provided visual and gestural cues that enabled them to interact smoothly. Gaze awareness among the collaborators in particular was used to convey cues in their interaction. When they used the shared drawing tool, they found it to be valuable in supporting distributed collaboration.

Users commented that the audio quality of the desktop conferencing prototype needed improvement. Because most team members used a speaker for audio output and an open mike for audio input, the system exhibited a considerable amount of audio echo. Those speaking often heard a delayed echo of their speech as it traveled to others' speakers and back through their microphones. The audio quality was worse in three-way conferencing, since mixing audio streams introduced even more echo, and the increased network traffic caused cutouts in the audio streams. Because of these problems, the team usually resorted to using telephone audio in three-way conferences. Although we provided headsets that eliminated the audio echo problem, all but one user found them too bothersome to use.

Additionally, our experiences with the desktop conferencing prototype indicated that the phone call model for establishing and managing conferences was too limited. Users were sometimes reluctant to use desktop conferencing to contact others because they could not tell in advance whether a person was available or interruptible. The prototype also did not have the equivalent of a phone answering machine to handle conference requests when no one was there, making it frustrating to try to contact someone. This problem was apparent in the many unsuccessful conference attempts found in the logs of prototype use. In addition to the 72 desktop conferences recorded, 96 attempts to conference were unsuccessful (recipient not in office to receive conference request, recipient's workstation not operational, recipient declined to accept conference request). It would be helpful to integrate desktop conferencing with other communication mechanisms, such as e-mail or voice mail, which could be used to leave a message after an unsuccessful attempt to conference.

The study also hinted at the value of the integration of tools. It was less likely that the team would use Show Me in the DCP minus video condition since it was no longer integrated with their medium for interactive communication (the phone). Tools such as a shared drawing space may not be used continuously throughout an interaction, but must be readily available when they are needed, or else users are less likely to expend the effort to access them. Environments that support interactive collaboration should integrate easy access to whatever shared tools the users commonly need to use.

Many of the design implications learned from this study have since been embodied in a research prototype called Montage (Tang & Rua, 1994). Montage provides a lightweight interface for making audio-video connections that is also integrated with other communication applications. Rather than being modeled on the phone call interface, Montage uses an interface metaphor of walking down hallways and peeking into offices to find someone available for interaction. It uses momentary, reciprocal video glances between computer desktops that provide easy access to full desktop video conferencing. If it is not a good time to interact, Montage offers quick access to browse an on-line calendar, send e-mail, or post an electronic note to help coordinate when to re-establish contact. A study of Montage in real use (Tang et al., 1994) found that the easier access and integration of Montage addressed many of the use issues identified by our earlier desktop conferencing prototype.

This desktop conferencing study was also a methodological learning experience in trying to combine different observational perspectives to understand the team's work activity and reaction to the prototype. Although the quasi-experimental structure of the study (three conditions, quantitative measures) did not yield many statistically significant results, it was helpful in identifying patterns and trends that we could then explore by analyzing video recorded examples of work activity and by interviewing the users for their perceptions. User perceptions elicited by the interviews also helped guide us in selecting samples of videotaped activity on which to focus our analysis and in suggesting explanations for patterns observed in the quantitative data. The multiple perspectives also provided a broader understanding of the activity that could not be found in any single observational method. In retrospect, it would have been even more useful to add a fourth condition to observe how the group returned to "normal" work activity after we removed the prototype.

The multiple observational perspectives also presented some new problems. Collecting multiple types of data added complexity to the data collection process and resulted in a vast amount of data. Since our primary commitment was to observing actual team work activity, we did not establish control conditions or exercise other manipulations often used in laboratory experiments to produce clean quantitative data for statistical comparison.

7.7   What we learned about multimedia-supported collaboration

What can we learn from our studies about designing multimedia technology to effectively support collaborative work? Two points clearly emerged from each of the three studies presented:

1.   users want video connections

2.   the quality of the audio connection is crucial.

It is also important to distinguish desktop conferencing from other types of communication media (e.g., face-to-face meetings, video conference room meetings, phone calls) to understand how it and other new multimedia collaboration technologies will be incorporated into everyday use with existing communication technologies.

Users want video

Each of the three studies clearly indicated that the users wanted to have a video capability so that they could have visual contact during their interaction. Why do the users want this video capability? Although these studies do not claim to definitively answer this question, they do present a variety of evidence that helps explain why users like video.

The video channel is clearly a valuable resource in mediating interpersonal interaction. Not only does the visual channel provide cues that facilitate the mechanics of turn-taking, but it also naturally affords gestures and other visual information that convey how much is being understood, reasons for pauses in speech, participants' attitudes, and other modifiers (e.g., humor, sarcasm) on what is being said. This support for interactional mechanisms make video-mediated communications more efficient, effortless, and effective. A richer communication channel affords greater mutual understanding among the participants, and we would expect it to help improve the quality of their collaborative work in the long term. Isaacs and Tang (1994) provide more analyses of the benefits (and limitations) of video from this same body of data.

Users' comments clearly show that they perceived added value from the video. Besides the specific benefits we identified in our analyses of video-mediated activity, users reported that the video capability made their interactions generally more satisfying. While the long-term effects of this perceived increased satisfaction are difficult to assess, they could have a cumulatively positive effect on the amount of interaction and mutual understanding over time. These user perceptions should play a significant role in guiding the design of technology to support collaboration.

Why did our studies find such a strong effect of video whereas the studies cited earlier (Ochsman & Chapanis, 1974; Gale, 1990) found none? Firstly, the previous studies focused on effects that were associated with the resulting product (e.g., quality of the result, time to complete the task). We found that the video channel affected the process of interaction (e.g., supporting turn-taking mechanisms, demonstrating understanding and attitudes). Although these effects on interpersonal communication have been hypothesized (Short et al., 1976) and recognized (Conrath et al., 1977; Gale, 1990) in earlier studies, this chapter presents specific evidence from real work activity of how video supports human interaction. While enhancing the interaction process may not have any measurable effect on the resulting product in the short term, we would expect tangible end product benefits over the span of weeks and months that is typical in real world work.

Secondly, the observational methods used in this research differed from those used in the previous studies. The previous studies analyzed the activity of artificial groups working on contrived tasks for an hour or so. The studies presented in this chapter examined the activity of actual working groups engaged in their real work activity over several weeks. Since audio and video tend to have the most effect on social, interpersonal communication, those effects would be most noticeable among a group in which social and personal relationships were well developed and exercised over time. Our ability to see how video supports social interaction was a direct result of studying actual working activity that had real social elements in it.

The value of video that we observed did not even include one of the inherent strengths of the video media. Video is good for showing and manipulating three-dimensional objects (e.g., a component to be manufactured, a shape to be designed), or viewing hazardous or difficult-to-reach work environments (e.g., unmanned space missions, neurosurgery – see Nardi et al., this volume). Since the groups studied in this research worked mainly with documents or computer software, they did not exercise this potential capability of video. We would expect that working teams in a domain that involved physical artifacts would find even greater value in video. As access to video-mediated communication broadens to more work environments (beyond select computer research facilities), this benefit of video will likely become more relevant.

Audio is crucial

In each of our three studies, audio quality was an issue. Audio plays a fundamental role in supporting human interaction, and users' expectations of audio are formed by their experiences in face-to-face and phone interactions. Technologies that degrade the audio channel (e.g., delays, echo, noisy audio quality) disrupt people's ability to smoothly interact with each other. Although the team using our desktop conferencing prototype was willing to endure the degraded audio to have the video capability, it was clearly the aspect they most wanted to see improved in the prototype.

Although the ideal is to strive for high fidelity audio and video, our experiences confirm that audio is relatively more important than video in supporting collaboration. Our desktop conferencing prototype made several trade-offs of degrading video performance in favor of preserving audio quality. If high network traffic prevented transmitting all of the audio-video data between sites, the video data degraded first (image froze) to allow as much audio data to get through before cutting out. Audio was delivered with minimal delay, even allowing the audio to arrive before the accompanying video image, disrupting audio-video synchrony. As long as network constraints require trade-offs to conserve bandwidth, our experiences indicate that degrading video quality before degrading audio quality provides a more usable experience.

Even with the anticipated explosion of bandwidth that information superhighways promise to deliver, bandwidth trade-offs will still be an issue in the near future. At the very least, there will be an extended transitional phase before high-bandwidth links become pervasive throughout the network. Furthermore, upgrading the infrastructure will also encourage more use and bandwidth demand, and it is unclear whether the infrastructure development will always outpace the increased demand for bandwidth. Wireless connections to mobile units and market demand for lower cost service will also perpetuate the need for bandwidth trade-off considerations. Although increasing the available bandwidth eliminates many of the current constraints on widespread adoption of multimedia technology, it also raises many new uncertainties.

Desktop conferencing is not face-to-face meeting is not video conferencing is not...

The data from our study of desktop conferencing demonstrated that it reduced certain amounts of other kinds of interaction (e.g., video conference room meetings, e-mail). Comments from the video conferencing room survey indicate that some users may like to think that video conference room meetings substitute for face-to-face meetings. However, these findings should not be taken to imply that desktop conferencing could completely replace face-to-face meetings, video conference room meetings, e-mail, or any other form of interaction. As discussed earlier, desktop conferencing is a distinct setting for collaboration and is unlikely to completely replace existing forms of interaction. The adoption of video conferencing rooms and other multimedia technology has suffered from marketing myths that promote them as replacements for face-to-face interaction (Egido, 1990).

Rather, we should strive to understand how new forms of interaction can be integrated with the existing ones into people's day-to-day work. By understanding how these new technologies augment, complement, and interact with people's existing work practice, we can design new technology that can be smoothly and naturally adopted. As we develop new technology for collaboration, more research is needed to understand existing collaborative practice as well as how users respond to the new technology in the context of their actual work. More research is needed into new issues that these technologies raise, such as the privacy concerns of having ubiquitously available audio and video and how to apply multimedia support to collaboration settings that are *non-cooperative*. By iteratively cycling between developing new technology and studying how people actually use that technology, we can both design better technology that is matched to users' needs and increase our understanding of human work activity.

Acknowledgements

We would like to acknowledge the other members of the Conferencing and Collaboration (COCO) group: David Gedye, Amy Pearl, Alan Ruberg, and Trevor Morris. They helped build the desktop conferencing prototype and provided many forms of support for this study. We thank the other participants in our regular video analysis sessions for the many insights and observations that they contributed: Monica Rua, Hagan Heller, Todd Macmillan, and Tom Jacobs. We thank Randy Smith and Jonathan Grudin for reviewing earlier versions of this chapter. The Digital Integrated Media Environment (DIME) group in Sun Microsystems Laboratories, Inc. developed the SBus card that enabled the COCO conferencing prototype. This research was conducted at Sun Microsystems Laboratories, Inc. We especially thank our anonymous participants in the study for giving us generous access to their daily work activity.

References

Bly, S. A. (1988). A use of drawing surfaces in different collaborative settings, *Proceedings of the Conference on Computer-Supported Cooperative Work*, Portland, OR, pp. 250–256.

Bly, S. A., Harrison, S. R. & Irwin, S. (1993). Media spaces: bringing people together in a video, audio, and computing environment, *Communications of the ACM,* **36**, (1), pp. 28–47.

Buxton, W. & Moran, T. (1990). EuroPARC's integrated interactive intermedia facility (IIIF): early experiences. In: S. Gibbs & A. A. Verrijn–Stuart (Eds.), *Multi–User Interfaces and Applications*, Amsterdam: Elsevier Science Publishers B.V.

Conrath, D. W., Dunn, E. V., Bloor, W. G., & Tranquada, B. (1977). A clinical evaluation of four alternative telemedicine systems, *Behavioral Science*, **22**, pp. 12–21.

Egido, C. (1990). Teleconferencing as a technology to support co-operative work: its possibilities and limitations. In: J. Galegher, R. E. Kraut, & C. Egido (Eds.), *Teamwork: Social and Technological Foundations of Cooperative Work*, Hillsdale, NJ: Lawrence Erlbaum Associates.

Falk, H. (1973). Picturephone and beyond, *IEEE Spectrum*, November, pp. 45–49.

Fish, R. S., Kraut, R. E., Root, R. W., & Rice, R. E. (1993). Video informal communication, *Communications of the ACM*, **36**, (1), pp. 48–61.

Francik, E., Rudman, S. E., Cooper, D., & Levine, S. (1991). Putting innovation to work: adoption strategies for multimedia communication systems, *Communications of the ACM*, **34**, (12), pp. 53–63.

Gale, S. (1990). Human aspects of interactive multimedia communication, *Interacting with Computers*, **2**, (2), pp. 175–189.

Gale, S. (1992). Desktop video conferencing: technical advances and evaluation issues, *Computer Communications*, **15**, (2), pp. 517–526.

Heath, C. & Luff, P. (1991). Disembodied conduct: communication through video in a multimedia office environment, *Proceedings of the Conference on Computer Human Interaction (CHI) '91*, New Orleans, LA, pp. 99–103.

Isaacs, E. A. & Tang, J. C. (1994). What video can and cannot do for collaboration: a case study, *Multimedia Systems*, **2**, (2), pp. 63–73.

Ishii, H. & Kobayashi, M. (1992). ClearBoard: a seamless medium for shared drawing and conversation with eye contact, *Proceedings of the Conference on Computer Human Interaction (CHI) '92*, Monterey, CA, pp. 525–532.

Kendon, A. (1986). Current issues in the study of gesture. In: J-L. Nespoulous, P. Perron, & A-R. Lecours (Eds.), *The Biological Foundations of Gestures: Motor and Semiotic Aspects*, Hillsdale, NJ: Lawrence Erlbaum Associates.

Krauss, R. M., Garlock, C. M., Bricker, P. D., & McMahon, L. E. (1977). The Role of audible and visible back-channel responses in interpersonal communication, *Journal of Personality and Social Psychology*, **35**, (7), pp. 523–529.

Masaki, S., Kanemaki, N., Tanigawa, H., Ichihara, H., & Shimamura, K. (1991). Personal multimedia-multipoint teleconference system for broadband ISDN. In: O. Spaniol and A. Danthine (Eds.), *High Speed Networking, III*, Amsterdam: Elsevier Science Publishers B.V.

Minneman, S. L., & Bly, S. A. (1991). Managing à trois: a study of a multi-user drawing tool in distributed design work, *Proceedings of the Conference on Computer Human Interaction (CHI) '91*, New Orleans, LA, pp. 217–224.

Mosier, J. N., & Tammaro, S. G. (In Press). Video teleconference use among geographically dispersed work groups: a field investigation of usage patterns and user preferences, *Journal of Organizational Computing*.

Ochsman, R. B., & Chapanis, A. (1974). The effects of 10 communication modes on the behavior of teams during co-operative problem-solving, *International Journal of Man-Machine Studies*, **6**, pp. 579–619.

Olson, M. H. & Bly, S. A. (1991). The portland experience: a report on a distributed research group, *International Journal of Man-Machine Systems*, **34**, (2), pp. 211–228. Reprinted in: S. Greenberg (Ed.), *Computer-supported Cooperative Work and Groupware*, London: Academic Press.

Pearl, A. (1992). *System Support for Integrated Desktop Video Conferencing*, Sun Microsystems Laboratories, Inc. Technical Report TR-92-4.

Root, R. W. (1988). Design of a multimedia vehicle for social browsing, *Proceedings of the Conference on Computer-Supported Cooperative Work*, Portland, OR, pp. 25–38.

Sacks, H., Schegloff, E., & Jefferson, G. (1974). A simplest systematics for the organization of turn-taking for conversation, *Language*, **50**, pp. 696–735.

Short, J.,Williams, E., & Christie, B. (1976). *The Social Psychology of Telecommunications*, London: John Wiley & Sons.

Smith, R. B., O'Shea, T., O'Malley, C., Scanlon, E., & Taylor, J. (1989). Preliminary experiments with a distributed, multimedia, problem solving environment, *Proceedings of the First European Conference on Computer Supported Cooperative Work: EC-CSCW '89*, London, UK, pp. 19–34. Reprinted in: J. Bowers & S. Benford (Eds.), *Studies in Computer Supported Cooperative Work: Theory Practice and Design*, Amsterdam: Elsevier Science Publishers B.V.

Stefik, M., Foster, G., Bobrow, D. G., Kahn, K., Lanning, S., & Suchman, L. (1988). Beyond the chalkboard: computer support for collaboration and problem solving in meetings, *Communications of the ACM*, (30), **1**, pp. 32–47. Reprinted in: I. Greif (Ed.), *Computer-Supported Cooperative Work: A Book of Readings*, San Mateo, CA: Morgan Kaufmann Publishers, Inc.

Tang, J. C. (1991a). Findings from observational studies of collaborative work, *International Journal of Man-Machine Studies*, **34**, (2), pp. 143–160. Reprinted in: S. Greenberg (Ed.), *Computer-supported Cooperative Work and Groupware*, London: Academic Press.

Tang, J. C. (1991b). Involving social scientists in the design of new technology. In: J. Karat (Ed.), *Taking Software Design Seriously: Practical Techniques for Human-Computer Interaction Design*, Boston: Academic Press.

Tang, J. C., & Minneman, S. L. (1991). VideoDraw: a video interface for collaborative drawing, *ACM Transactions on Information Systems*, **9**, (2), pp. 170–184.

Tang, J. C., & Rua, M. (1994). Montage: providing teleproximity for distributed groups, *Proceedings of the Conference on Computer Human Interaction (CHI) '94,* Boston, MA, pp. 37–43.

Tang, J. C., Isaacs, E. A., & Rua, M. (1994). Supporting distributed groups with a montage of lightweight interactions, *Proceedings of the Conference on Computer-Supported Cooperative Work (CSCW) '94,* Chapel Hill, NC.

Tatar, D. (1989). Using video-based observation to shape the design of a new technology, *SIGCHI Bulletin,* **21**, (2), pp. 108–111.

Watabe, K., Sakata, S., Maeno, K., Fukuoka, H., & Ohmori, T. (1990). Distributed multiparty desktop conferencing system: MERMAID, *Proceedings of the Conference on Computer-Supported Cooperative Work,* Los Angeles, CA, pp. 27–38.

Wilkes-Gibbs, D. (1986). *Collaborative Processes of Language Use in Conversation,* Unpublished Ph.D. dissertation, Stanford University.

Williams, E. (1977). Experimental comparisons of face-to-face and mediated communication: a review, *Psychological Bulletin,* **84**, (5), pp. 963–976.

8

From video-mediated communication to technologies for collaboration: re-configuring media space

Christian Heath, Paul Luff and Abigail Sellen

What of the hands? We require, promise, call, dismiss, threaten, pray, supplicate, deny, refuse, interrogate, admire, number, confess, repent, confound, blush, doubt, instruct, command, incite, encourage, swear, testify, accuse, condemn, absolve, abuse, despise, defy, flatter, applaud, bless, humiliate, mock, reconcile, recommend, exalt, entertain, congratulate, complain, grieve, despair, wonder, exclaim... There is not a motion that does not speak and in an intelligible language without discipline, and a public language that everyone understands.

(Montaigne, 1533–92)
See *Essays*, Book II Encyclopedia Britannica (1952) pp. 215-216

8.1   Introduction

Despite the optimism which has greeted successive advances in telecommunications over the past three decades, we are only now moving towards a stage at which organisations are attempting to exploit the enormous potential of recent developments in video technology. Whilst it can be argued that it is only within recent years that the technology has been robust or reasonable enough to exploit, it is interesting to note that even in cases where the technology has been deployed, there is little evidence to suggest that existing systems have proved particularly useful or even popular. It is not difficult, of course, to appeal to the local circumstances in each case to account for its relative failure, but it is worth adding that research both within the social and cognitive sciences has not succeeded in providing firm evidence for the advantages of audio-visual connectivity over the conventional telephone (cf.

Egido, 1990). There are the usual arguments concerning the significance of non-verbal behaviour in interpersonal communication and the ways in which it provides otherwise unobtainable insights into the person with whom one is talking, but given that we do not have too much difficulty talking on the telephone (and drawing inferences about another's character, will, Machiavellian intentions, and the like) it remains unclear what the visual channel adds. Indeed, we have been told that, in a large scale study of the use of video telephones by domestic users in a city in South Western France, many subscribers preferred to look at themselves whilst on the phone rather than the person with whom they were talking.

As yet, therefore, we have relatively little understanding of the characteristics of video-mediated communication and the contribution that remote visual, as well as audio access provides to physically distributed cooperative work. In this chapter we consider some of the limitations and difficulties that individuals encounter when using video technology. We do this first by describing our own naturalistic studies of people using "media spaces": computer-controlled networks of audio and video equipment designed to support collaboration among physically distributed colleagues. We focus on one media space in particular, namely EuroPARC's in-house system. We then supplement these findings with observations derived from studies of more conventional work settings, such as control rooms and medical practices. We then begin to explore the requirements for, and problems in, developing more sophisticated technological environments to enable individuals to collaborate remotely. These requirements form the basis of some experimental research which we will describe, in which we test and develop these ideas. We conclude by discussing how we might construct a more appropriate environment to support work at a distance.

8.2   Studies of video-mediated conduct

EuroPARC's media space: background and setting

In common with several other system research laboratories, Rank Xerox have in place an audio-visual infrastructure in their EuroPARC laboratory in Cambridge. This infrastructure allows scientists and administrative staff to establish visual and audible contact with each other, or to view public areas such as the commons area and the conference room. EuroPARC's offices straddle three floors, and in part the technology was introduced to facilitate informal contact and sociability between organisational personnel. The system basically consists of a camera, 14 inch monitor, speaker, and microphone in each office, with larger monitors in the public areas. The camera is typically placed either on top or is positioned to one side, roughly at a 120 degree angle, to their workstation (Figure 8.1). A flat PZM, multi-directional microphone is normally positioned on the desk by the workstation, operated by a foot pedal.

Over the past three years the infrastructure has become increasingly sophisticated, and we have experimented with various alternative configurations which might enhance contact and cooperation between EuroPARC's personnel. A number of these developments have been designed to provide "users" with more delicate ways of scanning the local environment or establishing connectivity (see, for example, Borning & Travers, 1991; and Gaver et al., 1992). Despite these technological developments, the most prevalent use of the system within EuroPARC is to maintain an open video connection between two physical domains, typically two offices. These "office shares" are often preserved over long periods of time (weeks and sometimes months). They provide two individuals based at different parts of building with continual video access to each other. Audio connections are normally switched off until one of the participants wishes to speak with the other.

A   B

Figure 8.1. Two offices using the audio-visual infrastructure at EuroPARC. In A, the camera and monitor are to the left of the workstation and the microphone is multi-directional, consisting of a small, flat metal plate on the wall, operated by a foot switch. B gives more detail of the common relationship between camera and monitor positions.

Methodological considerations

As part of the introduction and development of the EuroPARC media space, we undertook audio-visual recording of connections between individual offices. To diminish the potential influence of recording on the way people used the system, and to enable us to gain an overall picture of how frequently and for what purposes individuals used connections, we undertook "blanket" recording of a particular connection for up to two or three weeks. This data corpus was augmented by more conventional field observation both of connections and discussions in the laboratory concerning the system. We also collected audio-visual recordings of experimental systems, and the use of related technologies in environments other than EuroPARC, for example the Xerox Television (XTV) link between Britain and the USA.

Whilst our analytic orientation to the audio-visual materials and field observations was relatively catholic, it drew from recent developments in the social sciences, in particular, ethnomethodology and conversation analysis. In this approach, the emphasis is on the ways in which visual as well as vocal actions and activities are produced and rendered intelligible by participants themselves within the developing course of social interaction. In this kind of analysis, non-verbal behaviour is not treated in isolation from the co-occurring or surrounding verbal behaviour of the participants; indeed, visual and vocal conduct are treated as various means through which social actions in interaction are accomplished. Behaviour in interaction, whether visual, vocal, or a combination of both, is addressed in terms of the actions it performs *in situ* within the local configuration of activity. The meaning, or better, the sense of a particular piece of conduct, is embedded in the context at hand, accomplished in and through a social organisation which provides for the production and intelligibility of social actions and activities it performs.

In examining video-mediated communication, we had a particular interest in the ways in which participants were able to organise each others' involvement in the course of various activities and to coordinate their vocal and visual actions. In exploring the sequential organisation of the participants' actions (whether visual, vocal or a combination of both) we were also driven by an interest in various substantive concerns such as: how individuals established mutual engagement; the extent to which they were able to remain (peripherally) aware of each others' activities and environments; and whether video connectivity provided a suitable medium for accomplishing object-focused (such as screen or paper-based) collaborative tasks. Analysis developed on a case by case basis, in which we began by transcribing particular fragments of data. Using these fragments, we were able to identify particular phenomena. In this way we could compile sequences of particular types of conduct, build collections of candidate instances, and search for "deviant" cases. Comparing and contrasting our phenomena to instances found in more conventional face-to-face encounters, we slowly began to uncover some potentially interesting properties of communication mediated through audio-visual technologies (cf. Heath and Luff, 1991; Heath & Luff, 1992b).

Observations

Given the various, sometimes contradictory arguments concerning the significance of video to communication between physically distributed individuals, it is perhaps worth beginning by summarising the conclusions from our analysis concerning the contribution of real-time visual access to informal sociability and collaborative work. There are three such contributions worth mentioning.

The first is that, unlike a telephone or audio connection, at EuroPARC video provides the opportunity for individuals to assess visually the availability of a colleague before initiating contact. More precisely, the video channel not only allows an individual to discern whether a colleague is actually in his or her office, but also to assess more delicately the state of his or her current activity and whether it might be opportune to initiate contact. The infrastructure supports the possibility of momentarily glancing at a colleague before deciding whether it is opportune to establish engagement. In this way, video makes an important contribution not only to the awareness of others within a physically distributed work environment, but also to one's ability to respect the territorial rights and current work commitments of one's colleagues.

Second, once individuals have established contact with each other, video provides participants with the ability to coordinate talk with a range of other activities in which they might be simultaneously engaged. This aspect of video's contribution is particularly important to Computer Supported Cooperative Work (CSCW) where individuals are frequently undertaking screen-based activities whilst speaking with colleagues. Mutual visual access provides individuals with the ability to discern, to some extent, the ongoing organisation and demands of a colleague's activities, and thereby coordinate their interaction with the practical tasks at hand. Moreover, mutual visual access provides individuals with the ability to point at and refer to objects within the shared local milieu. Such facilities have become increasingly important in recent years as designers have begun to develop shared real-time interfaces (cf. Bly, 1988; Olson et al., 1990). Recent experiments (Olson & Olson, 1991; Smith et al., 1989) have demonstrated the importance of providing video for participants to coordinate simultaneous screen-based activities.

Third, the video channel provides participants in multi-party conversations with the ability to recognise who is speaking and to "track" the thread of the conversation. This is of particular importance where video-conferencing facilities support multi-party interactions and where each connection involves more than a single participant. In our analysis of multi-party audio-visual connections both at EuroPARC and the Xerox video-conferencing facility at Welwyn Garden City, we noted that video plays an important part in the allocation and coordination of speaker turns. The advantages of video in helping to identify and discriminate amongst speakers is also supported by experimental studies of multi-party video-conferencing systems (Sellen, forthcoming).

Despite these contributions, our observations of video-mediated communication suggest that this kind of technological medium provides a communicative environment which markedly differs from physical co-presence. In the following we will sketch some of the more significant differences between human conduct performed through technological media and actions and activities undertaken in face-to-face settings.

The insignificance of a look

In recent years a growing body of research has noted the ways in which looking at another person not only serves to provide certain information, but is itself a social action which engenders a response from the person who is being looked at (cf. Kendon, 1990; Goodwin, 1981; Heath, 1986). For example, all of us have been aware of being looked at by another within a public setting such as restaurant or a train, and felt the discomfort that another's gaze can cause. We are perhaps less aware of the ways in which we attempt to distract the other and avoid their gaze, by becoming "preoccupied" with a book we are reading or shielding our eyes with a gesture. On the other hand, a look may serve to encourage another to return their gaze, and having established a mutual orientation, allow the participants to move progressively into conversation or more generally focused interaction. Indeed, in research we conducted some years ago concerned with the medical consultation, we found the doctor would often initiate the business at hand in direct response to the patient turning towards him. In those particular cases, in the passing moment between the preliminaries of the consultation and discussing the patient's reason for visiting the doctor, a momentary look was enough to engender the doctor's initiating utterance. More generally, it has been found, throughout a range of ordinary settings, that turning and looking at another serves to elicit a response and most frequently a return of gaze from the person who is being looked at.

One of the interesting aspects of the ways in which gaze can serve to engender action, is that the person who is looked at, and responds, is not necessarily looking at the other. Whether in conversation or simply walking down the street, individuals are able to monitor peripherally the local environment, and in particular, others within the local milieu, and where necessary or appropriate, respond. Indeed, it would seem that our ability to remain sensitive to and monitor people's behaviour outside the direct line of our regard is a critical element of the ways in which we produce and coordinate our actions with each other, whether they are produced through visual conduct or talk.

When we began to look at video-mediated communication, there seemed to be some curious differences in the ways in which the participants looked at each and responded to each other's looks. In particular, we began to notice that whilst people would turn towards each other in the way they might in a co-present setting, their looks would often pass unnoticed by the person at whom they were looking. Moreover, it was not that the other was simply ignoring the look, since we knew from our research on face-to-face interaction that in "declining" another's gaze the recipient would frequently produce various actions to enable him to avoid the gaze of the other. Rather, in the cases at hand, one person would simply not notice that the other was looking at him, even where the other person upgraded, or exaggerated the look. The social and interactional significance of the look appears to be undermined by the technology; the look loses its sequential relevance.

For example, in the fragment illustrated in Figure 8.2 drawn from a recording of a video connection between a scientist and a member of the administration at EuroPARC, we find Maggie, the scientist, attempting to initiate contact with Jean. To do this, Maggie turns towards Jean and then waves. For more than ten seconds she stares at Jean but receives no response. Finally, Maggie looks away to her phone and dials Jean's number, summoning Jean to the telephone. Only when Jean replies to Maggie's greeting do the parties establish visual contact.

It is also curious that despite the relative failure of their looks and glances to engender a response from a colleague, they continue to attempt to use such devices to attract another's attention and initiate interaction.

In consequence, at least during the initial introduction of the media space into EuroPARC, we found that users frequently had to resort to more formal or explicit ways of initiating mutual engagement. Unlike co-presence where participants can delicately and progressively move, step by step, into a state of focused interaction, users would summon the other with a noise, as you might when calling someone on the telephone.

The articulation of talk and recipient insensitivity

Looking at another not only serves to initiate interaction, but plays an important part in the production and coordination of talk within an encounter. We have already mentioned how a look may encourage another to talk; gaze serving to display that the participant is not simply available but is also prepared to listen or "receive". During the course of talk speakers themselves are sensitive to the gaze of the person to whom they are talking and draw various inferences from the direction of the other's gaze concerning their involvement in the activity at hand. Indeed, it has been found that speakers have various devices for encouraging a co-participant to turn towards the speaker.

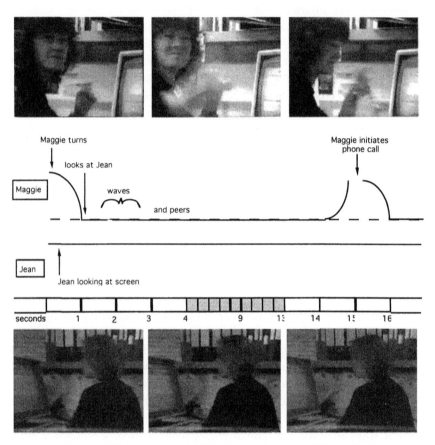

Figure 8.2. A fragment of activity between a scientist, Maggie (top), and a member of administrative staff, Jean (bottom). For presentation purposes, the gaze direction of each of the participants is indicated by a line. Gaze towards another is shown by the line moving towards a central dashed line; gaze away by their line moving away. In the above fragment, Jean's gaze remains fixed on the screen whilst Maggie first looks towards Jean and then, several seconds later, turns away.

These devices include speech perturbations such as pauses, the elongation of sounds, and various forms of self-editing and repair. They also include body movements such as gestures (cf. Goodwin, 1981; Heath, 1986). A critical element of the use and success of these various devices turns on the speaker's ability to encourage the recipient to reorientate, by looking at the co-participant. The speaker's gaze in many cases works with these various devices to establish a reorientation from the co-participant and thereby establish heightened involvement in the activity at hand.

The gaze of the speaker and the person to whom he is speaking therefore is consequential to the production of talk. For example, the speaker will often delay the onset of an utterance until they have secured the gaze of the recipient. Or, the speaker will stall the production of an utterance, withholding the gist of the talk, until they establish a reorientation from the recipient. Or, in some cases, a speaker will abandon the projected course of an utterance, and even a sequence of utterances such as a narrative, in the light of the failure to establish an appropriate orientation from the person to whom they are speaking. The production and articulation of talk in face-to-face interaction is embedded in, and interrelated with, the visual conduct of the participants; both talk and body movement inform the accomplishment of action and activity in interaction.

In consequence, the ineffectiveness of a look in video-mediated co-presence can be consequential for the production of talk and more generally the interaction between the participants.

In the following example we find the relative ineffectiveness of looking generating difficulties for the emergence of a conversation between two scientists at EuroPARC who are discussing a networking problem. We join the action as Ian initiates contact with Robert by enquiring what he should tell Marty, a colleague in the United States, to do:

```
1    I:    What I shall I tell Mar::ty↑ to do(hh).
2    (1.2)
3    R:    Er:°m::
4    (1.2)
5    R:    Let's see:: well first >first off I'd (.2) what I did
6          las: t night which seemed to (work) was send it tw::ice
7          under different names:: <an then she didn't (di::p:).
8    (1.6)
9    R:    en then she: could clean up the er::: (.8) line
10         noi:se.
11         (....)
12         (2.3)
13   R:    °thhh
14         (.3)
15   I:    O:k ay
16   R:    (Such a hak)
```

At the outset it can be noticed that Robert delays his reply to Ian's question firstly by pausing, then by producing "Er:°m::" (line 3), and then once again by pausing (line 4). Even when he does begin to reply, the actual answer is not immediately forthcoming; indeed, the gist of the reply appears pushed away from the beginning of the speaker's turn, by virtue of the preface "Let's see::" and various forms of speech perturbation, including a sound stretch ("see::"), a 0.2 second pause (line 5) and consecutive restarts "well first >first off I'd (.2) what". The speaker's actions and in particular his apparent difficulty in beginning his reply may be systematically related to the conduct of the (potential) recipient, and in particular with Robert's inability to secure his co-participant's gaze. The more detailed picture in Figure 8.3 might be helpful.

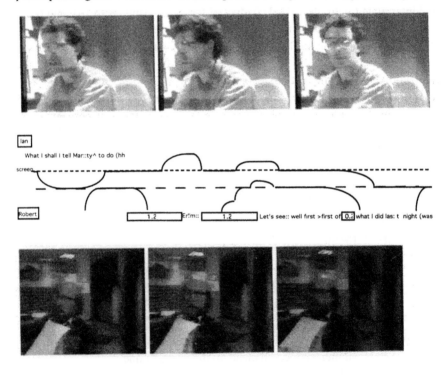

Figure 8.3. A fragment of interaction between Ian (top) and Robert (bottom) over a video-mediated "office-share" connection. Note, Ian's and Robert's talk is presented above and below the gaze line respectively. Intervals between utterances are in tenths of a second.

Withholding the reply fails to engender any reorientation from Ian, and following "Er:°m::", Robert begins progressively to shift his gaze towards Ian, as if attempting to encourage a reorientation whilst avoiding actually staring at his potential recipient. Both the withholding of the reply, and the subtle shifts in Robert's orientation fail to encourage any display of recipiency from the co-participant. Robert begins the preface "Let's see::" and looks directly towards his colleague. The alignment of gaze towards the co-participant, the preface, the sound stretch, the pause and the restarts are all devices which are regularly used to secure recipient alignment at the beginning of a turn. The pause appears to engender a response from Ian, and following his realignment of gaze from the screen to his colleague, the speaker begins the gist of his reply.

It is apparent therefore that, in this example, the respondent has various difficulties in securing the relevant form of co-participation from the potential recipient, ironically the party who initiated the interaction in the first place. The potential recipient displays little orientation to the speaker's successive attempts to secure his gaze. The difficulties faced by the speaker in attempting to secure a realignment from the recipient may derive from the relative ineffectiveness of his visual conduct and, in particular, the apparent inability of the co-participant to notice the successive shifts in orientation undertaken by the speaker. Unlike face-to-face, the relative scale and presentation of a speaker's more delicate shifts in orientation and gaze in a media space appear to pass unnoticed and thereby undermine the interactional significance of conventional devices to establish mutual orientation.

In passing, a further point should be mentioned. To provide individuals with the ability to vary their position whilst speaking with colleagues through the media space, we deliberately used multi-directional microphones to provide audio connections. These multi-directional microphones are designed to conceal relative changes in the direction of a sound within a circumscribed domain. In consequence, they mask changes in the sound level of the voice as a speaker changes his or her orientation. These changes may allow another to discern whether his colleague is changing his physical orientation, for example when the other is turning towards him. Thus, the relative ineffectiveness of a speaker's shift of gaze to engender response during the course of utterance may not only derive from the accessibility of their visual conduct, but also from the absence of changes in tone and loudness of the voice.

The impact of gesture

Other forms of bodily conduct movements, ranging from relatively gross shifts in postural orientation through to minor head nods and the like also accomplish, often in combination with talk, social actions and activities. They are "locally" or contextually significant, serving to engender or provide opportunities for particular actions from a co-participant. We have already mentioned, for example, how gestures can be used to elicit the gaze of the person to whom one is speaking, and how the utterance itself may be delayed until the gesture has accomplished its particular work. In some cases we find gestures accomplishing two or three actions simultaneously; the sequential relevance of the movement engendering particular responses from the co-participant at different points within the emergent of the activity. The significance of the participants' bodily conduct is accomplished within the developing course of the interaction and achieves its particular sequential significance then and there within the local configuration of action.

In video-mediated interaction, speakers use gestures as they might in face-to-face interaction. For example, in the following example (Figure 8.4) we find a lengthy description of an interface in which the speaker appears to encourage his recipient to participate.

The description itself is accompanied by a series of iconic or illustrative gestures through which Robert shows the operation of an icon in the interface. These include a side to side gesture occurring over "X an Y:::." (line 2) followed by an open palm movement from side to side with "were to be manipulated:" (line 6). Robert moves his palm down and flat as he utters "remain fixed" (line 8) and moves his second and third fingers down as he says "two:: (.) <three variables" (line 8). These gestures illustrate the ways in which the variables might be manipulated. Robert has the gaze of the recipient during much of this extract but only turns towards his co-participant during the final part of the description.

On the one hand, the speaker's gestures appear to be designed to provide a visual portrayal of the objects and actions mentioned in the talk (see for example, Birdwhistel, 1970; Bull, 1983; Ekman and Friessen, 1969; Schegloff, 1984). There is little evidence however, either in this fragment, or in numerous other instances of iconic gestures in video-mediated interaction, that the illustrative component successfully provides the co-participant with relevant or sequentially significant information. On the other hand the gestures also appear to be designed to encourage Ian to participate more actively in the description. They fail however to transform the way in which he is participating in the talk; indeed he provides little indication, despite various opportunities and encouragements to display that he is actually following the emergent description. Consequently, the speaker, who has been unable to encourage the recipient to indicate whether he agrees, disagrees or fails to follow the description, is then faced with having explicitly to elicit confirmation and clarification.

The relative inability of the speaker's visual conduct to effect some response from the recipient during the production of turns at talk is found elsewhere, amongst different users within the data corpus. Even relatively basic sequences that recur within face-to-face interaction, for example when a speaker uses a movement to elicit the gaze of a recipient and coordinates the production of an utterance with the receipt of gaze, tend to be absent from the materials at hand.

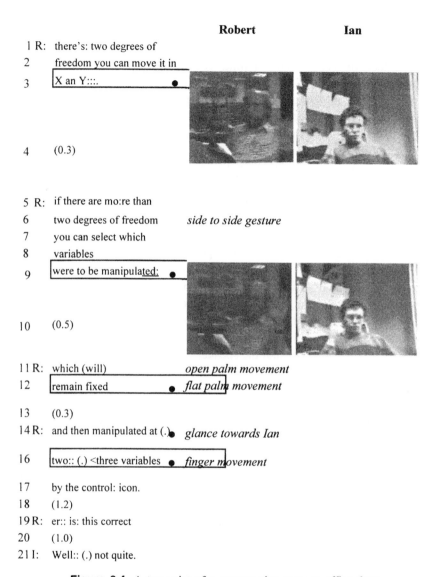

Robert   Ian

1 R: there's: two degrees of
2   freedom you can move it in
3   X an Y:::.   •

4   (0.3)

5 R: if there are mo:re than
6   two degrees of freedom   *side to side gesture*
7   you can select which
8   variables
9   were to be manipulated: •

10   (0.5)

11 R: which (will)   *open palm movement*
12   remain fixed   •   *flat palm movement*

13   (0.3)
14 R: and then manipulated at (.)• *glance towards Ian*

16   two:: (.) <three variables • *finger movement*

17   by the control: icon.
18   (1.2)
19 R: er:: is: this correct
20   (1.0)
21 I: Well:: (.) not quite.

Figure 8.4. A transcript of a conversation over an office-share connection between Ian and Robert.

Speakers continue to gesture and produce a range of bodily behaviour during the delivery of talk in video-mediated communication. Yet visual conduct largely fails to achieve its performative impact or sequential significance.

Asymmetries in video-mediated conduct

The foregoing analyses suggest that social interaction within a media space reveals asymmetries which, as far as we are aware, are neither found within face-to-face interaction nor in other technologically mediated forms of communication such as telephone calls. Indeed, even in the light of the growing corpus of literature concerned with asymmetries within various forms of institutional language use and interaction such as that in the medical consultation or in the courtroom, the distribution of communicative resources are particularly peculiar in video-mediated presence. For example, in institutional environments we find the incumbents of pre-established roles, such as doctor and patient, having differential access and influence to activity types throughout the course of an event. By contrast, in the materials at hand, the asymmetries parallel the categories of speaker and hearer and are in constant flux as the conversation and different forms of participation emerge. The asymmetries undermine the very possibility of accomplishing certain actions and activities.

Despite providing participants with the opportunity of monitoring the visual conduct of the other, and gearing the production of an activity to the behaviour of the potential recipient, media space and video-conferencing systems can systematically interfere with the interactional significance of non-vocal action and activity. On the one hand, the speaker, or more generally the interactant, has visual access to his or her co-participant. The speaker is able to monitor how the co-participant behaves whilst speaking to him or her and remains sensitive to the recipient's behaviour, state of involvement, and such like. But on the other hand, the resources upon which a speaker ordinarily relies to shape the ways in which a co-participant listens and attends to the talk appear to be interfered with by the technology. In video-mediated interaction, the speaker has visual access to the other but is, at least in part, communicatively impotent.

Incongruencies in the environment of action

The asymmetries we have outlined arise in the light of two, interrelated issues. Firstly, "recipients" have limited and distorted access to the visual conduct of the other. The other's conduct is available on a monitor which not only distorts the shape of a movement, transforming its temporal and spatial organisation, but also presents the image of the other *in toto*. It destroys the relative weighting of different aspects of an individual's conduct. Moreover the presentation of the other on a conventional monitor undermines the possibility of peripherally monitoring the different aspects of the co-participant's conduct. Secondly, an individual's limited and distorted access to the other and their local environment, undermines their ability to design and redesign movements such as gestures in order to secure their performative impact. These problems become more severe when one recognises that in contrast to physical co-presence, a person undertaking an action, such as speaking, cannot change their own bodily orientation in order to adjust their perception of the recipient and the local environment. The speaker is unable to see how his or her actions appear to the other, and in consequence, has relatively few resources to enable him or her to modify conduct in order to achieve a performative impact. It is not surprising therefore, that in reviewing the data corpus, one finds numerous instances of upgraded and exaggerated gestures and body movements as speakers attempt to achieve some impact on the way that others are participating in the activity, literally, at hand.

Our observations of EuroPARC's relatively sophisticated media space, as well as more conventional video-conferencing systems, have shown that such systems provide users with incongruent environments in which to communicate and collaborate.   Despite this incongruity, individuals presuppose the effectiveness of their conduct and assume that their frame of reference is "parallel" with the frame of reference of their co-participant. This presupposition of a common frame of reference and a reciprocity of perspectives is a foundation of socially organised conduct.

> Now it is a basic axiom of any interpretation of the common world and its objects that these various co-existing systems of coordinates can be transformed one into the other; I take it for granted, and I assume my fellow-man does the same, that I and my fellow-man would have typically the same experiences of the common world if we changed places, thus transforming my Here into his, and his – now to me a There – into mine.
>
> (Schutz, 1962, pp. 315–6)

In video-mediated presence, camera and monitor inevitably transform the environments of conduct, so that the bodily activity that one participant produces is rather different from the object received by the co-participant. The presupposition that one environment is commensurate with the other undermines the production and receipt of visual conduct and provides some explanation as to why gesture and other forms of bodily activity may be ineffectual when mediated through video rather than undertaken within a face-to-face, co-present social environment.

8.3   Collaborative work in other organizational settings

The difficulties that people have when using media spaces, and perhaps the general lack of enthusiasm for the technology, becomes clearer when one considers how collaborative work is organised in more conventional environments. Alongside our research of media space use, we have undertaken a series of naturalistic studies of work, interaction and technology in a range of organisational settings. These settings include line control rooms in London Underground (Heath & Luff 1992, 1994), primary health care (Greatbatch et al. 1993), architectural practices (Luff & Heath 1992), and news agencies (Heath & Nicholls, forthcoming).

Whilst the settings encompass a broad range of tasks and technologies, the studies reveal that collaborative work in more conventional environments appears to reveal generic features which are relevant to how individuals organise their own activities and coordinate their own contributions, in real time, with others. So for example, if we take the London Underground control rooms we find that personnel have developed a body of informal and tacit practices for distributing information to each other and coordinating simultaneously multiple activities. These practices allow personnel to distribute information to colleagues and to monitor each other's activities, whilst apparently engaged in a single, individual task. In this way, personnel coordinate their actions with each other and sustain a mutually compatible sense of the "business at hand" whilst managing their own specific responsibilities within a complex division of labour. The studies reveal the ways in which co-present collaborative work relies upon a complex body of interactional practices through which personnel "peripherally monitor" and participate in each other's actions and activities. Indeed, in such settings, it becomes increasingly difficult to demarcate the "individual" from the "collaborative" as personnel mutually sustain multiple activities which ebb and flow within various forms of co-participation and production.

More generally the studies reveal various aspects of collaborative work which are of relevance both to the design and deployment of media space as well as understanding the current limitations of such technologies. Of particular relevance are the findings that:

- Both focused and unfocused collaboration is largely accomplished not through direct face-to-face interaction, but through alignment towards the focal area of the activity, such as a document, where individuals coordinate their actions with others through "peripheral monitoring" of the others involvement in the activity "at hand". For example, much collaboration is undertaken side by side where the individuals are continuously sustaining a shared focus on an aspect of a screen or paper-based document, such as a section of an architectural drawing;
- Collaborative work relies upon individuals subtly and continuously adjusting their access to each other's activities to enable them to establish and sustain differential forms of co-participation in the tasks "at hand";

- Collaborative work involves the ongoing and seamless transition between individual and collaborative tasks, where personnel are simultaneously participating in multiple, interrelated activities;
- An individual's ability to contribute to the activities of others and fulfil their own responsibilities relies upon peripheral awareness and monitoring; in this way information can be gleaned from the concurrent activities of others within the "local milieu", and actions and activities can be implicitly coordinated with the emergent tasks of others;
- Much of the interaction through which individuals produce, interpret and coordinate actions and activities within co-present working environments is accomplished using various objects and artefacts, including paper and screen-based documents, telephones, and the like. The participants' activities are mediated and rendered visible through these objects and artefacts.

We can see, therefore, that video technology which primarily provides a face-to-face orientation to users, fails to support peripheral monitoring and peripheral participation, does not provide access to tools, artefacts and the users' "local" environments, and introduces unanticipated asymmetries into the interaction between users, is unlikely to support even the more basic forms of organisational work. However, on a more positive note, we can use these findings to guide us in how we might reconsider the design and deployment of video and telecommunication systems to provide a more appropriate environment for cooperative work, and more particularly to provide an environment which does not undermine human abilities and competencies.

8.4   Developing the work space

On the basis of the research we have described, we can begin to discern the limitations of a media space, at least as it is currently conceived. In part, these problems emerge as a result of assumptions which appear to inform the design of media spaces and related technologies such as video telephones and video-conferencing systems. One such overriding assumption appears to be that a face-to-face, head and shoulders view is the most important for interpersonal communication and collaboration.

Yet, as we have discussed, face-to-face interaction is only one amongst a variety of cooperative activities which take place. Indeed, in many settings, face-to-face interaction constitutes a relatively small part of working together, and is one amongst a diverse configuration of spatial and bodily arrangements through which personnel participate in each other's activities and accomplish the "business at hand". In working together, individuals are continually and seamlessly shaping their participation and involvement in each other's activities as the demands of the task(s) and the interaction emerge. Individuals not only coordinate their actions with each other through various artefacts such as documents (whether on paper or screen) but continually adjust their access to each other and the tasks in which they are engaged. Perhaps the most important element of this interactional work, is the ways in which individuals monitor each other's involvement in, or alignment to, an object or artefact. It is not simply a case of seeing what another is seeing, but rather seeing the other in relation to what he or she is looking at and doing. We need to consider ways of expanding access to the remote participant's activities, taking into account the flexible ways in which people accomplish collaborative tasks.

To explore some of these issues and in particular to consider the consequences of various ways of providing users with increased access to the remote space, we decided to undertake a series of experiments. The ultimate aim of the experiments was to inform the design of a system in which people could flexibly vary their access to their co-participants and their co-participant's activity and working environment. To do this, in collaboration with our colleague, William Gaver, we began by constructing two simple systems offering variable, expanded access. The purpose of experimenting with these systems was to explore some of the interactional consequences of providing users with variable accessibility: to find out what the possible advantages and disadvantages of different design solutions might be.

The multiple target video (MTV) studies

One of the obvious ways of expanding access into another's domain is simply to increase the number of views a participant has of the remote environment. Thus, it should be possible to enhance the capabilities of media spaces by adding cameras and positioning these so that an individual has more than just a single face-to-face view of his or her co-participants. Several commercial multimedia systems provide such possibilities, often by having an additional "document camera" pointed down onto the desk. However, the research we have outlined has suggested that having two views may still be limiting, being too restrictive and not providing a sense of colleagues' orientation to particular activities.

We therefore began by designing a system which offered more visual access: the Multiple Target Video (MTV) system. In the first of these experiments (MTV I), we offered different perspectives via four cameras: a conventional face-to-face view; a "desktop" camera to focus on the details of any activities on the work surface; a wider "in-context" view providing an image of the co-participant in relation to their work; and a "bird's eye" view giving access to the periphery of a colleague's environment. The difficulty for the design of such a system was how to display these different views to an individual.

In the first experiment, participants were given a single monitor to view their co-participant, and could change their view on the remote site by turning a knob. Thus, each participant could select for display on their monitor only one view at a time, doing so by sometimes momentarily passing through other views. To provide further information, each participant was also given a "feedback monitor" showing which view their co-participant had currently selected (see Figure 8.5).

In this experiment, the participants were given two tasks in collaboration with another colleague: the first was to draw a plan of their co-participant's office; and the second was to carry out a simple design task. In the design task, one of the participants, in the "design office", had a 3-D model of a room, complete with miniature furniture. The two participants' task was to agree on a layout for the room, subject to certain design constraints. The other person, in the "remote office", had to draw the final design. So that the individual in the remote office could see the model, one camera was used to focus on this model. This meant that the two participants did not have an identical range of views; only the individual in the "design office" had access to the bird's eye view.

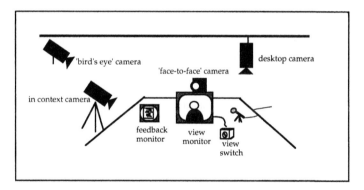

Figure 8.5. Schematic diagram of the configuration of the MTV I system using multiple cameras and a single monitor for each participant.

The experiment revealed some interesting results with regard to the use of the four different views.[1] For example, the face-to-face view was rarely used in the accomplishment of either task. Instead, participants mainly switched between the in-context, model, desk, and bird's eye views. Given the nature of the design task it is perhaps not surprising that the participants in the "remote office" focused on the view showing most details of the model.[2] It appears that the in-context and bird's eye cameras afforded similar possibilities for the subjects in the design office, allowing them to assess their colleague's orientation and to make sense of particular aspects of visual conduct, for example, gestures pointing to objects. Finally, some participants appeared to make use of the switch to track their colleagues as they moved around the room. It also seems that the intermediate views that appeared whilst the user switched between settings provided opportunities to monitor aspects of a colleague's conduct and see, momentarily, other features in their domain.

However, the participants in the experiment did have difficulties with the system. As might be expected given the previous analysis, the MTV I system did not appear to alleviate the asymmetries revealed by our prior study of video-mediated communication. Participants still had difficulties when establishing and re-establishing engagement, with perturbations in talk accompanying the beginning of turns, and with designing their gestures in the course of the interaction.

Moreover, the possibility of having different views of each other's domain appeared to exacerbate problems associated with these asymmetries. Because each person could select from multiple views, participants appeared to be even more uncertain about what view the other had chosen at any point in time. This fact, combined with the possibility that the other's perspective could be transformed at any moment, further undermined the presumption of a reciprocity of perspectives. It is perhaps not surprising that participants appeared to have difficulties both in achieving a common orientation to focused tasks and in managing the disengagement from collaborative activities. Participants often had to make apparent through talk their orientation to objects in the local environment and to the technology. For example, they had to reformulate directions given by their colleague, comment on their own movements and orientations and explicitly attempt to establish what the other could see. It seems that variable access to the other and their respective domain can make it more difficult for participants to preserve a sense of the (shifting) perspective of the other and to thereby coordinate their actions and activities with the contributions of their colleagues.

Interestingly, ascertaining the other's perspective did not seem to be alleviated by the presence of the feedback monitor, through which it was possible to find out what the other person was viewing. Instead, participants appeared to make use of this to refer to objects in their own domain, pointing to objects on the screen (such as their own documents) rather than pointing to those same objects in their local environment. Of course, this strategy was prone to difficulties, as pointing to the image on the feedback monitor was difficult, if not impossible for the remote person to see.

In addition to interfering with the establishment of a common frame of reference within which to work, the need to switch between views also appeared to be problematic because it precluded the ability to make a smooth and natural transition amongst views. Having to think about and negotiate the switch usually meant a break in the ongoing stream of activity. This may have presented enough of a distraction to discourage full use of the various views.

Whilst maintaining the effort to provide variable accessibility to another's domain, one possible solution to these difficulties was to remove the need for sequential access via a switch. In a second study, we used a system (MTV II) where each participant had multiple monitors each connected to a different camera in their colleague's office (Figure 8.6). In order to provide a symmetrical range of views for both participants, each person had three monitors showing an in-context view, a desktop view and a face-to-face view. The desktop view could be used either for viewing the model or a document. The wide angle previously provided by the bird's eye view was, in effect, provided by a wide angle, in-context view. The three monitors were arranged in both rooms in a similar fashion with the face-to-face view in the middle. This meant that a orientation towards the face-to-face view would also appear to a co-participant as a reorientation away from their in-context or desktop view, and *vice versa*. As both participants had access to all views simultaneously, there was no need for a feedback monitor. The tasks in this study were the same as those used in the first study.

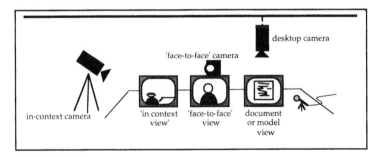

Figure 8.6. Schematic diagram of the configuration of the MTV II system using multiple cameras and multiple monitors for each participant.

Preliminary observations reveal that participants used all the views, and their pattern of looking at the different monitors indicates that they "switched" views much more frequently than in MTV I. It may be that by removing the necessity of having to switch views manually, it allows participants to use the available views more fully. Taking advantage of a different view was less cumbersome and did not require a break in the activity at hand.

Although they used all three views, participants oriented mainly to the desktop monitor when engaged in focused collaborative work, either to view documents or the model. However, the face-to-face view was found to be used much more frequently than in MTV I. During the course of the interaction participants would often glance briefly at each other between more prolonged sequences of looking at the model or document. Thus, although the face-to-face view was not looked at for long periods of time, it appeared to be pivotal as subjects tended to return to it frequently. Often, co-participants utilised the view in order briefly to glance at their colleague. At other times, and especially after periods of prolonged silence, the face-to-face view was utilised with the in-context view to assess the other person's involvement in the activity.

Despite the advantages of having multiple views simultaneously available, the MTV II system still presented problems for the participants. Separate, fixed cameras still failed to offer complete access to the remote space. In addition, there still appeared to be difficulty in ascertaining the other person's perspective as evidenced by conversations in which participants attempted to make their orientation to the other explicit. The lack of access to a shared space for working, such as the inability to point to a shared document or artefact, also presented a problem. These findings point out the issues which such simple experimental configurations fail to address, and clearly need to be considered in the design of future technologies.

Whilst the MTV experiments must be regarded as only preliminary attempts to build a more flexible environment for collaborative work, they are important in that they represent a break from the assumption that collaboration and communication are mainly face-to-face. This is an assumption that we believe has led to the impoverishment of much media space research. Multiple views of another's environment do appear to provide facilities for undertaking more complex and wide ranging collaborative work. However, the MTV studies have shown that design solutions which introduce variable access do this at the risk of imposing their own set of problems, as well as accentuating problems arising from the discontinuities and incongruencies that tend to be present in media space. It is important, however, to recognise these underlying problems, and to take them into account when envisaging how we might reconfigure media space. A more thorough understanding of the complex skills and competencies used by individuals in undertaking collaborative work can not only serve as a benchmark with which to evaluate our crude attempts to develop technologies, but provide an important resource in envisaging more innovative systems.

8.5   Conclusion

In the light of research concerned with interaction and collaboration both in a media space and more conventional working environments, it is not surprising that audio-visual connectivity has not been met with the excitement that we might have expected. Whilst we will undoubtedly find markets for the video-telephone and for video-conferencing facilities, as well as more sophisticated forms of connectivity, we may have to go some way before we develop a technology which can support more extensive forms of collaboration both within and across organisational environments. The limitations of current audio-visual infrastructures do not simply derive from the asymmetries that they inadvertently introduce into interpersonal communication; indeed, as we have suggested elsewhere (Heath and Luff 1992b), a certain insensitivity to another with whom one is intermittently working may have certain advantages in fulfilling one's own individual responsibilities. Rather, audio-visual connectivity, including the development of more sophisticated media spaces, has been primarily concerned with providing physically distributed personnel with face-to-face views of each other, whereas collaborative work across a range of organisational environments frequently involves access not simply to each other's physical domain but to the activities in which the participants are engaged. Those activities may be accomplished through a face-to-face orientation, but they also and routinely are mediated through a range of tools and artefacts including computer screens and paper documentation. The limitations of audio-visual connectivity, at least in its cruder forms, appears to derive, at least in part, from a misunderstanding of both collaboration and interpersonal communication in the work place. We need to consider perhaps, the forms of activity we are trying to support and the communicative and collaborative forms required to accomplish those activities in interaction with others in the work place.

In attempting to address some of the issues in the requirements for and development of a media space, we do confront some of the underlying "difficulties" which give rise to the peculiar forms of interpersonal conduct we find in communication mediated through audio-visual technologies. The relative insignificance of a look, the impotence of gestural activity, and their consequences for the articulation of talk, derive not only from the distorted presentation of the co-participants to each other, but also from the incongruent interactional environments provided by a media space. As Dourish et al. (1994) have recently argued, it may the case that some of the difficulties which derive from this incongruence are dealt with by an informal culture emerging amongst frequent users to manage the problems which arise in the operation of the system. This is undoubtedly the case. And yet, the interactional asymmetries which arise by virtue of the incongruent environments provided within a media space remain, and become increasingly severe, as we attempt to develop more sophisticated technology to support collaborative work. Indeed, as the MTV experiments demonstrate, the more we try to develop a technological environment to support collaboration and the variable access to each other's activities and the environments it necessitates, the more we can generate difficulties for users. Rather than rely upon the emergence of *ad hoc* informal culture to manage these problems, we need to explore systematically ways in which we can provide personnel with the resources with which to collaborate and participate, where necessary, in each other's activities, whilst unobtrusively preserving the individual's sensitivity to his own and his colleague's environment. If we can begin to address these issues and build a technology which can support task-based interaction and collaboration, then we might be surprised with the impact of media spaces and telecommunications on work and organisational life.

Acknowledgements

Part of the work reported in this chapter has been carried out on the MITS (Metaphors for Integrated Telecommunications Systems) Project funded by the EC RACE Programme (R2094). The MTV experiments were carried out in collaboration with Bill Gaver of Rank Xerox Research Centre Cambridge EuroPARC. We are also grateful to Wendy Mackay for assisting with the design of the MTV experiments. We would also like to thank Mike Molloy, Paul Dourish and others at Rank Xerox Cambridge EuroPARC, as well as Michel de Fornel, for help and support in our studies of the various audio-visual environments.

References

Birdwhistel, R. L. (1970). *Kinesics and Context: Essays on Body Motion Communication.* London: Allen Lane.

Bly, S. A. (1988). A use of drawing surfaces in different collaborative settings, *Proceedings of CSCW '88,* pp. 250–256.

Borning, A. & Travers, M. (1991). Two approaches to casual interaction over computer and video networks, *Proceedings of CHI '91,* pp. 13–19.

Bull, P. (1983). *Body Movement and Interpersonal Communication.* Chichester: John Wiley and Son.

Dourish, P., Adler, A., Bellotti, V. & Henderson, A. (1994). Your place or mine? Learning from long-term use of video-communication. Rank Xerox Cambridge EuroPARC Working Paper.

Egido, C. (1990). Teleconferencing as a technology to support cooperative work: its possibilities and limitations. In: Kraut, R. E., Galegher, J. and Egido, C. (eds.), *Intellectual Teamwork: Social and Technological Foundations of Cooperative Work,* New Jersey: Lawrence Erlbaum Associates.

Ekman, P. & Friessen, W. V. (1969). The repertoires of nonverbal behaviour: categories, origins, usage and coding, *Semiotica,* **1,** pp. 49–98.

Gaver, W. W., Moran, T., Maclean, A., Lovstrand, L., Dourish, P., Carter, K. A. & Buxton, W. (1992). Realizing a video environment: EuroPARC's RAVE system, *Proceedings of CHI '92,* pp. 27–35.

Gaver, W. W., Sellen, A., Heath, C. C. & Luff, P. (1993). One is not enough: multiple views in a media space, *Proceedings of INTERCHI '93,* pp. 335–341.

Goodwin, C. (1979). The interactional organisation of a turn at talk. In: G. Psathas (ed.), *Everyday Language: Studies in Ethnomethodology,* New York: Irvington.

Goodwin, C. (1981). *Conversational Organisation: Interaction between a Speaker and Hearer.* London: Academic Press.

Goodwin, C. (1986). Gesture as a resource for the organisation of mutual orientation. *Semiotica,* **62,** (1/2), pp. 29–49.

Goodwin, M. (1980). Processes of mutual monitoring implicated in the production of description sequences, *Sociological Inquiry,* **50,** pp. 303–317.

Goodwin, M. & Goodwin, C. (1986). Gesture and co-participation in the activity of searching for a word, *Semiotica,* **62,** (1/2), pp. 51–75.

Greatbatch, D., Luff, P., Heath, C. C. & Campion, P. (1993). Interpersonal communication and human-computer interaction: an examination of the use of computers in medical consultations, *Interacting With Computers,* **5,** (2), pp. 193–216.

Heath, C. C. (1982). The display of recipiency: an instance of a sequential relationship between speech and body movement. *Semiotica,* **42,** pp. 147–167.

Heath, C. C. (1984a). Interactional participation: the coordination of gesture speech and gaze. In: d'Orso Leonardie, P. and d'Orso Leonardie, V. (eds.), *Discourse Analysis and Natural Rhetoric,* Padua: Cleap Edition.

Heath, C. C. (1984b). Participation in the medical consultation: the coordination of verbal and nonverbal behaviour, *Journal of the Sociology of Health and Illness,* **6,** (3), pp. 311–338.

Heath, C. C. (1986). *Body movement and speech in medical interaction.* Cambridge: Cambridge University Press.

Heath, C. C. & Luff, P. (1991). Disembodied conduct: communication through video in a multimedia office environment, *Proceedings of CHI '91,* pp. 99–103.

Heath, C. C. & Luff, P. (1992a). Collaboration and control: crisis management and multimedia technology in London Underground line control rooms, *CSCW Journal,* **1,** (1–2), pp. 69–94.

Heath, C. C. & Luff, P. (1992b). Media space and communicative asymmetries: preliminary observations of video mediated interaction, *Human-Computer Interaction,* **7,** pp. 315–346.

Heath, C. C. & Luff, P. (1994). Converging activities: line control and passenger information on London Underground. In: Engestrom, Y. and Middleton, D. (eds.), *Distributed Cognition*, Cambridge University Press.

Heath, C. C. & Nicholls, G. N. (forthcoming). Animating Texts: selective renditions of news stories. In: Resnick, L. B. & R. Saljo (eds.) *Discourse, Tools and Reasoning.*

Heath, C. C., Jirotka, M., Luff, P. & Hindmarsh, J. (1993). Unpacking collaboration: the interactional organisation of trading in a city dealing room, *Proceedings of ECSCW 1993*, pp. 155–170.

Kendon, A. (1990). *Conducting interaction: Studies in the Behaviour of Social Interaction. Cambridge,* Cambridge University Press.

Luff, P. & Heath, C. C. (1993). System use and social organisation: observations on human computer interaction in an architectural practice. In: Button, G. (ed.), *Technology in Working Order,* London: Routledge.

Olson, G. M. and Olson, J. S. (1991). User-centered design of collaboration technology, *Journal of Organisational Computing,* 1: (1), pp. 61–83.

Olson, J. S., Olson, G. M., Mack, L. A. & Wellner, P. (1990). Concurrent editing: the group interface, *Proceedings of Interact '90 – Third IFIP Conference on Human-Computer Interaction*, pp. 835–840.

Reid, A. L. L. (1974). *TheImpact of Telecommunications Innovation on the Demand for Passenger Transportation.* Unpublished Ph.D. Thesis. University of London.

Schegloff, E. A. (1984). On some gestures' relation to talk, in structures of social action. In: Atkinson, J. M. & Heritage, J. C. (eds.), *Studies In Conversation Analysis*, Cambridge: Cambridge University Press.

Schutz, A. (1962). *Collected Papers: The Problem of Social Reality.* The Hague: Martinus Nijhoff.

Sellen, A. (1992). Speech patterns in video-mediated conversations, *Proceedings of CHI '92,* pp. 49–59.

Sellen, A. (forthcoming). Remote conversations: the effects of mediating talk with technology. *Human-Computer Interaction.*

Smith, R. B., O' Shea, T., O' Malley, C. & Taylor, J. S. (1989). Preliminary experiments with a distributed, multimedia problem solving environment, *Proceedings of First European Conference on Computer Supported Cooperative Work*, pp. 19–35.

Notes

1   See Gaver et al. (1993) for more details of the method and results of these experiments.

2   Although one 'remote' subject mainly opted for the in-context view that provided access to the co-participant in relation to the model.

9

The Electronic Agora

David Travis

9.1   Overview

In Athens, the Agora was the marketplace, but also a venue where citizens met to talk and gossip. We use this as a metaphor for a business meeting environment that is highly interactive and sociable, and which exploits the wealth of interpersonal skills that people already have. Compare the Agora with traditional video meetings: these are polite, with few interruptions. People wait their turn before speaking. The traditional face-to-face view in videotelephony makes it difficult to judge the body language of remote conferees. Issues such as these are responsible for the fact that users rate video meetings more akin to telephone meetings than to real meetings.

We argue that this is because conventional video support for remote collaborative work, including relatively sophisticated media spaces, offer restricted spatial access to local and remote users, limited possibilities to share documents, and are based on the misconception that collaborative work amongst business and professional people primarily involves face-to-face communication. In the Electronic Agora, video is ubiquitous and used to support the social and psychological elements of meetings. The aim is to provide remote conferees with many of the key proxemic cues that they would receive if physically present. We attempt this by using 'electronic surrogates' comprising a display, camera and speaker. These are placed in the positions normally occupied by physically present people: by the door, at the table, at the whiteboard, next to the overhead projector. This provides the remote user with a sense of the physical space, and shows different views of the meeting room, just as the user would get if physically present in the room carrying out these various tasks. Because the remote user can easily change position, users that are physically present gain a sense that the remote user is in the room, that is they gain a stronger sense of the other's social presence. In addition, remote conferees also have full access to the technological facilities in the meeting room, such as the whiteboard and the overhead projector. For example, a remote user can contribute to a brainstorming session on a whiteboard, and present slides and video footage from their local computer onto the overhead projector in the Agora.

9.2   Introduction

It is difficult to overstate the importance of interactive visual services as part of BT's future business. The convergence of computer technology, entertainment services and telephone networks is creating a host of new multimedia products and services. It is predicted that future telephone network traffic will be dominated by visual services, particularly videotelephony and switched-video services (Lyons, Jensen, & Hawker, 1993). Advanced applications and networks will have the potential to make visual services an attractive alternative to business travel and postal services and will increase the scope for remote or home working. World-wide, the revenue expected to be generated from visual telecommunications is estimated to be £13 billion by the end of the decade. Entertainment and interactive visual services for home users can be expected to be worth £17 billion in the first half of the next century.

Yet the uptake of video-mediated communication has been slow and the path of videoconferencing is littered with failures. It is worth considering AT&T's experience with the Picturephone in the 1970s. The development of the Picturephone is estimated to have cost $500 million, and had sufficient bandwidth needed for high resolution video communication. But despite this, the Picturephone was an expensive failure for AT&T, even though AT&T predicted, in its 1969 Annual Report, that 'With perhaps one million sets in use, Picturephone may be a billion-dollar business by 1980'. A key reason now identified for this is that the social and psychological 'drivers' and other related issues were not properly considered (Noll, 1992). Michael Noll (who was personally involved with the visual communications market research programme at AT&T) concluded that 'It is users and their behaviour, and not technology, that determine the use of teleconferencing'. Noll's report summarises a wide range of both scientific and market research conducted by AT&T prior and subsequent to the introduction of the Picturephone. It concludes that the single most important reason for the failure of the service was nothing to do with technology, but because it was produced without an understanding of human interpersonal communication behaviour and without a careful analysis of the types of communication where a visual image might be useful.

This is consistent with the work of numerous researchers who argue that existing videoconferencing systems make poor use of the user's rich set of existing interaction skills (Fish, Kraut, & Chalfonte, 1990; Dourish & Bly, 1992; Isaacs & Tang, 1993; Bly, Harrison, & Irwin, 1993; Buxton, 1995). Current systems make the user adapt in arbitrary ways to the technology.

The problem stems from the fact that when people communicate face-to-face they follow a complex set of rules, learnt by individuals over many years of 'playing the game' and by mankind over the course of evolutionary history. For example, Kraut, Lewis, & Swezey (1982) had speaker subjects watch a movie and then summarise it to two listeners. One of the listeners provided feedback, for example by asking questions, the other was merely an 'eavesdropper'. Feedback tailored the communication: that is, the listener who provided the feedback understood the movie better than the eavesdropper who listened to the conversation. This shows that speakers tune their behaviour to listeners, and there is considerable evidence to show that this occurs through moment-to-moment observation of listeners. In the classic monograph of Duncan & Fiske (1977), the argument is made persuasively that face-to-face interaction can be seen as having a definite organisation or structure, analogous to grammar in language. In a study of five-minute conversations, these authors identified nearly 50 different descriptive statistics, including turn-taking acts such as how long a person spoke for, back-channel behaviours such as nodding, as well as gazing, gesturing and even movements of the foot! An analysis of how this communication is part of our evolutionary history is provided by Watt (Chapter 12, this volume). Watt shows how the basic expressive regions of the face (the eyes and mouth) are used in conversation and the expression of mental state and emotions. He shows how these regions of the face can be easily localised in images of faces after processing by a model of human vision and argues that certain visual signals (for example the 'eyebrow flash', used as a signal of recognition) have evolved in tandem with the underlying visual mechanisms used in detection.

Looked at in this context, the challenge to mediated communication is to mediate without disrupting the visual grammar, or rules, of communication.

Yet existing video-mediated communication disrupts these rules on a number of levels. First, it frequently fails to transmit important conversational gambits such as hand gestures, because these may not be captured by the camera. Second, the camera may capture the cue, but the reproduced image may be too small and one-dimensional or too delayed for the cue to have an impact.   For example, Heath, Luff, & Sellen (in Chapter 8, this volume) describe the following interaction over a broadband video link:

> ..Maggie turns towards Jean and then waves. For more than ten seconds she stares at Jean but receives no response. Finally, Maggie looks away to her phone and dials Jean's number, summoning Jean to the telephone. Only when Jean replies to Maggie's greeting do the parties establish visual contact.

Similarly, Tang & Issacs (in Chapter 7, this volume) describe examples of 'just missed' glances, where one user looked up from her notes to glance at her remote collaborator, but after not receiving a reciprocal glance within the usual wait time, looked back down at her notes just before the remote collaborator looked up at his video display to glance at her. And on a third level, the technology may misrepresent the visual communication signals: that is, the visual cue is present and detected, but misperceived because of the technological limitations. Perhaps the most obvious example is gaze. Video-mediated communication reproduces gaze signals but offsets them depending on the degree of camera/monitor misalignment. This means that when a user is staring at the eyes of a remote user on the display screen, it looks as if they are looking to one side. On the other hand, when it looks as if the remote person is staring into your eyes they are actually staring into the camera. Although Ishii & Kobayashi (1992) have drawn a distinction between eye-contact (i.e. seeing eye-to-eye) and gaze awareness (being aware of where others are looking), it remains to be seen if a sense of gaze awareness is sufficient to enable effective and comfortable interaction. For example, Watt (this volume) argues that the eyebrows can influence the accuracy with which a viewer can judge where someone is looking. The eyebrows, in other words, offer the opportunity for seeing without using them simultaneously for signalling. Incorrect placement of the camera is likely to disrupt this cue.

Some examples of differences between face-to-face and traditional video-mediated communication are shown in Table 9.1. 'Traditional' means current commercial offerings (for a review, see Walder, 1994), that is, a single display screen on which remote participants are presented.

Short of human teleportation, it is clear that mediated-communication will never solve all of these problems. However, we are proceeding from the notion that systems that incorporate more of these types of cue will be more successful with users, and hence more successful commercially. With this aim in mind, we chose to design a video-mediated business meeting environment to capture as many of these cues as possible. Our aim has been to develop a meeting environment where video is ubiquitous and used to support the social and psychological elements of meetings. We argue that this is best achieved by reproducing in the mediated situation the visual information available to the viewer in the actual situation. We are interested in reproducing this visual information at a crude level (for example, spatial position of people and objects) and not at a detailed level (for example, high image fidelity). In fact, observations of people in naturalistic settings shows that much of the important information is processed through peripheral vision (e.g. Luff & Heath, 1993; Heath & Luff, 1991; Heath & Luff, 1992; Heath & Nicholls, 1995). This leads us to suggest that image quality is entirely the wrong parameter to optimise.

Face-to-face	**Video-mediated**
Field of view is variable, and easy to change	Field of view is fixed and difficult to change
Eye contact effortless	Eye contact problematic
Reciprocity holds: if you can see me, I can see you	Reciprocity may not hold: you can see me and I may not be able to see you
The physical distance separating speakers is "negotiated"	Speaker distance is not negotiated but determined by the placement of the camera and monitor
Voice perception predictable: I have a good idea of how my voice sounds to you	Voice perception unpredictable: I have no idea how my voice has been altered by the audio link nor how this interacts with the room acoustics
Gestures have full impact	Gestures may have no impact
Gaze useful to secure attention	Gaze not useful to secure attention
Feeling of intimacy	Feeling of 'distance'
Feeling of social and personal space	Feeling of restriction
Easy to share documents	Difficult to share documents

Table 9.1. Comparison of face-to-face and traditional video-mediated communication.

Our specific aim was to build an environment that would support business and professional users engaged in multi-party meetings. Part of the reason for doing this is that BT Laboratories is currently encouraging many of its managers and professional staff to work at home. Since meetings are such an integral part of working life we chose to design an environment which supported their needs. Our initial requirement was to support two remote users at different sites and two users at the local site (in fact, you will see that the system can easily be re-configured to support more remote and more local users). We set this objective for two reasons. First, about 55% of an average manager's day is spent in face-to-face communication, and about half of that time is spent in meetings with three or more people (Panko, 1992). Second, conventional videotelephony uses a single screen to represent the remote users and we argue below that this loses important visual information when more than one user is present. Hence, these systems are likely to be especially poor at supporting multi-party meetings.

We built our system on two fundamental design principles:

1. Remote conferees should have as much flexibility as physically present people. This means that as well as being able to occupy different parts of the room, they should have access to all of the technological facilities such as the whiteboard and the overhead projector.

2. Physically present conferees should not need to adapt their behaviour to achieve this objective. For example, they should not have to use a computer-based electronic whiteboard if they prefer to use a conventional whiteboard, nor should they be disallowed from presenting slides on an overhead projector.

9.3   The Electronic Agora

> The vision of a citizen-designed, citizen-controlled worldwide communications network is a vision of technological utopianism that could be called the vision of 'the electronic agora'. In the original democracy, Athens, the agora was the marketplace, and more—it was where citizens met to talk, gossip, argue, size each other up, find the weak spots in political ideas by debating them.
>
> (Rheingold, 1994, pp. 14–15)

Here Rheingold is talking about the Internet, but we have chosen to use the same analogy for video-based communication.

Joining the meeting

A typical meeting scenario might look like this. A meeting is called for 2pm and two people are already present in the meeting room. Just before 2pm there is a chime from the door, and Ben appears on surrogate 1 (see Figure 9.1). The camera attached to surrogate 1 gives Ben an establishing shot of the room, much as he would get if he were physically standing by the door (see Figure 9.2). This view is valuable to the remote conferee for a number of reasons. One key reason is that it makes clear who is in the room. Compare this with a direct face-to-face view, where it is not clear who is just out of camera view. This 'bird's eye' view makes it clear to Ben who is in earshot and provides information on the degree of privacy available for his conversation.

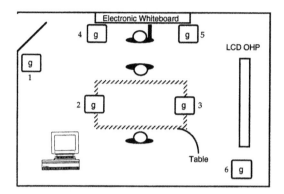

Figure 9.1. Plan of the Electronic Agora at BT Laboratories. Key:

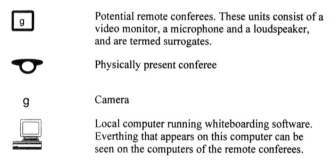

[g]	Potential remote conferees. These units consist of a video monitor, a microphone and a loudspeaker, and are termed surrogates.
⚬	Physically present conferee
g	Camera
🖥	Local computer running whiteboarding software. Everthing that appears on this computer can be seen on the computers of the remote conferees.

Now consider the view of the local participants. They see Ben appear by the door, much as they would do if he were physically entering the room. Compare this with the control access provided by other media spaces. A number of metaphors have been used including telephones, doors, rooms and hallways (e.g. Bly, et al., 1993; Dourish & Bly, 1992; Fish, et al., 1990; Gaver, et al., 1992; Ishii & Kobayashi, 1992; Isaacs & Tang, 1993). Yet in all these systems the image of the other appears directly on the screen in front of the local participants. In actual communication, there is an approach phase where, using peripheral vision, you realise that someone is attempting to engage you in conversation. This well-understood social convention is modelled in our system by physical location, just as in the real world.

Figure 9.2. Establishing shot of the room. The whiteboard can be seen on the left of the picture; the screen at the back of the room is displaying an image from the LCD panel connected to the computer.

Talking face-to-face

The people already in the room see Ben's video image and welcome him into the meeting, much as they would do if he were physically present. Ben chooses to take up the position at the table represented by surrogate 3, much as he would do if he were physically taking his seat at a table. Ben 'moves' position by using touchtones on his local videophone. Next, Dave appears on surrogate 1 and after a short welcome he moves to the position marked by surrogate 2 (see Figure 9.3).

This particular configuration is reminiscent of Buxton & Sellen's 'Hydra' system (see Sellen, 1992) and the 'Advanced presence videoconferencing system' of Hunter (1980) and Kelly (1982). For example, in Figure 9.3 it is clear to Ben that Dave has the floor because the physically present participants are looking at him. Compare this with other solutions to multi-party videotelephony such as the array method, where different participants are represented by different video windows on a single screen (Clark et al., 1994), or participants are segmented out from their backgrounds and placed in a synthetic environment by sophisticated chroma keying (Welsh, 1994; Boyer & Lukacs, 1995). In these systems, head turning cues cannot be used to pass the floor to another speaker and are replaced by small and insignificant changes of gaze. This is a classic example of how the 'visual grammar' of communication can be disrupted by technological mediation.

Figure 9.3. Ben's view of the meeting, showing Dave on surrogate 2.

Using the whiteboard

In a survey of videoconference room users (see Chapter 7, this volume), the need for a shared drawing surface stood out as the most commonly requested feature: 68% of the respondents mentioned it as a desired feature. There are currently some desktop videoconferencing systems that support this facility, but consider their implementation. The electronic whiteboard exists only on a computer and all users must adapt their behaviour in a number of ways. Most obviously, users must write on a screen with computer drawing tools or a keyboard. For anybody other than experienced computer-based designers, these tools do not lend themselves to handwriting or sketching.

But perhaps more importantly, with the electronic whiteboard conventional cues of social communication are lost. For example, in non-mediated meetings, when a user turns to the whiteboard he physically turns away from the other people in the meeting. When he chooses to engage somebody in conversation he turns toward him or her. This fundamental piece of social communication allows the user to move between different modes of communication: in this example, whiteboard mode and conversation mode. It is clear to all participants what the user is doing. This affordance is lost when the whiteboard is electronic: in a typical instantiation, the remote conferee and the whiteboard occupy different windows on the same screen. Only eye movements (10° at best) are needed to move between the different modes. Since direction of gaze cannot be judged reliably over a videolink (because the camera is offset from the centre of the screen), the remote conferee cannot judge what the user is doing.

For the participants in the Agora, the whiteboard is indistinguishable from a conventional whiteboard. The writing surface is the same, it uses a variety of different-coloured pens, and errors can be removed using an eraser. However, the output from the whiteboard can be directed towards a computer and then used by the remote participant as an electronic whiteboard. (Note that this is different from the desktop overlay system of Ishii et al., 1993, which blends the video image and the whiteboard image onto one screen.) In our example, Dave decides to take part in a brainstorming session with one of the people in the room. He then moves to surrogate 5, placed at about head height by the whiteboard, where the person running the brainstorm can use head turning cues to control the interaction, as would happen if Dave were physically present (see Figure 9.4a). For example, it is clear to Dave when Peter is using the whiteboard because he turns away from the surrogate and directs his attention to the board (see Figure 9.4b). When Peter turns his head back to Dave it is clear that he wishes to engage in conversation again. A proper whiteboard supports one of our fundamental design principles: it is important that physically present users do not have to reduce their behaviour to the lowest common denominator.

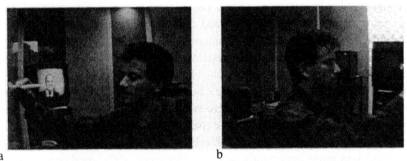

a   b

Figure 9.4. (a) Dave and Peter engage in a whiteboarding session (viewed from camera 4). (b) Dave's view.

The whiteboard session is captured on a local computer in real time and the image transmitted to both Ben and Dave. Of course, remote users are not able to physically write on the whiteboard in the Agora, but they can draw on the electronic copy.

Head turning cues are used naturally in our everyday communications but are lost in most instantiations of videoconferencing. In this example, non-verbal communication can be seen as an affordance (Gibson, 1979), directly perceived by others in the meeting room. In the Agora, the remote conferee effortlessly uses these affordances to decide what the user is doing. And in addition, the *local* user can judge whether the *remote* conferee is looking at him or looking at the electronic whiteboard, because the remote conferee must turn his head away from the camera to look at the electronic whiteboard image on his local computer screen.

Giving and watching a presentation

In a survey of videoconference room users (see chapter 7), 53% mentioned that one of the worst aspects was not being able to see overheads and other materials used in presentations. In the Agora, remote users can see the slides in perfect image quality on their local computer screens, and they can even place their own overheads on the screen. In our example, Ben is scheduled to present a review of his project and he achieves this by moving to surrogate 6, placed at about head height next to the projector screen. Since Ben has full access to all of the presentation facilities in the room, he transmits slides and video footage from his local computer and presents them on the LCD overhead projector panel. Dave has these slides appear in perfect quality on his local computer screen.

Figure 9.5. The presenter's view of the Agora.

9.4   Towards the notion of visual proxemics

Note that this use of multiple cameras builds on the findings from other studies (e.g. Gaver, et al., 1993) which show that, in a desktop system, users frequently switch between multiple available views if these are available. In our system, the surrogates are placed on flexible stands, allowing the conference space to be reconfigured. For example, monitors can be moved from the whiteboard to the table if more than two remote users are involved.

We have extended the notion of multiple views to the notion of visual proxemics: that is, we show how spatial relationships are used to support visual communication. Our initial findings suggest that this spatial dimension adds to the feeling of physical presence so desperately sought by videoconferencing systems.

9.5   Next steps

The next steps are to evaluate our design with people inside and outside BT. This will have two elements. First, we will collect qualitative data from actual usage as video communications become used more extensively within the unit. Second, we will embark on a formal research program to quantitatively evaluate the benefits of particular design decisions, such as the head turning cues at the whiteboard.

References

Bly, S., Harrison, S., & Irwin, S. (1993). Media Spaces: bringing people together in a video, audio and computing environment. *Communications of the ACM*, **36**, pp. 28–45.

Boyer, D. G. & Lukacs, M. E. (1995). The Personal Presence System – a wide area network resource for the real time composition of multipoint multimedia communications. In: *Proceedings of ACM Multimedia '94* (San Francisco, CA, USA, October 15–20, 1994) ACM, New York, pp. 453–460.

Buxton, W. (1995). Space-function integration and ubiquitous media. *Communications of the ACM*, To be published.

Clark, W. J., Burgess, G. D., Mason, T. I., Stubbington, N., & Dearne, S. (1994). *Continuous Presence Report* (Confidential No. 6280-20\TWCH\REP-001 Issue 1). British Telecommunications plc.

Dourish, P. & Bly, S. (1992). Portholes: supporting awareness in a distributed work group. In: *CHI '92*. Monterey, CA: ACM, pp. 541-547.

Duncan, S. & Fiske, D. W. (1977). *Face-to-face interaction: Research methods and theory*. Hillsdale, NJ: Erlbaum.

Fish, R., Kraut, R., & Chalfonte, B. (1990). The videowindow system in informal communication. *CSCW '90*, New York: ACM, pp. 1–12.

Gaver, W., Moran, T., MacLean, A., Lövstrand, L., Dourish, P., Carter, K., & Buxton, W. (1992). Realizing a video environment: EuroPARC's RAVE system. In: *CHI 92*. Monterey, CA: ACM, pp. 27–35.

Gaver, W. W., Sellen, A., Heath, C. C., & Luff, P. (1993). One is not enough: multiple views in a media space. In: *INTERCHI '93*. Netherlands: ACM, pp. 335–341.

Gibson, J. J. (1979). *The ecological approach to visual perception*. Boston: Houghton Mifflin.

Heath, C. & Luff, P. (1991). Disembodied conduct: communication through video in a multimedia office environment. In: *CHI '91*. New Orleans, LA: ACM, pp. 99–103.

Heath, C. C. & Luff, P. (1992). Collaboration and control: crisis management and multimedia technology in London Underground line control rooms. *CSCW*, **1** (1-2), pp. 69-94.

Heath, C. C. & Nicholls, G. M. (1995). Animating texts: selective readings of news stories. In: L. B. Resnick & R. Saljo (Eds.), *Discourse, Tools and Reasoning: Situated Cognition and Technologically Supported Environments*

Hunter, G. M. (1980). Teleconference in virtual space. In: S. H. Lavington (Eds.), *Information Processing 80*. North-Holland Publishing Company, pp. 1045–1048.

Isaacs, E. A. & Tang, J. C. (1993). What video can and can't do for collaboration: a case study. In: *ACM Multimedia '93*. Anaheim, CA: ACM, pp. 199–206.

Ishii, H. & Kobayashi, M. (1992). Clearboard: a seamless medium for shared drawing and conversation with eye contact. In: *CHI 92*. Monterey, CA: ACM, pp. 525–532.

Ishii, H., Arita, K., & Yagi, T. (1993). Beyond videophones: TeamWorkStation-2 for narrowband ISDN. In: D. D. Michelis, C. Simone, & K. Schmidt (Eds.), *3rd European Conference on CSCW*. Milan, Italy, pp. 325–340.

Kelly, C. W. (1982). An enhanced presence video teleconferencing system. In: *Computer Networks COMPCOM '82*, pp. 544–551.

Kraut, R. E., Lewis, S. H., & Swezey, L. W. (1982). Listener responsiveness and the coordination of conversation. *Journal of Personality and Social Psychology*, **43**, pp. 718–731.

Luff, P. & Heath, C. C. (1993). System use and social organisation: observations on human computer interaction in an architectural practice. In: G. Button (Eds.), *Technology in Working Order,* London: Routledge.

Lyons, M. H., Jensen, K. O., & Hawker, I. (1993). Traffic scenarios for the 21st century. *BT Technology Journal*, **11** (4), pp. 73–84.

Noll, A. M. (1992). Anatomy of a failure: Picturephone revisited. *Telecommunications Policy*(May/June), pp. 307–316.

Panko, R. R. (1992). Managerial communication patterns. *Journal of Organizational Computing*, **2** (1), pp. 95–122.

Rheingold, H. (1994). *The Virtual Community*. London: Secker & Warburg.

Sellen, A. J. (1992). Speech patterns in video-mediated conversations. In: *CHI '92*. Monterey, CA: ACM, pp. 49–59.

Walder, B. (1994). Being there. *Personal Computer*, October. pp. 232–259.

Welsh, B. (1994). *Enhanced desktop multipoint conferencing systems* (Confidential No. 5825-00/TECH/REP/004 Draft B). British Telecommunications plc.

Appendix: technical infrastructure

The main technical components of the Agora are shown in Figure 9.6. The key elements are the video server and surrogates, the LCD panel and the electronic whiteboard.

The heart of the Agora is a central video server controlling the surrogates. This connects directly to ISDN-2 and the remote user can select the surrogate by using DTMF tones on an ordinary telephone. For example, pressing button 2 moves the user to surrogate 2 on the desk, and pressing button 4 moves the user to surrogate 4 by the whiteboard (see Figure 9.1).

The remote user has a videophone and a separate computer. The videophone shows the view from the surrogate. The computer captures the computer screen in the Agora. The machine in the Agora is a mac, but the software package used to take control of the machine (Timbuktu) is compatible across platforms which means that the remote user can use either a Mac or a PC.

There is a minor constraint in deciding which surrogate is to be used for the whiteboarding session. This constraint arises from the desire to maintain veridical head turning cues for the local particpants. So, for example, if the remote user has his or her computer screen to the left of the videophone, the user should appear on surrogate 4. This is because the user will turn to the left to see the whiteboard on the computer screen, and it is important that this cue ('I am now looking at the whiteboard') is communicated accurately to the local participants. On the other hand, if the remote user has their computer screen to the right of their videophone, the user should appear on surrogate 5.

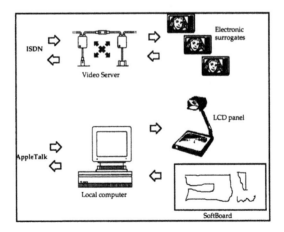

Figure 9.6. Schematic diagram of the technical infrastrucure of the Agora video server and surrogates.

Whiteboard

The whiteboard is a piece of commercially available hardware named 'SoftBoard' obtained from Microfield Graphics Inc. It has a 40 inch × 54 inch porcelain on steel writing surface and connects directly to a computer through a standard serial port.

Two laser scanners are used in the SoftBoard to collect data about the position and movement of a pen or eraser. The data are also used to detect the differences between the colours of the pens or the sizes of the erasers. All of these operations take place in real time, with the data being interpreted by a single TI 32026 Digital Signal Processor (running at 40 MHz) and forwarded in a compressed format via an RS-232 link (at 9600 baud) to the host computer. There are several keys to the sucessful operation of the laser scanners, which are made up from standard IR (780 nm) laser modules, multi-faceted scanner mirrors, and returned IR light collection and detection assemblies. The beams from the two scanners sweep across the writing surface, and the laser light reflected from any pen or eraser present is collected on its return path off the scanner mirror of origin and focused on the respective photodiode. Since both pens and erasers are equipped with encoded retro-reflectors, the modulated light being returned contains all the necessary information about their relative positions, motions and types. Gathering information from the two scanners at essentially the same time allows the exact positions of the pens and erasers to be tracked by triangulation anywhere on the writing surface.

LCD panel

We use a Sharp QA1150 colour video projection panel. This uses an active matrix TFT liquid crystal display to allow up to 185,000 colours to be displayed. When the panel is placed on an overhead projector, the text, graphics and other visuals produced by a computer can be enlarged. This enlarged information allows a group of people to view the screen, and is suitable for meeting room presentations. The projection panel has a built in video adapter, which outputs a composite video signal. There is also an external video monitor output connector, allowing a computer monitor to be connected for simultaneous display with the panel.

Timbuktu Pro & Apple Remote Access

The remote user dials in, using a modem over conventional telephone lines, and obtains access to the local network in the Human Factors Unit. Apple Remote Access ensures full security by using a dial-back procedure. Once connected to the network, the remote user then runs Timbuktu Pro to control or observe the computer in the Agora. Timbuktu Pro allows Macintosh and Windows users (connected through an AppleTalk network) to view each other's screens, operate each other's computers, and exchange files. This means that as far as the remote user is concerned, the image on the screen in the Agora is the screen of their local computer. The remote user can see graphical icons, the whiteboard software and any graphics presented on the screen. With the appropriate access permissions, the remote user can take full control of the screen. This allows him or her to run a (previously downloaded) presentation.

10

Video-as-data: turning away from talking heads

Bonnie A. Nardi, Heinrich Schwarz, Allan
Kuchinsky, Robert Leichner, Steve
Whittaker & Robert Sclabassi

10.1 Overview

Studies of video as a support for collaborative work have provided little hard evidence of its utility for either task performance or fostering telepresence, i.e. the conveyance of a face-to-face like social presence for remotely located participants. To date, most research on the value of video has concentrated on "talking heads" video in which the video images are of remote participants conferring or performing some task together. In contrast to talking heads video, we studied *video-as-data* in which video images of the *workspace* and *work objects* are the focus of interest, and convey critical information about the work. The use of video-as-data is intended to enhance task performance, rather than to provide telepresence. We studied the use of video during neurosurgery both within the operating room and at remote locations away from the operating room. The workspace shown in the video is the surgical field (brain or spine) that the surgeon is operating on. We discuss our findings on the use of live and recorded video and suggest extensions to video-as-data including its integration with computerized time-based information sources to educate and coordinate complex actions among distributed workgroups.

10.2   Introduction

The integration of video into groupware systems seems a logical next step in the quest for more effective computer support for collaborative work. Many such systems are currently under development, such as Portholes (Dourish & Bly, 1992), Cruiser (Fish et al., 1992), ClearBoard (Ishii & Kobayashi, 1992), SharedView (Kuzuoka, 1992), CAVECAT (Mantei et al., 1991), and Hydra (Sellen, 1992). (See Buxton, [1992] for an overview.) Videoconferencing systems in which participants gather in specially equipped conference rooms have been in existence for over 30 years (Egido, 1990). The Picturephone from Bell Laboratories was introduced at the 1964 World's Fair.

Talking heads video presents images of remote participants conferring or performing some task together. A large body of research has shown, however, that it does not enhance performance for a variety of tasks such as information transmission and collaborative problem solving (Chapanis, 1975; Egido, 1990; Gale, 1991; Short et al., 1976). Alternatively, investigators have been hopeful that talking heads video will foster *telepresence*,[1] that is, give users a rich physical and psychological sense of the other people with whom they are remotely interacting via cues obtained from gaze, gesture, facial expressions, body language (Gale, 1991; Short et al., 1976). But this has been difficult to achieve (Heath & Luff, 1991) and thus far little in the way of concrete value has been demonstrated for telepresence video (Chapanis, 1975; Egido, 1990; Gale, 1991; Short et al., 1976). For example, Egido (1990) reported on the history of videoconferencing and Picturephone, noting that videoconferencing remains "a small conglomeration of 'niche' markets." The Picturephone is a well-known failure, and while there are many possible reasons for this, Egido observed that trial use of Picturephone was met with

> disturbing reports of phenomena such as users' feelings of instant dislike toward parties they had never seen before, self-consciousness about "being on TV"......and resulting low acceptance.
>
> (Egido, 1990) (See also Noll, 1992)

What about "desktop video" systems such as Portholes (Dourish & Bly, 1992), CAVECAT (Mantei et al., 1991), Hydra (Sellen, 1992), Cruiser (Fish et al., 1992), and ClearBoard (Ishii & Kobayashi, 1992)? Portholes (Dourish & Bly, 1992) provides "awareness information" using slow scan video operating over local area or wide area networks to provide "visual snapshots" of selected workgroup members. The snapshots reveal information about the communication availability and current actions of workgroup members. CAVECAT (Mantei et al., 1991) is a media space which supports local area analogue audio and video connections for videophone and group conferencing. Hydra (Sellen, 1992) is a videophone designed to afford information about eye gaze, head turning, and spatially located speech for multiuser videoconferencing. Cruiser (Fish et al., 1992) is a videophone application that works in the local area using analogue technology. It includes "glance" features to determine others' communication availability as well as a "cruise" feature to simulate opportunistic communication encounters. ClearBoard (Ishii & Kobayashi, 1992) is a two person system that combines a drawing surface with visual information. It is centered around a shared workspace transmitted using analogue video and uses half-silvered mirrors to fuse the workspace with gaze and gesture information.

Will such systems prove a more successful application of video than traditional videoconferencing and Picturephone? Possibly they will, but to date there is little research to rely on for objective evaluation. Reports of the actual use of the desktop systems are often anecdotal and may involve both use and evaluation of the system by its developers and colleagues of the developers – a highly biased situation (e.g., Dourish & Bly, 1992; Mantei et al., 1991). A few systems have been tested in short trials on students or paid research subjects (e.g., Sellen, 1992; Fish et al., 1992), but the results have not been convincingly positive.

None of the current research systems as they are now configured provides strong evidence that video is an important support for collaborative work. For example, in a four-week trial of Cruiser it was found that Cruiser did not supply value added beyond telephone or email; Fish et al. (1992) reported that, "For the most part, people perceived and used [Cruiser] like a telephone or an electronic mail system . . ." Fish et al. suggest extensions to Cruiser which may improve its utility in the future, but it would be difficult to convince a disinterested observer of the value of video based on the implementations and related empirical findings of the current talking heads systems, as they are reported in the literature.

While available evidence on the utility of video for collaborative work promotes skepticism more than enthusiasm, does this mean that video is an unimportant technology for collaborative work? We believe that the answer is no for two reasons. First, current systems that attempt to facilitate telepresence have many problems such as lack of support for eye gaze or requiring a move to a special (expensively outfitted) room to utilize the technology. These problems will be overcome in time. Systems such as Hydra (Sellen, 1992) which support natural eye gaze and leave a small footprint on the desktop seem promising for remote meetings and informal conversations among four or fewer remotely located people. ClearBoard (Ishii & Kobayashi, 1992) also allows for gaze awareness and provides an innovative shared drawing space for two users. Once the technical challenges of the telepresence systems are met and the systems are more specialized to support specific tasks (just as ClearBoard supports intensive interaction between two people working closely together on a shared task), a more objective assessment of their worth will be possible. A large question will be the cost-effectiveness of telepresence video. Cost-effectiveness will have to be monitored as the technology and its price structure evolve over time.

Second, we think that video is a valuable support for collaborative work because a different aspect of video usage – *video-as-data* – has been in use for many years in medical and industrial settings and has become indispensable in many applications. Video-as-data stands in contrast to talking heads video: it is not used to support telepresence but rather provides images of the workspace –the "data"– to convey critical information about the work. People can see the work objects, and how they are changing and being manipulated within the work context. These images are used by teams of workers to coordinate demanding, highly technical tasks in real-time situations and to support research and technical training. For example, in power plants, live video of remote locations is used to monitor plant operations (Tani et al., 1992). Video is used in telerobotics and remote surveillance (Milgram et al., 1990).

The possibilities for extensions and enhancements to basic video capabilities are many. Milgram et al. (1990) have a system that combines stereoscopic video and stereoscopic computer graphics so that users can point to, measure and annotate objects within the video. Tani et al. (1992) have proposed "object-oriented video" in which the real-world objects in the video become computer-based objects that can be manipulated so that users will be able to reference, overlay, highlight, and annotate them, as well as use the objects for control and information browsing. In Tani et al.'s prototype system for power plants, users can, for example, point to a burner on a boiler in the live video and bring up a document that explains how the ignition system of the boiler works. By pointing to a pipe on a live video they can view a graph that shows the amount of fuel running through the pipe. Users can get a more detailed video or related video of an object by pointing to the object, obviating the need to directly control remote cameras. Users can control remote devices through direct manipulation techniques such as clicking and dragging; for example, "pushing" a button on the video image engages a real button on the remote device (Tani et al., 1992). Such uses of video are quite distinctive from talking heads video, and open up a whole new realm of video-based applications.

In this chapter we report on an ethnographic study of the use of video-as-data in a medical setting, where live color video is used to coordinate team activity during neurosurgery and both live and recorded video are used for training in neurosurgery. During the critical parts of neurosurgery, such as the removal of a brain tumor, the neurosurgeon looks through a stereoscopic microscope to view the brain as he[2] works. A video camera comounted with the optics of the microscope displays a video image of what the surgeon sees on a monitor on a cable TV link. Thus everyone in the operating room (hereinafter abbreviated "OR," the term used in the hospital) can see what the surgeon sees, though the video image is 2D and is a somewhat smaller view of the surgical field than what the surgeon sees. This technology has been in existence (though not universally available) for over twenty years, and is now an indispensable part of OR activity in many hospitals. A microphone mounted on the microscope provides audio capability for remote broadcast.

We examine the ways in which the live video image coordinates the work activities of the many neurosurgical team members. The technical complexity of neurosurgery is remarkable, and in the teaching hospital setting that we studied, the neurosurgical team includes an attending neurosurgeon, resident or fellow neurosurgeon(s), surgical technician, scrub nurse, circulating nurse, nurse-anesthetist, anesthesiologist, neurophysiologist, neurotechnician and sometimes an anethesiology resident. We also examine how the live video in the OR promotes education: student nurses, medical students, residents, fellows, and visiting neurophysiologists and physicians[3] are often present in the OR during an operation. In addition, we studied the use of remote video and audio facilities to enable remote collaboration during neurosurgery.

Our main argument is that video-as-data is an important application of video technology in computer-based systems, and that we should not lose sight of its potential by over-focusing on talking heads video, and in particular, by placing too much emphasis on the lack of demonstrated utility of talking heads systems to date. We will describe how live video coordinates tasks within the OR, provides critical educational opportunities, and is used for remote monitoring by neurophysiologists. We discuss the extensions to both live and recorded video which will be useful for research, training, diagnostic, legal, and archival purposes across a broad range of applications that potentially go far beyond the medical domain. In particular, the need to integrate and synchronize video images with other time-based data sources will be critical.

10.3 Methodology

We conducted an ethnographic study comprised of observations in the OR; audio-taped, semi-structured interviews; informal interaction (such as going to lunch with informants[4] and casual conversation in hallways, offices, etc.); and "shadowing." The shadowing technique involved following around a single individual for several days to track and record his or her activity in as much detail as possible. We used this technique with the neurophysiologists to study their use of the remote video. We had originally hoped to quantify this information in terms of times-per-task, but because of the complexities of hospital life we would have needed at least 3–6 months of shadowing to iron out anomalies and make statistically valid statements. The shadowing was nevertheless very informative as we learned a great deal about the daily activities of neurophysiologists and had many opportunities for informal conversation.

The fieldwork team included six investigators – three psychologists, two anthropologists, and one computer scientist. A total of 14 person-weeks of fieldwork was conducted. One investigator was in the field for five weeks and one for three weeks (the anthropologists). During these weeks the observations and some shadowing were done, as well as many of the interviews. The other investigators contributed interviews and shadowing. Over 500 pages of transcripts resulted from interviews with about 35 informants.

The operating room

It is necessary to provide some background on work flow and work roles in the operating room to be able to make sense of the discussion of the use of the video in the next section of the chapter. Our observations were conducted in the operating room during a series of brain and spine surgeries. In some cases we observed complete surgeries and in others we spent a period of hours in the OR (neurosurgeries can last from about 5 to 24 hours). While it might seem odd that we were allowed in the operating room, the staff was accustomed to visitors because we were at a teaching hospital. We donned "scrubs" (soft, loose, cotton clothing) and masks, exactly the same as that worn by all operating room personnel, and our presence was inconspicuous.

At the beginning of an operation the patient is tranquilized, anesthetized and connected to a variety of monitors and drips. The attending anesthesiologist plans the general course of the anesthesia to be used for the operation, and is usually present during the "prep" period. The attending anesthesiologist works with the nurse-anesthetist and/or resident anesthesiologist to administer the anesthesia and insert the appropriate intravenous lines for blood and a catheter for urine. After the initial set-up, the attending anesthesiologist generally leaves the OR to attend to another operation or to take care of other tasks. The resident and/or nurse-anesthetist then monitor the patient's basic physiological functions: heart rate, blood gases, blood pressure, breathing, urine concentration, etc. The attending anesthesiologist returns to the OR when necessary. He can be reached by phone via his pager, and he makes "check-in" visits to see how things are going.

The beginning of the operation is also the time when the patient, after being anesthetized, is connected to the electrodes that will be used to monitor muscle and nerve activity. Neurophysiological monitoring is a relatively recent innovation in neurosurgery which reduces morbidity by constantly tracking and providing feedback on central nervous system activity to see that it is maintained within acceptable parameters. During neurosurgery, there is a high risk of damage due to the surgery itself; for example, cutting, stretching or compressing a nerve, or cutting off the blood supply to parts of the brain. Neurophysiological monitoring helps prevent such events.

The neurophysiologist and neurotechnician apply the electrodes which provide "evoked potential" data. Throughout the course of the operation the patient is given electrical stimulation (electrical potential for activity is actually evoked by stimulation) to make sure that muscles and nerves are responding appropriately and are not being damaged by the surgery. The neurophysiologist supervises the neurotechnician and all on-going cases and is ultimately responsible for the interpretation of the neurophysiological data. The neurotechnician does the more routine monitoring. She sits in front of a computer screen viewing data from a networked computer system that processes the neurophysiological data, showing it as plotted line graphs.

The neurophysiological data can also be viewed in other locations outside the OR because the graphs can be displayed on remote nodes on the networked computer system. The networked system allows neurophysiologists to monitor operations remotely from many nodes: their offices, other operating rooms, or conference rooms where the system is installed. The system can display all of the neurophysiological data for any operating room where the system is connected. A neurophysiologist, when on call, thus usually spends a part of the day in the various ORs and a part of the day in his office, monitoring the evoked potentials via the computer displays. Neurophysiologists typically monitor as many as six operations concurrently (they have a back-up person assigned to help in case of overload). When not in the OR, they communicate with the neurotechnician in the OR via telephone.

After the prepping of the patient, the neurophysiologist, like the attending anesthesiologist, may leave the OR to go to other operations that he is monitoring. Or he may go back to his office to monitor the operation remotely. If during the course of the operation, the neurotechnician suspects a problem, she reports it to the surgeon. She may also telephone the neurophysiologist if he is not in the OR at the time. The neurophysiologist then returns to the OR to evaluate the data and possibly communicate with other members of the surgical team such as the attending neurosurgeon or anesthesiologist.

After the prep, the patient is "opened" – that is, the incision made – by the resident or neurosurgical fellow. The resident or fellow then continues to cut and drill until he is down to the point in the brain or spine where the most delicate surgery is required; for example, the brain tissue that must be "picked through" to reach a tumor, aneurysm or blood vessel compressing a nerve. At this point the attending neurosurgeon arrives in the OR to take over. Often the procedures used by the attending neurosurgeon are "micro-procedures," i.e.

those requiring the use of the microscope.   The resident or fellow neurosurgeon watches the operation through a second (2D) lens on the microscope, while the attending neurosurgeon views the surgical field through the main stereoscopic lens.   When the microscope is being used, the video is on as well, so those in the OR can watch the surgery on the TV monitor. The audio portion of the system is on as soon as the microscope is turned on, typically at the beginning of the operation, long before the microscope is needed. A recent innovation is that some neurophysiologists have a cable TV link in their offices so that they can access video and audio broadcast from the OR. This enables them to see the microscope video and hear much of what is said and done in the OR. The operation may or may not be recorded, according to the discretion of the attending neurosurgeon.

Throughout the surgery the scrub nurse hands the surgeon the instruments and supplies that he requests. The circulating nurse makes sure that the scrub nurse has everything she needs; the circulating nurse is a bridge between the sterile operating area and non-sterile areas of the OR. At the hospital we studied, scrub nurses and circulating nurses are cross-trained, so each can do the other's job.

When the attending neurosurgeon has finished his work, the patient is "closed" – that is, the incision is repaired – by the resident or fellow. The patient is revived from the anesthesia in the OR and asked to wiggle his toes and say something. He is then wheeled to recovery.

In addition to the visual displays used to monitor physiology and neurophysiology function, some of the equipment provides (intentionally or not) auditory cues to the progress of the operation or the patient's state. For example, the suction device tells everyone in the OR how much blood is being suctioned; a lot of blood might indicate a problem. The audio broadcast to remote locations clearly transmits the sounds of much of the OR equipment.

10.4   Findings

Video is used in the neurosurgical setting to *coordinate* and *educate*. In this section we examine how the live video supports task coordination and education within the OR. We also report preliminary findings on the use of remote video and audio in the offices of neurophysiologists.

Task coordination in the operating room

"Coordination" is distinct from communication and from collaboration. By coordination we mean the smooth enactment of actions requiring more than one person, or requiring information from another's actions. Collaboration, by contrast, is at a higher level of abstraction than an action, and involves shared goals and the enactment of a web of actions that allows goals to be fulfilled. Communication refers to the transmission of information. We do not have space here to fully explore these concepts, but they are delimited in activity theory (see Nardi, [1992] for an overview of activity theory and a bibliography).

The live video is used in the OR to coordinate activity during the most critical part of the surgery when the neurosurgeon is working deep in the brain or spine on very small structures that he sees only by looking through the microscope. In a sense, even though OR personnel are co-located, the video provides "remote" access; the surgical field is invisible, without an intervening technology, to all but the surgeons. The video is used by the scrub nurse, anesthesiologist, nurse-anesthetist, circulating nurse, neuro-physiologist, and neurotechnician.

The most important function of the live video in the OR is to allow the scrub nurse to anticipate which instruments and supplies the surgeon will need. As one scrub nurse said, the video is "the only indication we have of what's going on in the [patient's] head."

The TV monitor is on a movable cart, and its position changes depending on the orientation and position of the patient, which depends on the kind of operation being performed. The circulating nurse positions the monitor so that the scrub nurse has an unimpeded view.

During the critical parts of the surgery, events move very quickly, and the surgeon must be able to work steadily and without interruption. He changes instruments as often as every few seconds, and he needs to work in tight coordination with the scrub nurse who is selecting an instrument from over one hundred instruments arrayed on the sterile table near the operating table. The scrub nurse may also need to hand the surgeon one of hundreds of types of supplies (sutures, sponges, teflon pads, etc.) brought to her by the circulating nurse. The work of a neurosurgical operation is extremely detailed and fast-paced and the better idea the scrub nurse has of the surgeon's needs, the more smoothly the operation proceeds. Even with the video, the surgeon calls out the instrument or supply he needs next, but the ability of the nurse to anticipate what the neurosurgeon will want is considered very important by OR personnel. One neurosurgeon used a sports metaphor to explain how the video supports neurosurgeon-scrub nurse coordination:

Neurosurgeon:
 . . . an operation is like team work, [for example], ice hockey – the center brings the puck around, and the forward goes to the appropriate position, and the puck is coming in and he hits it.

Surgeon and scrub nurse:
> it's mutual team work . . . So a good scrub nurse looks at the video and knows what's coming next – instrument in and out, instrument giving and taking. It's all team work, [like] sports activity. So if you don't have the video, there's no way to do so [i.e. coordinate activity quickly]. . . So it's uniform, harmonious work.

As she watches the video, the scrub nurse is tracking the course of the operation and looking for unusual events to which she must respond with the correct instrument or supply. For example, she may know that the surgeon is approaching a time in the operation when a clip will be needed. Or she may see the surgeon nick some tissue, in which case a cautery device will likely be called for to repair the nick.

The scrub nurse's effective use of the video depends on her own knowledge and understanding of what she is seeing; the presence of the video image is not a guarantee that she will be able to anticipate the surgeon's needs and respond quickly. There is an interaction between her level of expertise and understanding, and the presence of the video in the environment. As one neurosurgeon explained:

Neurosurgeon:
> . . . Some scrub nurses are excellent when they look at the video, they know what's next and they are very good. But other scrub nurses are not at that level yet, so [I] have to tell her what I need and even if she's looking, [she] is not at level yet, so it is more time consuming.

Because the scrub nurse is listening to the surgeon, selecting instruments and supplies and handing them to the surgeon, her use of the video involves very quick glances at the monitor to see what is happening. All the more reason she must instantly understand what she is seeing.

In contrast to the scrub nurse's quick glances at the monitor, the others in the OR who watch the video may watch it intently for long stretches of time. Their use of the video helps them keep track of the progress of the surgery, but generally they do not rely on the video for split-second reactions as does the scrub nurse. Anesthesiologists, nurse-anesthetists, circulating nurses, and neurotechnicians watch the video in part to remain attentive to the surgery, to maintain interest and concentration at times when they may have very little to do. For example:

Interviewer:
> . . . What does [the video] tell you about what you have to do?

Anesthesiologist:
> In the neurosurgical procedure, the microscopic part actually is quite long and boring usually for us because once we get to that part of it. . . .the patient usually is very stable. . . .It's nice to see where they are, how much longer are

they going to be. Is he [the surgeon] still dissecting or is he [finishing] up? I don't have to ask the surgeon that.

Many anesthesiologists, nurse-anesthetists, circulating nurses, and neurotechnicians commented that watching the video was "interesting" and that it was much better than just sitting there with nothing to do. The video thus alleviates boredom and provides a focal point of attention that helps maintain shared awareness of the work being done by the surgeon.

This is critical because events can change very quickly during an operation. Suddenly what is seen on the video monitor can dictate that someone take action or that a new interpretation of an event applies. OR personnel look for a variety of events such as the placement of a retractor or clip, where the surgeon is drilling, if there is bleeding, how close to a tumor the surgeon is. For example, a nurse-anesthetist explained that anesthetic requirements vary depending on the surgeon's actions:

Nurse-anesthetist:
    . . . The anesthetic requirements [for] drilling through bone are different from the anesthetic requirements when they are working inside the head, where there are not pain fibers.

In this example, the actions of anesthesia personnel must be coordinated with those of the surgeon, and depend critically on what he is doing at a given moment in the surgical field. The video provides this information to anesthesia personnel.

Neurophysiologists and neurotechnicians interpret the graphs they watch on the computer display in concert with events shown on the video. One neurotechnician explained that they can "decipher the responses better" when they can see what the surgeon is doing; for example, when a retractor is placed, a delayed response may result which should not necessarily be attributed to nerve damage, but may have been caused by the retractor itself. Interpreting the neurophysiological data is difficult because its meaning can be affected by signal noise, the type and amount of anesthesia used, surgical events, and random variation. The video provides an important source of visual information for making better inferences in a highly interpretive task. Again, the use of the video allows tasks to be coordinated appropriately by supplying neurophysiologists and neurotechnicians with crucial information about the neurosurgeon's actions.

Education in the operating room

At a teaching hospital, education is of critical importance. Anesthesiology and neurosurgical residents, and fellows, student nurses, and neurophysiologists-

and neurotechnicians-in-training observe or take part in operations as a critical part of their education. While the neurosurgical resident or fellow uses the second 2D lens on the microscope to view the operation when the attending neurosurgeon is operating, others in the room watch the video on the large monitor. We observed students, residents and fellows training at the hospital watching the video, and also visiting students, residents and fellows from other hospitals. On several occasions they entered the OR, parked themselves in front of the video monitor and watched for the duration of the micro-procedures (which may go on for several hours).

Many of the operations performed at the hospital we studied are highly innovative. The OR, therefore, accommodates neurosurgeons, anesthesiologists and neuro-physiologists, many of them eminent in their own specialties, from other institutions around the world who come to learn about the new procedures. One of their main activities in the OR is to watch the video. In this way the video provides support for observational learning.

The use of remote video and audio to monitor operations

Much of the time the physical presence of the attending neurosurgeon or neurophysiologist is not needed in the OR. An extension to the networked computer system is now being tested to support the remote monitoring of operations by supplementing the neurophysiological plotted line data with audio and video. Only a few such multimedia links are functional in the current system (for neurophysiologists), so our findings about their use are preliminary at this time. The idea behind the remote audio and video is that neurophysiologists and neurosurgeons can make better use of their time in their offices monitoring multiple operations, or working on other tasks such as research, taking calls from patients, or attending meetings. They will also be able to remotely monitor operations in other ORs from the OR they happen to be in at a given time. Using the remote monitoring, neurophysiologists and neurosurgeons should be able to simultaneously monitor a larger number of operations, spreading scarce expertise over a greater area and making more efficient use of their time.

What kinds of information do the video and audio provide to neurophysiologists? The remote video provides the kind of information provided by the video within the OR, as described above. Neurophysiologists can interpret the graphic data more easily with the addition of the video information. They can anticipate what will happen next in the surgery and generally keep track of what is going on in the surgery at a particular moment. For example, one neurophysiologist explained:

Neurophysiologist:
> One time I was watching the remote video and I could see that the surgeon was in trouble, that he was having a problem, like there was a big bleed, for instance. Then I would go to the operating room.

The remote audio provides additional information from two sources: (1) what is being said in the OR, (2) the overall atmosphere in the OR. Together, the audio and video provide a much more complete picture of OR activity than the plotted line graphs alone:

Neurophysiologist:
> When you look at the computer data by itself [from a remote location], it seems to be one dimensional. When you add the rest of it [audio and video], you get a very rich picture of what's going on [in the OR].

The audio information is very important in the remote situation. The neurosurgeon often explains what he is doing or discusses his anticipated actions with the other neurosurgeon(s). Anesthesia personnel discuss the patient's physiological function. This information is useful to the neurophysiologist: the progress of, and plans for, the operation revealed by the comments of the neurosurgeons, and physiological data revealed by the comments of the anesthesia team, help him to interpret the neurophysiological data he is looking at, and to anticipate what will happen next.

In many cases, the neurophysiologist actually has better access to what is being said when he is in a remote location than when he is in the OR. Within the OR, it is sometimes difficult to hear clearly what is being said because of the noise of equipment and random conversations. There may even be a radio playing. Listening to the audio in a remote location, by contrast, one gets a clear transmission of what the neurosurgeons and the anesthesia personnel are saying, as they are positioned closest to the microscope (on which the microphone is mounted). One neurophysiologist explained:

Neurophysiologist:
> In fact, the audio is better over the network than it is in the operating room because you can't hear what the surgeons are saying in the operating room so if you don't know the case, you kind of guess what they're doing. With the audio, you know exactly what they are doing. . . Because they talk to each other about the steps they are going to take. So you can really anticipate what potentially might happen.

This is an example of "beyond being there" (Hollan & Stornetta, 1992) where at least one aspect of being remote is preferable to being co-located.

The audio also allows the remotely located neurophysiologist to hear what the neurotechnician is telling the surgeon, and how the surgeon responds to that information. The neurophysiologist can see for himself what the neurotechnician sees on the graphs, but the response of the neurosurgeon is very important. The neurosurgeon may say that he's not doing anything that might be causing a problem, that he doesn't understand the response, or that he will change an action he is taking. He may say nothing at all. These responses are of great interest to the neurophysiologist. The neurophysiologist may not agree with what he hears the neurotechnician tell the surgeon:

Neurophysiologist:
In that case, I heard the technician say something to the surgeon that I didn't agree with. . . [He] said there was a change in the response. There wasn't.

Interviewer:
. . . So what did you do, you called?

Neurophysiologist:
Called right away. . .Told the surgeon there was no change.

Here the audio information directly influences the neurophysiologist's behavior: he telephones the OR to provide a different interpretation of the neurophysiological data than that given by the neurotechnician.

Other audio information provides an overall impression of the atmosphere in the OR. The surgeon's voice may sound nervous, or there may be a dead silence indicating a tense moment in the operation. As one neurophysiologist said:

Neurophysiologist:
The microphone is very close to the surgeon so I can really get a good feeling for whether he feels like the case is going well or not. . . you can hear it from his voice. You can hear how much activity is in the room, whether the people are scrambling.

Again, this information influences the neurophysiologist's behavior, in this case his decision as to whether to go to the OR from his office:

Neurophysiologist:
Well, if people are agitating, there's a lot going on. I probably would have a much lower threshold for going to the room because I'm alerted then that there's something going on in the room, and that's maybe an opportunity for me to make a significant contribution.

Our preliminary findings indicate that the information from the remote multimedia sources concerning the course of the surgery, the surgeon's observed and anticipated actions, the content of key comments made by personnel such as the neurotechnician, and the overall atmosphere in the OR allow the remotely located neurophysiologist to perform his job more efficiently and effectively. He can better plan and coordinate his visits to the

OR because he has richer information with which to decide when he needs to visit a particular OR, or whether he wants to place a telephone call. If he does need to go to the OR, he arrives with better information about the status of the operation. If the neurophysiologist is communicating with the neurotechnician via the telephone, again he has a better idea of what is happening in the operation if he has the video and audio data in addition to the graphs of neurophysiological function.

The use of remote multimedia facilities does not eliminate the need for neurophysiologists to be physically present in the OR for at least part of the operation. Rather, it redistributes their allocation of time across ORs, their offices and other locations in the hospital such as conference rooms. The use of multimedia appears to give neurophysiologists more flexibility to move about the hospital on an as-needed basis, rather than to stay tied exclusively to a small number of ORs.

10.5 Discussion

We were struck by the extent to which the use of video-as-data in the operating room and in remote locations serves a number of highly varied functions. The overall goal of the video is to provide a window into the unseeable world of the surgical field, but the uses to which the surgical information is put, and the way the information is gathered, vary greatly depending on the specific tasks associated with the differing roles within the operating room or remote offices. As we have seen, the video image can coordinate fast-paced exchanges of instruments and supplies between neurosurgeon and scrub nurse; it can serve as a means of maintaining attention and focus over long stretches of time during which some OR personnel are relatively inactive; it helps OR personnel to choose the correct action or interpretation depending on the event portrayed in the video; it educates a variety of medical personnel; and the video plus audio may allow neurophysiologists and neurosurgeons to decide when their presence is needed in the OR from a remote location. The use of video in neurosurgery shows the utility of one well-chosen artifact, and the many activities it permits and coordinates. It demonstrates the utility of video-as-data, in contrast to telepresence video.

Looking more closely, we see that the use of video in the neurosurgical context is quite different than some of our standard notions of what it means to support collaborative work; rather than facilitating direct interpersonal communication (as many CSCW systems are intended to do), in many crucial instances, the video permits individuals to work *independently*, actually obviating or reducing the need for interpersonal communication. The video supplies enough information so that the need for interpersonal communication is reduced or eliminated, and individuals can figure out what they need to know based on the video itself, circumventing the need to talk to or gesture at someone. Thus we may find that in settings where video is data, the provision of visual information at key moments provides a different channel of communication than that which would be provided through verbal, gestural or written communication. Rather than facilitating collaboration through interpersonal interaction, the video itself informs OR personnel of the collaboration – in the sense of tasks that need to be performed to advance the work – that is needed. Collaboration and coordination are enabled as each member of the neurosurgery team interprets the visual information, and proceeds to do his or her job based upon an interpretation of that information. The video data, plus individual knowledge and understanding, combine to produce an interpretation that leads to the desired collaboration, with little or no interpersonal interaction.

Similar arguments have been made for other types of shared workspaces. Studies of document editing and design show that a crucial function of a shared document or design is to support coordination; a shared visual object enables remote participants to *see* where others are currently focusing their attention or making modifications. This can happen without the need for conversation (Whittaker et al., 1993).

In other cases, the content of the video image becomes the basis for discussion and interaction, another aspect of its use as a shared workspace. For example, we observed a nurse-anesthetist in the OR watching the video with a student nurse-anesthetist and describing to her the progress of the operation. Indeed, we ourselves profited from explanations in which the video was a key point of reference as OR personnel educated us about many aspects of neurosurgery. Visitors, residents, fellows, etc. also discuss what is being shown on the video monitor.

Video-as-data may change our sense of what it means to be "remote" or "colocated." In the OR, even though people are colocated, the surgical field is remote, because it is invisible to anyone not looking directly through the microscope. The surgical field is accessible only through the video to most OR personnel. Thus it is not necessarily the location of *people* that is important in the video-as-data situation, but rather of the *workspace*. Aural information in the OR, on the other hand, is not remote, so we have a situation in which the aural and visual have different values for the dimension of colocation. One can imagine other such situations; for example the repair of a delicate piece of machinery with many small parts might be a situation in which a view of the workspace is remote, while aural information is not. For neurosurgery, we also have a "beyond being there" situation in which the aural information may be richer in the remote location, via broadcast audio, as we described for the remote audio used by the neurophysiologists.

10.6   Future directions

Video-as-data applications open up a whole new realm of video-based applications, especially if the right video analysis tools are provided. For example, for educational applications, students could use video-as-data to *analyze* and *problem solve*, not merely to passively view video images. If video-based educational software is to be more than just educational television, students need tools that will help them to actively engage the material they are working with. Once we see that video goes well beyond talking heads, we can begin to supply the kinds of tools that will take advantage of video-as-data, and that will make video into an interactive medium supporting analysis and problem solving.

For the medical application we studied, we found that recorded video is already used for classroom teaching and to review events in past operations. Integration of video with other computerized time-based data is the next critical step. Uniform storage, access, and presentation methods for data are needed. Means of visualizing complex relationships between datasets of varying types will support research and teaching. Medical personnel in our study underscored the need for future tools that will allow for the synchronization of video with other data sources, in particular the instrument data relevant to a particular specialty. Anesthesiologists, for example, want to see the video images synchronized with the physiological data they monitor such as blood pressure, blood gases, heart rate, pulse, temperature. Such observations could be done during an operation, with video and instrument data they had just recorded. The synchronized datasets could also then be used for post hoc analysis and for training purposes. Neurophysiologists want to see video synchronized with the many measures of nerve and muscle response that they monitor. Capabilities are needed that will enable users to "scroll through" a video/instrument dataset, finding a particular video event, or instrument event, or a particular time, so that they can then view all related contemporaneous data for the event or time.

It would also be useful for users to scroll through different datasets at different rates to capture latency in cause and effect relations between variables. For example, a neurophysiologist might want to scroll back through a videotape to find an event that took place a minute or two ago, such as the placement of a clip, which might just now be causing a reaction in the patient which would show up in the neurophysiological data seen in the plotted line graphs. Scrolling at different rates in different datasets might also be done in studying the recorded operation and related data, after the fact, to try to ascertain delayed effects of surgical events.

Again, it is easy to see how the provision of such analytical capabilities will have wide educational applicability in many domains. Students trying to understand complex relationships among many variables would have a vivid graphic image with which to visualize events. At the same time, the more abstract quantitative measures would be made more intelligible, giving students help with difficult concepts. Animation would be an interesting substitute for actual video in some applications where a video image is not available and a simulation is needed, e.g., to analyze what happens when a bridge collapses. The idea of seeing the image as data to be analyzed against other variables is the same in both cases and similar tools would be appropriate. It would also be possible to compare animated simulation information with actual video test data, i.e., testing the data of the real object against the simulations run during the design phase. There are many exciting possibilities then, for using video to *analyze data* and to support complex problem solving activities. The integration of video-as-data with other data sources will be useful in many applications for analysis, training, legal, and archival purposes. Users of such technology will want to be able to edit, browse, search, annotate, overlay, highlight, timestamp, and display video data.

Of course, the manipulation of large amounts of relatively unstructured information presents a novel set of problems, particularly those related to indexing, search, and retrieval of video information. The user must be able to specify in a clear way what he or she is looking for. Unlike text systems and conventional database systems, where keywords to aid search may be generated automatically, keywords used today to describe the contents of video must be generated manually. This is labor intensive and error prone and may also introduce sources of bias as the description of content is subject to interpretation. For dynamically changing stores of video data, this task becomes particularly complex.

The alternative of content-based search and retrieval is promising, but remains an open research area. One needs to consider which features of the video information are represented, how these features are extracted, and how an index and search structure based on these features is computed. Often some level of user involvement is needed in the indexing; the effectiveness of the indexing mechanism, and the resulting level of ease with which a user can browse and navigate through the video information, may be thus dependent upon the level of sophistication of the user.

Our findings about the importance of the on-going use of video-as-data in a real work setting with demanding requirements (as opposed to brief experiments or testing within research labs) should encourage us to pursue our understanding of how video-as-data can be extended and used in other work settings. Within medicine, video is used in many kinds of surgery including orthopedic surgery, plastic surgery and general surgery that employs micro-procedures. Non-medical applications of video-as-data could include monitoring and diagnostic tasks in complex mechanical or electrical systems such as the Space Station, power plants, or automated factories; and training for many aspects of using, designing, monitoring, and repairing such systems. Real estate agents might show properties remotely. Attorneys are making increasing use of video data in courtroom presentations, such as the Rodney King video. There are many potential applications for video-as-data.

Whether such extensions to video-as-data will be cost-effective remains to be seen; video is an expensive technology. Current applications of video-as-data such as the present study, the power plant applications described by Tani et al. (1992), and Kuzuoka's work (Kuzuoka, 1992) suggest that there is tremendous potential for video to enhance collaborative work. Future research should go beyond talking heads to recognize the value of video-as-data, and should be concerned with offering good video utility in a cost-effective manner.

Acknowledgments

We would like to thank Erik Geelhoed and Bob Simon for their help with data collection. Steve Gale's previous work on the project was of great value. Robin Jeffries, Jim Miller, Vicki O'Day, and Andreas Paepcke gave insightful comments on earlier drafts. At the hospital we thank the secretaries who helped us to track down and schedule interviews with peripatetic medical personnel. Our many informants in the hospital generously allowed us to follow them around, ask endless questions, and watch them for hours on end at their jobs. For their good cheer and thoughtful answers to our questions, we offer grateful thanks.

References

Buxton, W. (1992). Telepresence: integrating shared task and shared person spaces. *Proceedings of Graphics Interface'92* (Vancouver, 11-15 May, 1992), pp. 123–129.

Chapanis, A. (1975). Interactive human communication. *Scientific American*, **232**, pp. 36–42.

Dourish, P. & Bly, S. (1992). Portholes: supporting awareness in a distributed work group. *Proceedings CHI'92* Monterey, 3–7 May, 1992, pp. 541–547.

Egido, C. (1990). Teleconferencing as a technology to support cooperative work. In: J. Galegher, R. Kraut, & C. Egido, (Eds.). *Intellectual Teamwork*. Lawrence Erlbaum Associates, Hillsdale, NJ.

Gale, S. (1991). Adding audio and video to an office environment. In: J. Bowers and S. Benford (Eds.), *Studies in Computer Supported Cooperative Work: Theory, Practice and Design*. North-Holland: Amsterdam.

Fish, R., Kraut, R., Root, R., & Rice, R. (1992). Evaluating video as technology for informal communication. *Proceedings CHI'92* Monterey, 3–7 May, 1992, pp. 37–48.

Heath, C. & Luff, P. (1991). Disembodied conduct: communication through video in a multimedia office environment. *Proceedings CHI'91* New Orleans, 27 April–2 May, 1991, pp. 99–103.

Hollan, J. & Stornetta, S. (1992). Beyond being there. *Proceedings CHI'92*, Monterey, 3–7 May, 1992, pp. 119–125.

Ishii, H., & Kobayashi, M. (1992). ClearBoard: a seamless medium for shared drawing and conversation with eye contact. *Proceedings CHI'92*, Monterey, 3–7 May, 1992, pp. 525–532.

Kuzuoka, H. (1992). Spatial workspace collaboration: A SharedView video support system for a remote collaboration capability. *Proceedings CHI'92*. (Monterey, 3-7 May, 1992), pp. 533-540.

Mantei, M., Baeker, R., Sellen, A. Buxton, W., Milligan, T., & Wellman, B. (1991). Experiences in the use of a media space. *Proceedings CHI'91*, New Orleans, 27 April–2 May, 1991, pp. 203–215.

Milgram, P., Drascic, D., & Grodski, J. (1990). A virtual stereoscopic pointer for a real three dimensional video world. *Proceedings Interact'90*, pp. 695–700.

Nardi, B. (1992). Studying context: A comparison of activity theory, situated action models, and distributed cognition. *Proceedings, St. Petersburg Human Computer Interaction Workshop*, St. Petersburg, Russia. 4–8 August, 1992, pp. 352–359.

Noll, M. (1992). Anatomy of a failure: Picturephone revisited. *Telecommunications Policy*, pp. 307--316.

Sellen, A. (1992). Speech patterns in video-mediated conversations. *Proceedings CHI'92*, Monterey, 3–7 May, 1992, pp. 49–59.

Short, J., Williams, E., & Christie, B. (1976). *The Social Psychology of Telecommunications*. John Wiley & Sons: London.

Tani, M., Yamaashi, K., Tanikoshi, K. Futakawa, M., & Tanifuji, S. (1992). Object-oriented video: interaction with real-world objects through live video. *Proceedings CHI'92*, Monterey, 3–7 May, 1992, pp. 593–598.

Whittaker, S., Geelhoed, E. & Robinson, E. (1993). Shared workspaces: how do they work and when are they useful. *International Journal of Man Machine Studies* **39**, pp. 813-842.

Notes

1   The term "telepresence" does not yet have a firm definition, and people use it in different ways. There is a need for a word to precisely denote remote *human* presence, as opposed to virtual reality or remote shared task space.   It is in the sense of human presence that we use telepresence. Used in this way, telepresence resonates with terms in common usage such as "social presence," "stage presence" and simply "presence." Webster's defines the latter as "a quality of poise and effectiveness that enables a performer to achieve a close relationship with his audience," which is very much like what we are trying to achieve via technology for remotely located participants.

2   Our use of the pronoun "he" is strictly for convenience' sake; any other construction would make it very awkward to describe individual roles in the operating room. We alternate he and she as generics.

3   Neurophysiologists usually have Ph.D.'s not M.D.'s., though some have an M.D. degree.

4   In ethnographic studies, participants are called "informants" in the sense that they are to *inform* the investigator, rather than that the investigator is to *subject* participants to an experiment (as in psychology), in which case they are subjects. (The American Psychological Association has recently recommended the use of the word "participant" in lieu of subject.) The essential notion is that the investigator is ignorant of the understandings possessed by the informant, but wishes to learn as much as possible through interaction and observation.

11

The role of the face in face-to-face communication: implications for videotelephony

Vicki Bruce

11.1 Introduction

Adults can communicate quite adequately by telephone, but a great deal of importance is lost when speakers cannot interact with each other face-to-face. One obvious limitation of remote communication is that the speakers do not have shared access to what they are talking about. Compare how easy it is to construct or negotiate changes to a document or a design when all parties are present compared with using telephones or current electronic mail systems. However, face-to-face interaction also provides more subtle advantages – because the face itself provides important information that can aid communication. In this chapter I will review the different uses that are made of information from the face in social interaction, and consider what image quality, resolution and synchrony are likely to be needed in order for such information to be usable when face-to-face interaction is achieved via video. The pressure in the development of current videophones seems to have been to produce high quality colour images, but at some sacrifice to synchrony when used over current limited bandwidth phone lines. Here I will argue that for most uses made of facial information, one-bit per pixel images may suffice to convey the important social signals, but that good synchrony is likely to be more crucial for communication efficiency.

A good deal of past research has demonstrated that face perception and recognition is possible even when the information content of the images is considerably reduced through changing the spatial resolution. For example, Bachmann (1991) demonstrated that identification of face images was affected very little when spatial quantisation was reduced from 74 down to only 18 pixels, of 16 grey-levels, horizontally across the face. In this article I will concentrate on effects of the information content at the level of individual pixels, comparing the effectiveness of line-drawn and full colour images.

11.2   Person identification

The face is the most reliable cue to person identification. In the absence of the face, other cues such as voice and name must be used to identify speakers at the start of a telephone conversation. Once the identities of the parties are known, however, it would seem that there is little further need to identify a person during a conversation. This is true for two-way conversations, but in tele-conferencing, speakers must introduce themselves by name each time they speak. This is unnatural and reduces the efficiency of communication. If video-telephony were used for conferencing the ability of all participants to see who was speaking would be a considerable advantage over voice-only systems. What is known about the representations used for person identification to suggest the optimal way to display faces for mutual identification?

Early research on the identification of faces shown in different formats suggested that face recognition was significantly impaired if faces were shown in line drawings rather than photographs. Davies, Ellis and Shepherd (1978) compared the identification of famous faces shown in photographs with drawings of these same faces obtained by tracing around all the facial features and adding lines for wrinkles, skin-folds, etc. Identification of these elaborate line drawings was only 47% compared with 90% correct identification of the original photographic images. Identification performance dropped even further, to only 23% correct, when simple line drawings tracing only the face features were used. These results suggest that one-bit per pixel face images are very difficult to identify. However, our own recent research has shown that such images can be very good representations for identity, provided that the black and white images preserve information about the relative light and dark areas of the face.

Our research (Bruce et al, 1992) was motivated by the algorithm developed by Pearson and Robinson (1985) for real-time videotelephony using one-bit per pixel images. Pearson and Robinson developed an algorithm for producing a computer-generated drawing of a face (and hands, since the application was developed primarily for use by deaf signers). The algorithm generated drawings ("cartoons") of faces which were remarkably similar to those created by a human artist invited to sketch the same frame of video, and appeared to be extremely good representations of the people shown. Pearson and Robinson's

(1985) algorithm comprised two components. The first, "valledge" component produced a sketch of places where there were large changes in surface orientation relative to the viewer (e.g. around the edges of the nose) and where there were major contrast changes (e.g. between hair and forehead). In effect, the valledge component produced a representation of "edges" rather similar to that which might be obtained by a person tracing the outlines of the face features.   The second, "threshold" component preserved the pattern of light and dark from the original image by drawing in black any area which was darker than a certain grey level in the original.   Bruce et al (1992) compared the identification of famous faces shown in full grey-level images with those shown in valledges alone, thresholds alone, or the full cartoons comprising both valledge and threshold components.

Relative to the identification rates obtained with the full images (100%), the full cartoons were identified 93% correctly, the threshold images 77% and the valledge images 67%. We therefore confirmed the poverty of representations showing only "edges", but showed that the addition of the threshold component made one-bit per pixel drawings of faces almost as good as the original images for identification.   At a theoretical level it is interesting to enquire how the addition of the threshold component conveys this benefit. The threshold component conveys information about "pigmentation" (whether hair is dark or blonde, for example) and also about patterns of shading. Images showing thresholds alone look much more three-dimensional than those showing valledges alone.   On the basis of just these data we cannot distinguish which of these sources of information provides the advantage or whether both may be important. Other research conducted in our laboratory suggests that it is the pigmentation information which may be more crucial for identification than shading, but further work is needed on this (Bruce and Langton, 1994). Our results suggest that one-bit per pixel images preserving the pattern of dark and light could be a very efficient format for facial identification.   Can such images also suffice for other, more communicative uses made of face information?

11.3 Emotional expressions

A second use made of the information from the face lies in our perception of emotions from facial expressions. We may be able to use tone of voice during a telephone conversation to tell us whether a person sounds pleased or disappointed with the news we are conveying, but the face may provide an important additional source of such information. The relative importance of face compared with voice or context for emotional interpretation is not clear, though Ekman (1982) suggests it is misleading to ask how much information is conveyed by "separate" channels when normally these co-exist. Ekman and his associates (see Ekman, 1992) have shown that people across all cultures tested appear to be able to categorise about seven different facial expressions reliably from posed photographs (happiness, sadness, surprise, disgust, anger, fear and "interest"), though the classification of emotions from spontaneous dynamic presentations has been less extensively investigated.

Ekman and Freisen (1978) described the different "facial actions" which characterise different emotional expressions, and presumably it is the perceived configuration of these different muscle groups that allows observers to categorise different expressions. Paramey (1993) has shown that line drawings of faces obtained from original images by tracing appear to give rise to very similar expression perception to the images themselves, again suggesting that one-bit per pixel video images might suffice for interpersonal perception of emotion. Moreover, Paramey's line-drawn images did not contain anything equivalent to the threshold component we described above, so that the eyebrows for example were outlined but not portrayed as dark, yet despite this appeared relatively good at conveying emotional expression. These data suggest that the information conveyed by patterns of light and dark (the threshold component of Pearson and Robinson's algorithm) may be less important for the classification of expressions than for identification. This may reflect the relative ease of the expression classification task compared with that of individual identification (where thousands of different faces may be known compared with only 6 or 7 expression types), and forms another example of the independence of expression processing from identification (see Bruce and Young, 1986; Young & Bruce, 1991 for further discussion).

However, in expression perception the timing as well as the final posture of the face movements is important. Some expressions flicker rapidly across the face lasting as little as 200 ms. Such "micro-expressions" may be lost at video rates of only five frames per second. Ekman and Friesen (1982) have analysed differences between spontaneous and deliberate or "deceptive" smiles, and shown that deceptive smiles are more asymmetrical in terms of the muscle movements involved and are also timed differently. Deceptive smiles have shorter onset times, irregular offset times, and are either relatively short or long in duration compared with spontaneous smiles. A more extensive investigation by Hess and Kleck (1990) suggested that differences in timing between spontaneous and posed expressions are found more clearly when actors are explicitly required to pose an expression which is deceptive about their underlying emotional state, for example smiling while watching a disgusting video film. If there are physical differences between genuine and "deceptive" expressions, it is reasonable to enquire whether observers can distinguish one from the other. Preliminary evidence reported by Ekman (1992) suggests that observers can distinguish genuine from posed smiles from a series of face images, though it is not clear whether this judgement can be made when the smile is embedded in the richer context of everyday communication. To the extent that people can distinguish genuine from deceptive facial expressions in everyday communication, video telecommunication is likely to provide a richer source of accurate interpersonal information than the voice channel alone.   From the somewhat limited evidence available it may be that the accurate timing of the display is as important as the fidelity of the image.

11.4   Speech perception

Face perception helps us to decipher speech. All of us lip-read, not just those who are hard of hearing. This can be demonstrated in a number of ways, but most directly by showing that speech can be deciphered at a much lower signal-to-noise ratio when the speaker's face can be seen than when only the vocal channel is available.   Adding face to voice has an effect which allows a listener to tolerate an additional 4–6 dB of noise to achieve the same level of intelligibility when seeing compared with only hearing a speaker (Summerfield, 1992), where each decibel of signal-to-noise ratio gained can improve intelligibility by 10–15%.   These figures indicate that at certain levels of noise, seeing the face can allow a listener to "hear" otherwise unintelligible speech.   Information from vision may therefore be particularly important for speech perception when the auditory channel is noisy, as it can be during telecommunication, either because of signal limitations, or because of competing noise from the external environment in which the communication is taking place.   Information from vision neatly complements that available by audition alone.

Phonetic distinctions such as place of articulation which are difficult to hear are easy to see.   Thus it is hard to hear the difference between "em" and "en", or "eff" and "ess" unless the speaker can be seen, explaining why it so often proves necessary to spell out postal codes when giving an address via telephone, and why such information is often misheard.   A more dramatic demonstration that lip-reading is an obligatory component of speech perception is given by the "McGurk" effect, where conflicting speech information presented via the face and voice may be "heard" in a way which appears to combine information from both channels (McGurk and MacDonald, 1976). For example, if lips say "ga" and voce says "ba" the percept is commonly of "da".

What information from the face is required to confer the usual benefits of audio-visual speech perception? McGrath (1985; discussed by Summerfield, 1992) compared the accuracy of identifying vowels by lip-reading when subjects could see the whole face, with those obtained when a moving schematic face was shown (Brooke and Summerfield, 1983), in which the main face features were shown, including teeth in some conditions of the experiment. Without the teeth, the schematic face vowels could be identified on 51% of trials. With the teeth drawn in on the schematic face, performance rose to 57% correct. Performance was similar in comparison conditions where only the lips (shown with luminous lipstick) or lips plus teeth (lipstick plus ultra-violet illumination) were shown to observers, from which identification of 50% and 56% of vowels respectively were obtained. This suggests that the schematic face provides the same information to observers as the isolated information from lips and teeth in a real face. However, these levels of performance are well below those obtained from a real face, where 78% of vowels can be recognised. This suggests that information additional to that from the lips and teeth contributes to "lip"-reading. Summerfield (1992) suggests that this additional information may include perception of the tongue or wrinkling and protrusion of the lips. Moreover, when the schematic faces were combined with auditory speech sounds, there was a much reduced incidence of McGurk illusory blends, subjects tending to report what they heard uninfluenced by the seen schematic face. Again this suggests that a simple line-drawing of the kind used will not convey the usual benefits of audio-visual perception. It would be interesting to know whether "cartoon" faces produced using Pearson and Robinson's (1985) algorithm would be lip-read more accurately than the schematic faces used by McGrath. Until such experiments have been done it is too early to know whether a one-bit per pixel face image could convey the usual benefits of audio-visual speech perception. For now, the evidence seems to suggest that higher-information images of faces may be needed if video images are to be helpful for deciphering speech.

However, the synchrony of voice and face is crucial if audio-visual speech benefits are to be obtained. Summerfield (1992) reviews evidence which shows that integration of audio and visual channels can occur up to delays of about 80 ms. Longer delays can be tolerated if the audio channel lags behind the visual channel than vice versa, probably because the response latencies in the retina are considerably longer than in the cochlea. Summerfield suggests that a delay of up to 80 ms is tolerated so that the sight and sound of events occurring at some distance from the observer are perceived as synchronous, given that sound takes longer to reach the observer than light. We can therefore see that the parameters within which audio-visual synchrony is achieved may arise as a result of a rather complex set of constraints from the physical properties of the signals and the biological properties of the observer. Although these constraints mean that the observer is quite tolerant of small lags between audio and visual signals, the current generation of videophones used over the narrow bandwith PSTN network introduce greater delays than this. For this reason, when users select video mode, a delay is introduced into the audio as well as the visual signal to maintain their synchrony. Unfortunately, this means that the synchrony between the two users of the system is destroyed, so that there is a delay in feedback from the listener, much as there used to be in transatlantic telephone conversations. We do not yet know what effect this loss of interpersonal synchrony has on the efficacy of discourse, or on the acceptability of the system. Nor is it clear that the result – speech and video synchronised, but with video running at only a few frames per second – does provide a signal from which audio-visual integration takes place.

11.5 Gaze

In addition to information from the lips and mouth, a number of other facial gestures convey information important for mutual understanding in conversation, for example nodding and shaking of the head. Gaze patterns provide an extremely important and rich set of social signals which help to regulate conversation as well as expressing intimacy and social control (see Kleinke, 1986). Conversants signal their "turns" within a conversation by gaze, and gaze patterns may also reveal to an observer where another person is attending. Humans are remarkably accurate at detecting changes in gaze direction (Watt, 1992, and see chapter 12). It is currently not known whether accuracy at tasks of gaze detection would be sacrificed if "schematic" faces were used in such tasks, since comparisons have not been made between the accuracy of gaze perception from line-drawings and photographs, for example. Anecdotally, however, it seems easy to discriminate gaze direction from schematic drawings of faces, and a number of developmental psychologists have made use of such drawings in their research into gaze perception in infancy and childhood. Although detecting gaze direction from a full-face image might seem relatively straightforward, since it could be achieved by assessing the degree of deviation of the pupils from the axis of facial symmetry, such a task becomes much more complex when head angle also varies, particularly as perceived gaze direction must take account of head angle in a rather subtle way.

The timing of face gestures again may be crucial for their interpretation. The prolonged stare means something different from the brief glance. Gestural movements can be very rapid indeed. The movements which punctuate speech may be as brief as 50 ms, a duration that may be lost at low video frame rates, or whose implications may be too late if there is much by way of lag in the signal.

11.6 Communicating with and without the face

Although we make use of the face in all these various ways in normal, face-to-face interaction, it is quite clear that the face is not necessary for human interaction.   Can we observe advantages for communicative efficiency when people can see as well as hear each other over and above those that might be expected from lip-reading? Research in social psychology has shown that restricting an interaction to the telephone can have subtle effects on the outcomes of negotiations. For example, Stephenson, Ayling and Rutter (1976) suggested that people were more likely to be hostile or critical over the telephone than when interacting face to face. In simulated, two-person bargaining situations it has also been shown that the side with the stronger case, as measured by the relative number and strength of the arguments assigned to each bargainer, tended to win more often by telephone than face-to-face (e.g. Morley and Stephenson, 1969).

Social psychologists have tended to interpret differences between the two situations in terms of social psychological mechanisms such as the depersonalisation which results when speakers and hearers cannot see each other. More recently, however, the comparison between face-to-face and unseen communication success has been taken up by cognitive psychologists. In research conducted at the University of Glasgow, within the ESRC's Human Communication Research Centre, Anderson and her colleagues have found substantial advantages when people can see each other in terms of efficiency of dialogue. This research has made use of the "map task" which has been used extensively in psycholinguistic research as a way of eliciting dialogue whose successfulness can be objectively assessed (e.g. see Anderson et al, 1992). In the task, one member of a pair of subjects (the information sender, S) tries to describe a route to the other member (the information receiver, R) who has to reproduce the route on his or her own map. S and R can hear, and in some conditions see, each other, but cannot see each other's maps. The landmarks shown on the two maps have some differences, and the two dialogue partners therefore have to work together to try to decipher these differences and produce a route which is accurate despite these. The task therefore elicits quite natural, yet task-directed dialogue. An example of the kind of discourse that results in this task would be:

S: "Keep the swamp to your left and head towards the gorillas"
R: "I haven't got gorillas"
S: "Have you a swamp?"
R: "Mmmm"
S: "Well keep it to your left"
R: "What do you mean left.... left of the path I'm drawing?"
S: "The path"
R: "OK"

Eventually, as a result of the dialogue, R draws a route through the map, and the deviation of the produced route from the target route (shown on S's map) can be calculated. Boyle, Anderson and Newlands (1994) showed that when S and R could see as well as hear each other, they required considerably less dialogue to produce performance of equivalent accuracy to that obtained when S and R were hidden from each other's view. When the two partners could see each other, they used about 20% fewer words and there were fewer "turns" (alternations from one speaker to another). Dialogue was also much smoother, with fewer interruptions, when the partners could see each other. It seems that the face can be used to synchronise dialogue, and to signal comprehension or disagreement, and if the face and/or other non-verbal gestures are absent, words must be used instead. This finding itself suggests that multimedia communications systems which allow collaborators to see as well as hear each other when engaged in problem solving tasks could promote more efficient (as well as more satisfactory, perhaps) performance. However, this depends on exactly what aspects of seeing the partner are important, and how this information may be preserved on screen. In current work in laboratories at Nottingham and Glasgow we are exploring the circumstances which give rise to these benefits, and will consider the implications of our results for the design of video telecommunication. Our preliminary results suggest that the advantages of face-to-face communication do not transfer to video-mediated communication, and we are currently trying to analyse the reasons for this. We are also examining the effects upon dialogue of communication via the current generation of video telephones, where the demands of image compression down current, limited bandwidth telephone lines have resulted in some delays between the messages sent and received in conversation. The map task provides an objective way to assess the effects of such delays on performance.

Findings such as those above suggest that non-verbal discourse information may provide an important supplement to that provided by the voice. We do not yet know how non-verbal and verbal information is combined in comprehension, nor do we know whether non-verbal information substitutes for, complements or adds to information obtained in the vocal channel. As part of our project work in Nottingham, Steve Langton is currently investigating how information from face and hand gestures is combined with that provided by voice, by setting these in conflict and examining the patterns of interference that are obtained from one medium to the other.

11.7   Conclusions

I have described the multitude of uses made of the information from the face in social interaction. For identification and expression perception, discrimination of one-bit per pixel images (if appropriately constructed) can produce performance near that of full face images. For lip-reading the situation is currently less clear, and for gaze it is untested. Research systematically addressed at the information content of images required for different aspects of face communication could show whether the current move towards full colour image resolution is necessary. This may be important, because we have seen that for several of the uses made of facial information, the precise timing of the movements, and the synchrony between participants, could be crucial. Where there are limitations in bandwidth, it might be better to sacrifice image quality for better timing and synchrony: again systematic research could help to answer such questions.

Acknowledgements

Some of the research described in this chapter is funded by the Economic and Social Research Council (Grant R000233560) to Claire O'Malley, Vicki Bruce and Anne Anderson at the Universities of Nottingham, Stirling and Glasgow.

References

Anderson, A. H. (1992). The human communication research centre dialogue database. *Journal of Child Language,* **19**, pp. 711–716.

Bachmann, T. (1991). Identification of spatially quantised tachistoscopic images if faces: how many pixels does it take to carry identity? *European Journal of Cognitive Psychology,* **3**, pp. 87–103.

Boyle, E., Anderson, A. H. & Newlands, A. (1994). The effects of eye contact on dialogue and performance in a cooperative problem-solving task. *Language and Speech.*

Brooke, N. M. & Summerfield, A. Q. (1983). Analysis, synthesis and perception of visible articulatory movements. *Journal of Phonetics,* **11**, pp. 63–76.

Bruce, V. & Langton, S. (1994). The use of pigmentation and shading information in recognising the sex and identities of faces. Manuscript under review.

Bruce, V. & Young, A. W. (1986). Understanding face recognition. *British Journal of Psychology,* **77**, pp. 305–327.

Bruce, V., Hanna, E., Dench, N., Healey, P. & Burton, M. (1992). The importance of 'mass' in line drawings of faces. *Applied Cognitive Psychology,* **6**, pp. 619–628.

Davies, G. M., Ellis, H. D. & Shepherd, J.W. (1978). Face recognition accuracy as a function of mode of representation. *Journal of Applied Psychology*, **63**, pp. 180–187.

Ekman, P. (1982). *Emotion And The Human Face: Second edition*, Cambridge University Press, Cambridge.

Ekman, P. (1992). Facial expressions of emotion: an old controversy and new findings. *Philosophical Transactions of the Royal Society of London*, **B335**, pp. 63–69.

Ekman, P. & Freisen, W. V. (1978). *Facial Action Coding System*. Consulting Psychologists Press, Palo Alto, CA.

Ekman, P. & Friesen, W. V. (1982). Felt, false and miserable smiles, *Journal of Nonverbal Behaviour*, **6**, pp. 238–252.

Hess, U. & Kleck, R. E. (1990). Differentiating emotion elicited and deliberate facial expressions. *European Journal of Social Psychology*, **20**, pp. 369–385.

Kleinke, C. L. (1986). Gaze and eye contact: a research review, *Psychological Bulletin*, **100**, pp. 78–100.

McGurk, H. & MacDonald, J.W. (1976). Hearing lips and seeing voices, *Nature*, **264**, pp. 126–130.

Morley, I. M. & Stephenson, G. M. (1969). Interpersonal and inter-party exchange: a laboratory simulation of an industrial negotiation at the plant level, *British Journal of Psychology*, **60**, pp. 543–545.

Paramey, G. (1993). Schematic faces: could they convey emotional meaning? Paper presented to the Experimental Psychology Society. April, 1993, Cambridge.

Pearson, D. E. & Robinson, J. A. (1985). Visual communication at very low data-rates. *Proceedings of the IEEE,* **73**, pp. 795–811.

Stephenson, G. M., Ayling, K. & Rutter, D. R. (1976). The role of visual communication in social exchange, *British Journal of Social and Clinical Psychology*, **15**, pp. 113–120.

Summerfield, Q. (1992). Lipreading and audio-visual speech perception. *Philosophical Transactions of the Royal Society of London*, **B335**, pp. 71–78.

Watt, R.J. (1992). Faces and vision. In: V. Bruce & M. Burton (Eds), *Processing Images of Faces*, Ablex, Norwood, New Jersey.

Young, A.W. & Bruce, V. (1991). Perceptual categories and the computation of grandmother. *European Journal of Cognitive Psychology*, **3**, pp. 5–50.

12

An examination of the visual aspects of human facial gesture

Roger J. Watt

The purpose of this chapter is to describe some results that have been obtained from an examination of images of human faces. These results are part of a general study of the relationship of the structure of human vision to its function in some common visual tasks. The general approach is to use simulations of human visual processing in combination with minimal special purpose decision rules in order to provide information that is directly applicable to a given task. It is not difficult, technically, to create reasonable computer models of the initial stages of human vision and then to apply these models to digitized naturally obtained images. This chapter describes the findings of doing so for facial images and images of facial gestures.

The plan of the chapter is as follows. It starts by examining the common facial gestures. Next, the general method for the visual analysis is described, and a commentary is made on its relationship to visual processing in the human brain. A sample human face image is used to illustrate this. Next, the general pattern of response to images of human faces will be considered. This section can be regarded as being a consideration of the basic physical structure of faces and their interaction with light. This is then followed by an examination of how images of faces change as facial gestures are produced – the emphasis is on the spatial aspects of facial gestures. Finally, it is shown that this approach can throw fresh light on how facial gestures can be understood within the context of a signalling system.

A number of simplifications have been made to both of the issues: human vision and facial gestures. For human vision, the emphasis is on those parts of the process that are concerned with simple form information. Depth perception through stereopsis is not required for the present discussion, nor is colour and texture perception. For facial gestures, the complete set of different gestures is large in size and complicated in its structure. Many facial gestures involve much of the face and all appear to be subjected to varying degrees of emphatic modulation. For present purposes in studying the visual aspects of facial gestures, it is convenient to treat the facial gesturing organs individually and in small neighbouring clusters. In particular, it will be shown to be visually simpler to treat the area from just beneath the lower lip (i.e. including the shadow under that lip) to just above the base of the nose as a single cluster, and the area from just below the eye to just above the eyebrow as another single cluster.

12.1   Facial gestures

Many facial signals are not gestures. The face signals the sex, the age and the identity of the face's owner. These are not changing (at least over the time course of perception). There are many facial gestures that involve movements of parts of the face that are perceptible. Three facial organs are mobile enough to serve dynamic expressive functions – the mouth, the eyes and the eyebrows. These are taken in turn.

The mouth

The human mouth is quite a remarkable piece of engineering. It serves three obvious functions: breathing, eating and speaking. When we speak, we open and close our mouth in a way that depends on what we are saying and how we are saying it. If you are sitting in a noisy train, then even though you cannot hear anything, it's easy to see if someone is speaking by watching their face. Mouths open and close for many reasons, but if a person is speaking, then there is a characteristic type of jerkiness to it that you do not see otherwise. The movements of our mouth play a further role in speech: the different speech sounds that are created by changing the shape of the vocal tract structures at the front of the mouth are naturally visible and therefore useful for lip-reading.

Lip-reading is a skill that we all have, although it is more practised in people whose hearing is impaired. It is simple to show that most people can get some extra information from being able to watch a speaker's mouth. An experiment was carried out by MacLeod and Summerfield (1987) to measure just how much extra information could be picked up by people. They took a group of normal subjects, and played spoken sentences to them. After each sentence the subject was required to repeat the sentence back to the experimenter. In some presentations, the subjects only heard the sentence and in others, the subjects could watch the speaker at the same time. MacLeod and

Summerfield measured the amount of noise that could just be tolerated without markedly impairing the ability of subjects to report the sentence correctly. They found that the maximum noise level for correctly reporting the sentence was higher when subjects were able to see as well as hear the speech than when they could only hear the sounds. Different subjects showed different degrees of benefit from seeing the speech and were presumably more or less practised and skilled at lip-reading, although the range of different performances was not very great.

An earlier study, by Erber (1974), had provided some information about the conditions under which lip-reading is possible. The main purpose of this study was to discover how deaf children should be seated around the teacher in a classroom, and where the teacher should be put, relative to the daylight at the windows. Erber measured the proportion of words that could be lip-read successfully by profoundly deaf children at various distances and directions from the speaker and for different types of illumination of the face. The illumination did not have very much effect, but the other two factors did. In the best conditions, 2 m from the speaker and a full-face view, the children could get more than 80% of the words correct. This performance fell if the children were seeing the profile of the face. Performance also fell with increasing distance although, for a distance of 7 m, the children were still able to get around 60% of the words correct.

One major way in which lip-reading can contribute to the process of understanding speech concerns the vowel sounds. Although these are quite distinctive and different from each other as sounds, they also lead to visible cues on the face that we can use in adverse acoustic situations. Brooke and Summerfield (1983) obtained video recordings of people as they pronounced various vowel-consonant-vowel syllables. The speakers were simultaneously filmed in full-face and in profile view, so that the full three-dimensional movements of many points on the face could be measured. The main movements of the lips were found to be a simple opening of the mouth, so that the mouth area increased and a stretching or shrinking horizontally so that the mouth is elongated and flattened or is rounded.

McGrath, Summerfield and Brooke (1984) followed this study up with experiments to assess what aspects of lip-reading people actually use to distinguish between vowels. Subjects were shown videos of speakers pronouncing syllables of the form b-vowel-b (e.g. bib), but with no sound. The subjects' accuracy in reporting the vowel was then measured for all the different possible vowels. Subjects were told to guess if they did not know. The videos were of three types. Subjects saw either the full face, or the lips and teeth, or just the lips (UV light and fluorescent dye were used to make these latter two tapes).

Their first basic finding was that subjects can do well at identifying vowels from the visual appearance of a face (70+% correct for an image sequence of the full face). Performance was poorer if only the lips and teeth are visible (55% correct) and slightly poorer still for displays in which only the lips are visible. Multidimensional scaling was used to find out how the confusions that subjects make can be described. Earlier work by Montgomery and Jackson (1983) had identified two important aspects of the visual appearance of the mouth: the extent to which the mouth was rounded or elongated and where the tongue was in the mouth. The study of McGrath et al. identified mouth rounded/elongated as an important variable that allows subjects to identify the vowel that is being pronounced. They also identified the overall opening of the mouth and the duration of the mouth movement as important cues.

In lip-reading, we are very good at distinguishing between several broad classes of consonant. Some consonants are produced by closing and then opening the two lips (the so-called bilabial consonants, such as p, b, m). Others are produced by the lower lip contacting the upper teeth (the labio-dentals, such as f and v). Another group is produced by the tip of the tongue touching the upper teeth (the linguo-dentals, such as th). All of these groups can be visually discriminated from each other because the articulation of the consonant involves visible structures. Consonants that are produced by articulation at various places farther back in the vocal tract are much harder to tell apart visually. In this latter group, however, there is another distinction that can be seen. Some consonant sounds are generated with a secondary articulation. One such secondary articulation can be seen because it involves a rounding of the lips (examples are s and sh).

The eyes

Our eyes have an obvious function, seeing. When we look at something, then we tend to turn our head to face that thing, and to move our eyes so that they are pointing directly at the object in question. If our eyes were fixed in their sockets, then it would be necessary to move the whole book in front of you as you read, or to move your whole head from word to word.

When we look at something, we turn our eyes directly towards that thing for as long as it takes to see what it is we want to see or until the eyes have to be diverted to something else. This is necessary because the central part of our vision is capable of extracting much more detailed and accurate information than is the periphery of our vision. Typically it takes several tenths of a second to capture enough information about some object and to decide where to look next. This means that our eyes tend to hop around a scene stopping for periods of between a quarter of a second to a second. Obviously, the more time that is spent looking at one particular object, the more information we are extracting from that object and, presumably, the more interested in that object we are.

When the object that we are looking at is another person, then the amount of interest that we are showing could be very important to them and to others for a variety of reasons. An experiment by Ellsworth, Carlsmith and Henson (1972) shows this very clearly. An experimenter, riding a motor scooter, arranged to arrive first at a red traffic light. When a car drew alongside, the experimenter turned to stare directly at the driver until the traffic signal turned green. The time taken for the driver to cross the road junction was then measured. The timings obtained by this technique were compared with an equivalent set of timings obtained in the same way, except that the experimenter merely glanced at the driver before looking away again. The basic result was that drivers drove away faster (by about 15%) if they had been stared at than if they had not been stared at.

Clearly, looking at someone else's face, and especially at their eyes is a powerful social signal. Whether we look or not, and if we do for how long and how frequently are all significant indicators of the type of relationship that exists at that moment. In the case of a normal interaction between two people, there is a typical pattern of eye behaviour, especially useful for the regulation of conversation. It is often found that listeners tend to look at a speaker's face more often than the speakers look at the listener's face (Argyle and Cook, 1976). When you speak to somebody, you have a natural tendency to look at that person and especially to look at their eyes. There are several good reasons for this. Their eyes will give you an indication of whether they are paying attention to you or to something or someone else. While I am talking to you, I expect you to be watching my mouth for the purposes of lip-reading. If you look up into my eyes, then that signals to me that you have stopped lip-reading, and perhaps have stopped listening as well.

Kendon (1967) has reported a detailed examination of where people look during a conversation. In his study, pairs of students were engaged in a getting to know you one-to-one conversation for between 5 and 16 minutes. As they interacted, they were filmed for subsequent analysis. In this type of conversation, the topics were usually about one or other of the participants. Kendon presents some data on the looking behaviour of subjects in various different contexts within such a conversation.

The first and simplest observation is that the subjects did tend to look at one another. More interesting was the more detailed looking behaviour at critical points in the conversation. Kendon calls the person who is being discussed (presumably the person speaking because the two people didn't know each other) P, and the other person Q. When P draws to the end of a natural phrase in what is being said, he or she is more likely to look directly at Q than whilst in the middle of a phrase. Conversely if P hesitates whilst speaking, then he or she is less likely to look at Q until resuming speaking.

All of this makes good sense as a mechanism for controlling who speaks and when. By looking at the listener when a phrase has ended, some reaction can be obtained if the listener has a reaction to offer. If the listener will only speak when looked at, then an interruption is prevented by looking away during a hesitation. The important point here is that by looking at the listener, the speaker is showing a readiness to be interrupted. By looking away, the speaker is showing an unwillingness to be interrupted yet. The showing has to be visible – the listener must be able to catch the message. It is important for us to be able to see with some accuracy where someone is looking.

Because patterns of gaze show typical distributions, with few lasting longer than a second or so, any deviation from normal behaviour can usually be associated with an unusual form of interaction. People tend to gaze at another's face more when they are being persuasive, deceptive, ingratiating, or assertive (see Kleinke, 1986 for a review). People also tend to judge another person by their pattern of gazing, attributing attentiveness, competence, credibility and powerfulness to others.

The eyebrows

Compared with the mouth and the eyes and their very obvious functions, the eyebrows seem to be something that was left behind when we became smooth-skinned organisms. There has been speculation from time to time, (for example the eyebrows were thought to shield the eyes from drops of water – sweat or rain – running off the forehead) but no suggestion has really made sense. The eyebrows have several communicative functions, however, as well as being important in making us recognizable.

Our eyebrows are mobile features on the face. They can move up and down, and to a limited extent side to side. They can also change their shape, becoming more or less arched. The eyebrows are a very visible feature on the face. In pale-skinned races, they can have a considerable colour difference compared to the skin above. In all races, the forehead is quite a shiny surface and tends to appear bright and glossy. Against this, the texture of the eyebrows is rather dull. The eyebrows also protrude from the surface of the face, tending to add prominence.

The eyebrows are involved in signalling during conversation and they also convey messages about our emotional state (although not on their own). The fullest examination of how we use our eyebrows has been undertaken by Ekman and Friesen (1978) and Ekman (1979). By a careful study of the muscles of the face and by observation of people's eyebrows, Ekman has identified seven visibly distinctive actions that eyebrows can make.

A slightly simpler classification is to consider only two basic actions: eyebrows up (Ekman's Action Unit 1+2) and eyebrows down (Action Unit 4). When we do this, then a fairly simple account of the use of eyebrows for signalling some of our emotions can be attempted: 1+2 generally corresponds to surprise and interest; 4 generally corresponds to anger and distress. These are opposites in emotional as well as eyebrow position terms. As Ekman notes, these two extremes should be least confused. Action Units 1+2 and 4 can be used for various different purposes in the course of a conversation, by both the speaker and the listener.

A speaker will use eyebrows to add emphasis to what is being said and to add some form of punctuation. A specific instance of the latter is the frequent use of eyebrow Action Units 1+2 or 4 to mark the end of a question. Ekman notes some preliminary evidence that an eyebrow action is particularly likely to be used at the end of a question if the question does not begin with an interrogatory word (what, where, who, when, which). In these circumstances, action 1+2 is the most likely. If a speaker hesitates, engaging in a word search, then it is important to prevent the listener from taking over speaking. The speaker will also not look at the listener. Ekman offers some evidence that Action Unit 4 may also be used in this situation, or, alternatively, 1+2 with the eyes directed right up in the air.

The listener may also use the two eyebrow actions 1+2 and 4 during conversation. Generally, 1+2 is thought to be used to signal understanding and perhaps agreement with what is being said. Action Unit 4, on the other hand, probably carries a signal of incomprehension, literally or metaphorically to signal disbelief.

There is one other important eyebrow signal that must be mentioned. This is the eyebrow flash, a gesture of greeting, originally reported by Eibl-Eibesfeldt (1972). In this the eyebrows are raised (Action Unit 1+2) for a small fraction of a second and then dropped. This signal is generally held to be a message of recognition.

12.2 Visual processing – general method

It is convenient to use three different forms of visual representation, or data structure, to explain the processes that are used to model the initial stages of human vision. These forms of representation are to be understood as logically distinct devices that carry very different types of information about the input image. These three different forms are the minimum required to be able to obtain specific information about objects in the image.

Image algebra

A digitized image is represented as a matrix of numerical values. Each value corresponds to the luminance value of a point in the image. The spatial layout of the values in the matrix maps on to the continuous spatial dimensions of the optical image. Each pixel is thus a spatially localized sample.

The first set of operations that the visual system performs keeps the information within this spatial matrix form. This set of operations will be referred to as image algebra operations, to emphasize that the representation format is that of the sampled image, and the main considerations are to do with image patterns at this stage. Two are of significance for present purposes.

1 The first image algebra operation is a form of local contrast gain control. The goal of this computation is to render the image so that local mean luminance and local standard deviation of luminance are relatively uniform across the image. This is significant for images that have significantly directional illumination, especially if that illumination is from the side. Details of an algorithm that we have found to be suitable are given in Watt (1994).

2 The second relevant image algebra operation is convolution with a set of spatial scale and orientation selective filters. The generic filter function used in these studies is a filter that is the product of a second derivative of a Gaussian in one direction and a plain Gaussian in the orthogonal direction:

$$f(x, y) = (1 - y^2)e^{-(x^2 + y^2)}$$

where the filter coordinate system (x,y) is mapped on to the image coordinate system subject to three parameters: an orientation (rotation), a spatial scale (isotropic dilation) and an elongation (dilation in the direction at right angles to the direction of differentiation). The elongation is always set to a value of 3.0 in the work described here. The other two parameters are used to define a set of filters covering the space of orientations and spatial scales.

Image description

All that is made explicit in the image form of representation is the value of a pixel at a specified location. This is rarely, if ever, a useful form of information. It therefore follows that a further form of representation must be used to make explicit information that is more useful.

In a filtered image, the mean value can be regarded as the expected value – the least informative. Deviations away from the expected value carry the information. For the filters considered here, the expected value of the response is zero, and so deviations away from zero carry the information. These deviations away from zero tend to lie in spatially extended areas so that a filtered image can be broken down into a set of zero-bounded regions, within which the response is consistently positive or negative. These zero-bounded regions are treated as the most primitive pattern structure in the filtered image. Zero-bounded regions are called blobs for short.

Each blob is described by a list of parameters which form a descriptive sentence. The intention of such a list is to make explicit all the useful information about the blob that it describes. The complete set of descriptive sentences – the image description – is intended to make explicit all the useful information that is available from the outputs of each filter. The parameters that are chosen for exposition in this chapter are explained in more detail in Watt (1991). These parameters are measurements of the region mass (response strength), centroid (position), length, width, and orientation.

The complete set of region descriptions is known as an image description. An image description makes explicit a wide range of information about structures within the image. In this respect, it is a more useful representation than is an image. It is termed an image description because it describes structures within the image. The extent to which these structures are related to the form and layout of objects in the image depends on the nature of the filtering stages that precede this stage.

Visual description

The descriptive sentences, one per region, are all of equal status within the image description. Since this representation is a set, there are no explicit relationships between sentences. However, a single blob description is most unlikely to correspond to a whole object. Accordingly, it becomes necessary to compute which sentences might arise from common objects and then to group together those sentences into subset structures. This operation can be expressed by giving the rules which are used to determine which descriptive sentences might belong with which.

Many objects have an axis of some sort. Objects that can be described at an appropriate scale and approximation by a generalized cylinder have an natural axis (Marr, 1977; Marr and Nishihara, 1978). Objects that have some degree of bilateral symmetry have a natural axis (Marr, 1982; Watt, 1991). Objects that move in a particular direction (necessarily) have an axis in that direction (Watt, 1991). A common consequence of this is that, at the appropriate spatial scale, there exists a set of parallel blobs all aligned on a common axis that runs through their centres that is oriented at or near to right angles to the orientations of the blobs.

Therefore it follows that one rule that can be used to group together blobs that, by virtue of being aligned along a common orthogonal axis, might reasonably arise from the existence of an object in the image. We now see how such a rule might be worked out.

If we were to take the output of any particular oriented filter, then for any two blobs, which would necessarily be more-or-less parallel, there would be a common axis. It is necessary to be more restrictive than this. A sensible grouping can be proposed where one or more of the following additional conditions are met:

• The axis is more nearly at right angles to the blob orientations

• The blobs share similar values on other parameters, especially scale and elongation

• The blobs are not widely spaced on the axis

• More than two blobs are aligned on the same axis.

From such a list of conditions it is possible to devise a rule that can be used to group together certain blobs into a cluster. It should be noted that, with the exception of the last of these conditions, each is a measure of similarity between the blobs on some simple dimension such as position on either spatial dimension (with the coordinate system rotated to be aligned with the orientation of the blobs). Details are given in Watt (1994).

Obviously, there is a need for more than one such grouping rule. For present purposes, this one alone will be sufficient. This stage of representation, where descriptive sentences are clustered into groups (which implies that certain types of relationships between them are now explicit), is called a visual description, because the entities that are described by the clusters of descriptive sentences, and the processes that can be used to create the clusters are determined by knowledge and constraints that relate to objects not images.

12.3 Images of the human face and vision

The consequences of filtering an image of a face at various spatial scales and orientations are shown in Figure 12.1. Significant visual structures are found only at certain spatial scales and orientations (with respect to the face). In general, oblique orientations are of little additional value beyond the information that can be obtained from horizontal and vertical filters. There are basically only two types of response pattern in the range of filter outputs at different spatial scales: a fine scale structure that highlights facial features; and a coarse spatial scale structure that captures the gross structure of the face. The pattern illustrated is quite typical for faces under the normal range of illumination conditions.

Coarse spatial scales

At the coarsest spatial scales, the response of the horizontal and vertical filters is a simple set of parallel, aligned blobs:

The horizontal blobs form a reliable pattern which can be specified as a sequence, starting from the top, of light, dark, light, dark, light.

The first blob of the sequence, a light blob, is generated by the broad shiny area of the forehead – this can be missing if the person has hair that covers the forehead.

The second blob, a dark one, arises from the dark region of the face around the eyebrows and eye sockets. It is extremely reliable, being found in all face images we have examined, including those of people wearing spectacles.

The third blob, which arises from the shiny prominent surface on the cheek bones and the tip of the nose (which are normally aligned) is extremely reliable.

The fourth member of this sequence, a dark blob, may be missing – it is primarily generated by dark areas at the base of the nose and around the lips. For some mouth postures, this blob will be too weak to be reliably detected.

The final blob in the sequence, a light one, is reliably found and is caused by the chin area.

Whist this is the basic sequence there are a few potential variations caused by different parts of the face being visible. As well as missing blobs, it is also possible that there will be additional blobs present. These will naturally arise at either end of the sequence where the face is contrasted against some background. They may also arise internally if the scale chosen is somewhat too fine.

It is simple to relate these blobs in the horizontal and vertical filters to particular facial features. They arise because of the surface properties and the shape of the face. The forehead, cheek bones and tip of the nose, and the chin are the major convex areas of the face.

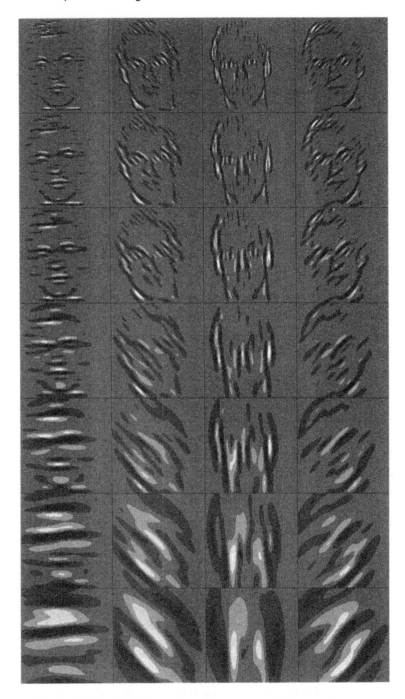

Figure 12.1. This figure shows the reponses of filters at four different orientations and seven different spatial scales to a typical image of a face. Notice the major response patterns that are found in the coarse horizontal filter and in fine horizontal and vertical filters.

The first two of these areas are also highly specular regions, presumably being well endowed with sebaceous glands. The forehead and cheek bones and the nose all present surfaces that are extended vertically for some considerable distance and that are all oriented with a slight upwards tilt. The effect of these arrangements is that, under illumination that is generally from above or from the front, but not from beneath, these areas of the face will reflect light more than other parts of the face which are either not specular (such as the eyebrows) or are likely to be shaded (such as the base of the nose).

The pattern of vertical blobs is less interesting. The outer ones clearly delimit the extent of the face laterally, and the large central one is generated by the nose and possibly any vertical furrowing of the forehead. The sequence of blob polarities is obviously more variable, depending on which side of the face the illumination is coming from. Since side lighting from either direction is equally likely, the polarity of blobs cannot be specified.

It is worth noting that the pattern of blobs so described has a number of characteristics that are functionally important. As was stressed above, a sequence of parallel, aligned blobs in a filtered image is a useful indicator that some form of object may be present. It seems likely that a sequence of seven such blobs (five plus two outer edge blobs) will be rare even as a response to an object. It therefore follows that the structure of the face is a highly salient visual object.

Fine spatial scales

At the finer scales, approximately two octaves smaller in spatial scale than the coarse scales considered above, there are similarly salient visual response structures. These structures bear an obvious relationship to the facial features that are involved in human communication. It is convenient to split the face up into three smaller areas. These areas are found automatically by the grouping rules in the visual description process. Two correspond to the eyes/eyebrows (left and right) and the third corresponds to the base on the nose and the mouth (including lips, tongue and teeth, if visible). In each of these regions a set of aligned, parallel stripes are found. In each case the exact sequence of stripes in the pattern depends on the facial expression. However, if we take a neutral expression to start with, then we can see the basic patterns.

Starting with the region around the eye and eyebrows, the neutral expression produces a set of alternating light and dark horizontal stripes which can be readily traced to structures such as the eyebrow. A pattern of five, three light stripes with two interleaved dark stripes in between, is normal although the lower two stripes are both small and relatively weak. The eyes themselves also give rise to a small pattern of aligned vertical stripes, with the eyeball itself creating a triplet of light, dark, light.

The region around the mouth is also represented by a pattern of alternating light and dark stripes. As will be seen in the next section, the number of stripes depends on which mouth structures are visible. Interestingly the base of the nose produces a reliable dark response. This is extremely useful since the base of the nose is the only prominent, non-mobile feature on the face, and can thus serve as a location reference for the other features.

Hypothetical visual processing of face images

Watt (1987) showed that the human visual system processes spatial information in a sequence starting with information available at coarse spatial scales and progressing to finer spatial scales over a period of around a second or so. It was hypothesized that this represented a process that was assigning spatial locations to image features through iterative processing within a spatial scale. The present observations provide a very clear indication of how this might work.

Dakin and Watt (1995) have shown that once the basic coarse-scale pattern of stripes has been identified, the image description of the stripes can be used to locate the finer scale features with 100% success. The rule is basically to use the light stripes to bracket regions of the image. It follows that the coarse-scale pattern, as well as being a readily detectable environmental signal, contains a personal code for the layout of the person's face. This point is illustrated in Figure 12.2.

Figure 12.2. This figure shows the basic process of finding the patterns of response that are significant in perceiving the face and the facial gesture.

12.4   Facial gestures and face images

We can now turn to consider the relationship between the face image and facial gestures. Ideally, this study would use sequences of images obtained under natural conditions and obtained with several different people's face. Such a study is presently under way in my laboratory, but so far only preliminary results can be reported.

A series of 15 different images of the face of one individual were obtained. These 15 included: two neutral conditions: mouth closed, mouth open; the pronunciation of three vowels sounds: /cool/ /kill/ /keel/; the pronunciation of four consonant sounds: /f/ /th/ /p/ /sh/; three eye directions: down, slightly to the right, and far to the right; three different eyebrow conditions: lowered in a frown, raised in surprise and raised in a smile.

Figure 12.3 shows the 15 images of the preliminary study reported here. The images were obtained under good lighting conditions, with a dark background so that image processing would be straightforward. The images were obtained to illustrrate the range of facial postures that the mouth, eyes and eyebrows could make, rather than with the intention of being natural examples of particular gestures.

The coarse-scale responses in filtered images did not show any notable variations, and so the discussion will focus on the fine-scale responses.

The mouth

The mouth shows a number of variations in the different images. Responses of small horizontal filters to the mouth region are shown in Figure 12.4. These are all in line with the discussion of the use of the mouth in facial gestures above. The response to the base of the nose and the mouth is generally combined into a single entity by the grouping process that selects stripes that are aligned on a common axis. It is therefore simplest to treat this entity as a whole rather than trying to subdivide it into its constituent parts: the nose and the mouth.

This complex of stripes always has at least two dark stripes and may have up to five. If there are only two dark stripes then the mouth is closed and the stripes correspond to the base of the nose and the mouth. If there are five then they correspond to the base of the nose, the top lip, the gap between the teeth (or the tongue if it is visible), the lower lip and the shadow beneath the bottom lip. In between these there will be light stripes. One light stripe will lie between each pair of dark stripes, except that the gap between the base of the nose and the upper lip may be sufficiently large for there to be a second light stripe. The lowest stripe of the sequence is dark if the lower lip is protruded and light otherwise. From the number of stripes that are found, the parts of the mouth structure that are visible can be deduced.

Another variable that is of use is the width of the widest dark stripe. The widest dark stripe is generally the second one down, corresponding to the upper lip, or to the mouth, if it is closed. This width takes on one of just two values in the set of images obtained. The two values differ by a factor of about 1.5 – a substntial difference. Clearly the mouth will vary between these two limits, but it seems likely that they represent "states".

Figure 12.3. This figure shows the set of basic facial gestures used in the preliminary study.

There are three basic parameters that can be used to distinguish mouth gestures. First, the number of stripes in the sequence ranges from 6 to 9. Second, the lowest stripe may be dark or light. Third the widest stripe may be large or small. Each combination could be found, making 16 possibilities in all. In the set of 15 images of this study, two combinations are missing. These would correspond to a wide, closed mouth with non-protruding lips and a wide and open mouth with protruding lips. Both might be thought of as extreme expressions.

The eyes and eyebrows

The key to understanding the effects of changes in this region of the face is gained by appreciating how movements of the eyes from side to side changes the response blobs. The main effect is on the small vertical blob sequence that the iris and sclera of the eye give rise to. This sequence is in the order light, dark, light. As the eye turns, the ratio of the amplitudes of the two light stripes changes. This appears to be a sensitive cue to the direction that the eye is pointing in. As the eye approaches the extreme turn in the socket, one of the two light stripes eventually vanishes. These responses are illustrated in Figure 12.5.

The precision with which a visual system can measure the eye direction from the ratio cue will depend on the overall amplitude of the response of the small vertical filters. As this overall amplitude is reduced, the signal to noise ratio worsens and more time for inspection would be needed.

In examining the 15 images of facial expressions, two different factors have been found to influence the amplitude of the response to the eye itself. The first of these is the separation of the eyelids. The wider apart the eyelids are the stronger the response because more of the eyeball is visible. A secondary and less intuitive effect is a direct effect of the eyebrows.

The eyebrows can be raised with or without the eyelids also being more separated. If the eyelids are kept close together, as in a smile, then the eye signal is kept quite weak. If the eyebrows are raised and the eyelids are made more separated than normal, then the strength of the response of the visual mechanism to the eyeball is increased. The increase is greater than can be attributed solely to the eyelids, and so there is an effect of the eyebrows themselves.

Figure 12. 6 illustrates the two effects of eyelids and eyebrows.

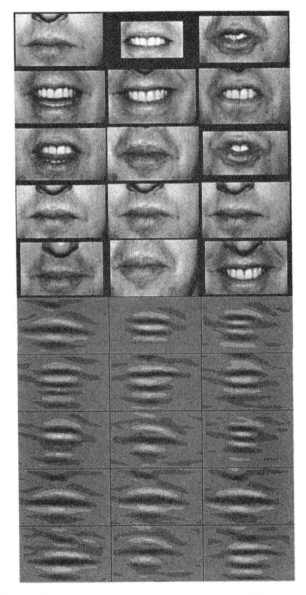

Figure 12.4. The responses to the mouth in various different facial gestures.

12.5   The use of facial gestures

The three regions of the face: the mouth, the eyes and the eyebrows plus forehead constitute three devices for sending out fairly rapid signals to other people who are watching for them. Taken as a single whole, they can make a coordinated system for controlling interactions between people. As I engage in a conversation with someone, there is a natural sequence in the flow of information between us. Initially, some very gross decisions have to be made about the nature of the interaction that we might have. These are determined by the age of the other person, their sex, whether I know them and so on. The next step is to begin to set a context for the conversation and this can be determined in part by how the other person appears to be feeling. Facial gestures of mental state become very important therefore at this stage. It is also necessary to ensure that both parties to the conversation are ready for it to start – there is nothing more embarrassing than speaking to someone who is not listening. Once the conversation starts, then facial gestures are involved in regulating who speaks and when. They are also involved in providing a form of commentary to run alongside the spoken word.

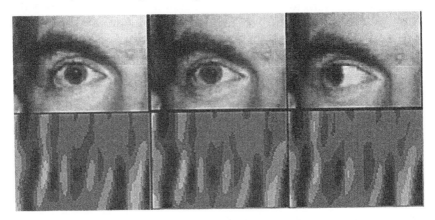

Figure 12.5. The reponse of vertical filters as the eye is turned to one side.

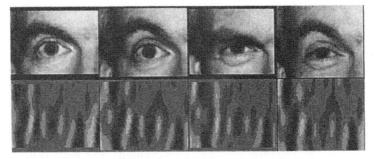

Figure 12.6. The vertical responses over the eyeball are shown for four different eye states: normal, eyebrows down, eyebrows up with eyelids close together and eyebrows up with eyelids widely separated.

It can be seen that there are three systems of communication. The first system is the system that is used to start to aid and to regulate conversation between two or more people. This is a highly dynamic system of signalling and can be analyzed in the same way as communication between a network of computers. The second system is used by us to convey something of our present state; our emotions determine how we will react to other people, and will signal this with our face. For completeness, it is worth noting that there is a third system that is involved in identifying information about a person – how old they are, whether they are male of female, what race they belong to and so on. There has been less work than one would like that has been concerned with these complete signalling systems and much of what follows here is speculative.

We can now turn to consider these issues of facial gestures as parts of systems of communication. No one of the facial structures is a complete signalling system in its own right; all messages that our faces send are part of a communication process that involves all parts of the face.

Expression of mental state

Compared with the facial gestures used in conversation, the facial expression of mental state, especially emotion, is straightforward. The eyebrows and the mouth both play a role in this. These are suitable facial features to use because they can be seen from considerable distances. The messages "I am angry/happy/sad/fearful" are obviously ones that will generally need to be transmitted over reasonable distances.

Since these gestures use the same facial features that are used for regulating conversation, the possibility of confusion should perhaps exist. There is one major difference however that serves to distinguish between the two classes of message. A still picture of an angry expression makes sense in that we can recognize the message. By contrast, a still picture of someone saying ABA (apart from the obvious impossibility) is not recognizable in that way. The facial gestures involved in signalling mental state will typically be more slowly changing, so that we can rather think of the facial gesture as a state. In conversation the gestures are rapid and we should really think of them as facial movements rather than facial states.

Conversation

Two people are engaged in earnest conversation. The topic is difficult, and language is stretched to its expressive capacity. The scope for misunderstanding, for a failure of communication, is very considerable. The need for continually monitoring how the conversation is proceeding is likewise considerable.

The speaker could speak with eyes shut so that no distractions would disrupt the flow of words and the pattern of thought. However, the speaker would have no idea whether they were speaking at an appropriate speed and with an appropriate degree of explanation for the listener to follow what was being said. Feedback is necessary, and so the speaker watches the listener for signals indicating a reaction. It is better for the listener not to have to deliver that reaction orally. We find it very difficult to listen and speak at the same time and so verbal reaction would have to be confined to moments when the speaker was quiet. This would slow the conversation down very considerably. Hence the feedback is visual.

Likewise, the listener could engage in the conversation with eyes shut but a sequence of words on their own can be mildly ambiguous, and the speaker is likely to be using facial gestures to help resolve the ambiguities. At a basic level, mouth gestures can go some distance towards disambiguating some speech sounds. Equally important, other facial gestures are used to provide emphases, punctuation and to indicate subtleties in the language.

When it comes to deciding that the speaker and listener should reverse roles, then there has to be common assent. This will always require some degree of negotiation. As we have seen above, the eyes are particularly useful for doing this. The role of the eyes in conversation is obviously of high significance. When the speaker looks up at the listener, this is an indication of a readiness to yield the airwaves. Conversely a look away is an indication of a desire to keep the airwaves. When the listener looks away, the speaker could well assume that the communication shared is in danger of being closed. Conversation is often only likely to start when two people have looked at each other.

The role of the eyebrows makes very interesting sense. Various different people have wondered whether there is any significant relationship between the eyebrows raised and eyebrows lowered gestures and their different patterns of usage. It has been suggested, for example, that the effect of eyebrows on the extent of the visual field might explain why eyebrows lowered is a more negative signal than eyebrows raised (Blurton-Jones and Konner, 1971). It has been suggested that the eyes are held more steady in the eye-sockets when the eyebrows are lowered and are able to move more quickly when the eyebrows are raised (Darwin, 1872). There is a much simpler account, if the accuracy with which a watcher can judge where someone else is looking, and more particularly whether the watcher is being looked at, can be influenced by the eyebrows. Let us assume that by lowering the eyebrows, the direction of gaze is somewhat concealed, and that by raising the eyebrows, the direction of gaze is made very visible. We can now see that the eyebrows could play a regulatory role in supervising the signalling. If a speaker raised the eyebrows during conversation, this would allow the recipient clearer access to the "over to you" signal from the eyes. If the listener raised the eyebrows, indicating agreement or surprise, then this would perhaps allow the speaker to see that the listener's eyes are looking for an "over to you" signal. Frowns would work in the opposite way in each case.

The eyebrows offer the opportunity to use the eyes for seeing without using them simultaneously for signalling, if or when it is desired to conceal the direction of gaze. The eyebrow flash greeting gesture can also be seen as a mechanism for allowing the recipient clearer access to the "I am looking at you" signal.

The signalling system involved in the regulation of conversation has performance characteristics that are quite specific. It has a rate of communication that is fairly rapid, to be matched to the conversational needs. It has a range of communication that can be relatively restricted: it only needs to involve the people conversing and they are very likely to be near to each other. It can also be quite directional: the signals only need to be sent in one direction because the people are likely to be facing each other. These requirements are well matched by the visual apparatus.

12.6 Summary

The face contains three basic regions that are expressive: the mouth and the two eyes. These regions are used in conversation and in the expression of mental state and emotion.

These regions can be readily localized in images of faces after processing by simulations of human visual perceptual mechanisms. The changes that normal facial expressions give rise to are both readily visible and easily analyzed by simulations of human visual processing. At least certain aspects of the function of the eyebrows can be understood as being ways of modulating the readiness with which an observer can discriminate eye direction.

Acknowledgements

This work was supported by research grants from SERC. Steve Dakin and Ian Paterson have helped with software and other assistance and have offered very useful discussions on the topics presented here.

References

Argyle. M, & Cook, R. (1976). *Gaze and Mutual Gaze.* Cambridge University Press.

Blurton-Jones, N. G. & Konner, M. J. (1971). An experiment on eyebrow-raising and visual search in children. *Journal of Child Psychology and Psychiatry,* **11**, pp. 233–240.

Brooke, N. M. & Summerfield, A. Q., (1983). Analysis, synthesis and perception of visible articulatory movements. *Journal of Phonetics,* **11**, pp. 63–76.

Dakin, S. C. & Watt, R. J. (1995). A simple relationship between the structure of the human face and the human visual system, (In preparation).

Darwin, C. (1872). The Expression of the Emotions in Man and Animals. New York: Philosophical Library.

Eibl-Eibesfeldt, I. (1972). Similarities and differences between cultures in expressive movements. In: R. A. Hindle (Ed.), *Non-verbal Communication,* Cambridge University Press.

Ekman, P. (1979). About brows: emotion and conversational signals. In: M. von Cranach, K. Foppa, W. Lepenies & D. Ploog (Eds.), *Human Ethology.* Cambridge University Press.

Ekman, P. & Friesen, W. V. (1978). *The Facial Action Coding System.* Consulting Psychologist's Press, Palo Alto.

Ellsworth, P. C., Carlsmith, J. M., & Henson, A. (1972). The stare as a stimulus to flight in human subjects: a series of field experiments. *Journal of Personality and Social Psychology,* **21**, pp. 302–311.

Erber, N. P. (1974). Effects of angle, distance and illumination on visual reception of speech by profoundly deaf children. *Journal of Speech and Hearing Research,* **17**, pp. 99–112.

Kendon, A. (1967). Some functions of gaze-direction in social interaction. *Acta Psychologica,* **26**, pp. 22–63.

Kleinke, C. L. (1986). Gaze and eye contact: a research review. *Psychological Bulletin,* **100**, pp. 78–100.

MacLeod & Summerfield, A. Q. (1987). Quantifying the contribution of vision to speech perception in noise. British Journal of Audiology, 21, pp. 131–141.

Marr, D. C. (1977). Analysis of occluding contour. *Proceedings of Royal Society of London,* **B197**, pp. 441–475.

Marr, D. C. (1982). *Vision.* Freeman: San Fransisco.

Marr, D. C. & Nishihara, H. K. (1978). Representation and recognition of the spatial organisation of three-dimensional shapes. *Proceedings of Royal Society of London,* **B200,** pp. 269–294.

Mc Grath, M., Summerfield, A. Q., & Brooke, N. M. (1984). Roles of lips and teeth in lip-reading vowels. *Proceedings of the Institute of Acoustics,* **6,** pp. 401–408.

Montgomery, A. A. & Jackson, P. L. (1983). Physical characteristics of the lips underlying vowel lip-reading preformance. *Journal of Acoustical Society of America,* **73,** pp. 2134–2144.

Watt, R. J. (1987). Scanning from coarse to fine scales in the human visual system after onset of a stimulus. *Journal of Optical Society of America,* **4A,** pp. 2006–2021.

Watt, R. J. (1991). *Understanding Vision.* Academic Press, London.

Watt, R. J. (1994). A computational examination of image segmentation and the initial stages of human vision, *Perception,* pp. 383–398.

13

Interdisciplinary approaches to multimedia research

Andrew Monk

In this book there are chapters from computer scientists, psychologists and ethnographers and it is not difficult to think of other areas of research that have made contributions to our understanding of the relationship between computers and their users. The investigators working in each of these areas of research use different concepts and apply different criteria to their work. These concepts and criteria are collectively agreed upon amongst themselves. Such a body of shared concepts and criteria can be described as a "discipline". The normal way of learning a discipline is through some sort of apprenticeship such as a degree course.

This chapter is concerned with the problems of integrating work from different disciplines. Two conclusions are drawn. (a) Scientists who justify their work as of significance to the design of some practical artefact have an obligation to encapsulate the understanding achieved through their investigations as procedures that can be used in design. (b) Design teams that consist of individuals with varying disciplinary backgrounds have great potential if those individuals can come to understand the concepts and values of their colleagues. Both these conclusions require some degree of compromise of disciplinary rigour.

13.1 Why does travel "broaden the mind"?

Travel is a useful analogy for thinking about the advantages and drawbacks of interdisciplinary approaches to research. Travel is said to broaden the mind. Readers of this chapter who enjoy travelling to foreign parts may agree with this. Coming into contact with people and artefacts from a different culture and history is indeed fascinating. Contact with an alternative set of values and assumptions serves to make one aware of many of the assumptions and values of one's own culture that one would not otherwise think about. Thus travel broadens the mind by allowing one to evaluate the normally implicit assumptions brought to any situation by virtue of one's own background.

Scientific disciplines are very much like national cultures. They are determined by history and they in turn determine the values and behaviour of a community, in this case a community of scientists. The values defined by a discipline are criteria for deciding what is good and bad research. By behaviour I mean the methods and procedures that derive from these criteria.

Returning to the travel analogy, anyone lucky enough to spend a prolonged period immersed in someone else's culture and language will know that the differences between cultures are not just a matter of degree. It is not the case that everyone recognises the same basic concepts but that some put different emphases on them. The concepts themselves differ. Sometimes there are parallel but subtly different concepts in one's own culture. Sometimes the new concepts one learns are entirely foreign. This makes understanding someone else's culture very hard work. Understanding someone else's scientific discipline is similarly difficult. The normal way of learning a discipline is through a lengthy apprenticeship such as a degree course. Most scientists do first and second degrees in a single discipline before they are qualified as researchers. This may be anything between three and ten years of full time work. What hope then for the scientist in an interdisciplinary research team who would like to understand the point of view of a team member from a quite different discipline? Does she have to do another three years training before they can work together? If they are to fully understand one another the answer is probably yes! Thankfully, people can work together without fully understanding each other's points of view. However, the effort involved in inter disciplinary research should not be underestimated. The scientists involved must be aware that their understanding of each other may be extremely limited at first and that each has a duty to explain. The scientist explaining her research should consider herself a host to the other team members who are visitors to her "country". Certain allowances are made to visitors from foreign lands but there is an obligation on both sides to work hard at achieving an understanding.

13.2   A brief tour

Good travel guides start of with some background on the country concerned. This will include some history and an attempt to capture the things that are important to people of the country that the visitor will need to understand. In this section I will attempt a very brief guide to three scientific disciplines that may be applied to obtain an understanding of how people communicate using information technology. My aim is to give a flavour of what these disciplines have to offer. I should also emphasise that I am a psychologist by training who has worked closely with computer scientists for many years and ethnographers to a smaller extent. This gives me a particular viewpoint which will be very apparent to researchers with other backgrounds. It should also be said that there are other disciplines with valuable contributions to make that have been omitted (ergonomics, management science, artificial intelligence, linguistics, graphic design and so on). The researcher who wants a fuller and wider guide book is referred to Gilbert and Monk (1995).

Computer science

Multimedia application developments are being implemented using techniques developed by computer scientists for building all kinds of systems. Computer science is a relatively new discipline that has grown out of engineering and mathematics. This history is very apparent in the way computer scientists think about their subject. One assumption that computer scientists take from engineering is that building a system is preceded by two other activities. As well as creating the artefact itself, the implementation, there will also be a requirements document and a specification. The requirements document describes what the implementation has to achieve. As with any other serious undertaking in engineering, in between writing the requirements and building the implementation a blue print or specification is built. This is because the implementation is extremely difficult to change. The specification is built to be changed, that is, to be evaluated, analysed and improved as much as possible before construction begins.

A major concern in computer science is the problem of abstraction. Computer systems can be extremely complex. Reasoning about a specification that included all the detail of the final implementation is impossible and so models are built that make explicit certain aspects of the design and abstract over others. For example, one may see these scientists reasoning about the high level structure or "architecture" of a design by drawing boxes connected with lines. The major contribution computer scientists have made is to develop abstractions and notations with sound mathematical bases that allow proof and automatic analysis. This area of research is known as "formal methods".

The above may give a false impression of what computer scientists do. It is not the case that researchers in computer science departments spend all their time devising new generally applicable abstractions and that building specific applications is left to the practitioners and engineers. Most computer scientists come into the discipline because they enjoy programming and building working artefacts is a large part of their work. Building a working system serves to demonstrate what can be done and provides a testing ground for the abstractions they use. There is another more subtle reason for building systems in a research environment. Invention proceeds in small steps not in large bounds as is sometimes assumed (Carroll et al., 1991). It was not James Watt's observation of a kettle that inspired his steam engine. His work capitalised on the experience of others with existing atmospheric engines. Sometimes it is only by building something and using it that one can see new uses or how it may be improved.

This book may not be about the engineering problems involved in building systems but computer scientists still have a great deal to contribute, both through the demonstration systems they create and through the abstractions they have developed. Several chapters in this volume describe activities in the former category. The latter activity, that is applying the formal abstractions developed by computer scientists to this area is only just beginning (but see the work of Dix 1992). For example, a major concern in formal methods is how to describe communication between independent processes. It would be surprising if this well developed work had no insights to contribute to our thinking about communicating human agents.

Psychology

Psychologists are also concerned with abstraction and models but here there is a strong additional emphasis on measurement. The psychologist's world is divided into hypothesis and data. The models provide the hypothesis and the data then provide evidence for or against it. This emphasis on hypothesis testing is a product of the subject's long and chequered history. Early psychologists were criticised as being arm-chair theorists with untestable theories. Because these theories had no mathematical basis they could not even be defended on the normal grounds of formal consistency or completeness. Due to its historical association with the arts through philosophy, psychoanalysis and so forth psychology has not traditionally attracted mathematically oriented theorists and so the reaction to this criticism, until recently, was mainly to develop methods for the measurement of behaviour and ways of testing rather simple hypotheses. More recently, computers have made available abstractions that make it possible to construct formal theories of how behaviour arises. The use of computers in psychology has also attracted scientists with rather different orientations to theory construction. The nation of psychology is divided between the old hands who measure and manipulate and a new band of separatists who model. It is to be hoped that this new faction can be integrated into the larger community as time goes by.

As indicated above the major concern of psychologists is measurement and hypothesis testing, that is, the construction of experiments. Psychologists are taught a variety of craft skills and formal techniques that allow them to distinguish alternative explanations to various phenomena. One of the essential problems with behavioural data is measurement error. In contrast to most physical measurements which are highly reliable, behavioural measurements are not. The same measurement made on different individuals in the same situation may give results that vary considerably. There is thus always the possibility that a result has occurred by chance. Statistical tests are carried out to rule out this possibility so that results can be generalised from samples to populations.

By ingenuity in constructing experimental controls and through applying these statistical techniques, psychologists have been able to make generalisable statements about phenomena in a variety of areas of human and animal behaviour. Most relevant to much of this book is cognitive psychology, perception, and the work on the behaviour of individuals interacting with others known under the rubric of "social psychology".

The experimental methods developed by psychologists are also eminently suitable for answering practical questions. Take for example the numerous experiments carried out in the late sixties and early seventies comparing different ways of communicating (e.g., writing, typing, audio only, video and face-to-face) when completing a joint task (see for example Williams 1977).

Turning to the relatively new field of computer modelling in psychology, there is relevant work in the area of computational linguistics. This is concerned with modelling the way in which we comprehend and produce verbal utterances. These are cognitive models (loosely, concerned with thinking) in that they describe internal representations and algorithms for generating them. Some would criticise these models as being too cognitive at the expense of providing an explanation of action. The applied problem of communication systems has provided a strong stimulus to provide models that account for action as well as cognition and one can expect interesting developments in the next few years in this area.

Ethnography

Literally speaking ethnography is to write culture. Here the data is all important. An ethnographer tries to record everything that could be relevant. In particular, they are not just concerned with what people say and do but the context which gives these behaviours meaning. For this reason choosing the right naturalistic setting for data collection is important. Experimental control and manipulation are hard to interpret in this framework because the context that gives behaviour meaning is artificially created by the scientist. Indeed, ethnographers react against the idea of coming to data with a strong hypothesis to be tested. A good ethnographer lets what is interesting emerge from the data.

Ethnography comes from sociology and anthropology. The emphasis on freeing interpretation from prior ideas and theories may to some extent be a reaction to other approaches to sociology which are heavily constrained within a particular ideological framework. The other characteristic of this discipline, that comes from this history, is the idea of socially constructed meaning. The ethnographer is not simply attempting to make a faithful record of some social behaviour, though this is important. The record also characterises what the behaviour meant to the people involved. Ethnomethodology goes further and tries to describe the structures or methods by which people achieve meaning. Conversation analysis, CA for short, for example painstakingly records the precise structure of overlap and pausing in speech to tease out the structures by which people communicate. The picture that emerges of the complex synchronised dance which is conversation is fascinating and enlightening.

The notion of socially constructed meaning is often contrasted with more cognitive notions of meaning. Social meaning is constructed at the level of the group whereas cognitive notions of meaning are concerned with the internal representations generated by an individual. This contrast is often associated with a belief that cognitive approaches to meaning are necessarily "positivist" whereas social meaning is "interpretive". A positivist account assumes some single objective reality that has to be represented. An interpretive account assumes that there are any number of ways of constructing "reality" and that communities construct systems of meaning to achieve certain social ends. This is a false association. It is possible to imagine positivist accounts of meaning at the level of the group and, in point of fact, most cognitive accounts of meaning can be viewed as interpretive in the mechanisms they propose for learning.

Ethnographers have much to contribute when it comes to the design of interactive multimedia systems. Their observational studies of communities using prototype systems have already been most influential. In the future one might also expect the more microscopic analyses of CA to bear fruit.

13.3   How to achieve understanding

Just as sketches of national characters are of necessity caricatures and over generalisations, the accounts of computer science, psychology and ethnography given above will be similarly wanting. Nevertheless, I hope it is clear that scientists coming from these three disciplines: (a) have something individual and of value to offer and (b) have very different ways of looking at a practical question, such as the one we are concerned with in this volume. How then should we combine contributions from these disciplines? Two possibilities will be considered: encapsulation and interdisciplinary work.

The word encapsulation comes from engineering and describes the process of translating a research finding into a form in which it can readily be used to answer practical problems. For example, the results of research into the absorption of nitrogen in the body of deep sea divers might be a set of complex differential equations. For the practical purpose of calculating decompression steps, these results are encapsulated as measurement procedures and tables that a diver can use without a full understanding of the research. This can only be done by approximation. The tables will not be anywhere near as accurate as the original model but, because the purpose of the table is known, it is possible to approximate and then add appropriate safety margins. Scientists who justify their research in terms of its practical worth have an obligation to encapsulate their results. In the context of this volume this probably means outlining procedures for design and design guidelines. Unfortunately many scientists are reluctant to do this. The discipline teaches that certain criteria have to be upheld in reporting results and the process of approximation involved in encapsulation violates these criteria.

Interdisciplinary work is even more difficult for the purist. Having worked in the field of human computer interaction for many years I have observed myself and many other scientists coming to terms with being in an interdisciplinary team. There are three discernible stages that one goes through. The first may be characterised as the "*look at me this is how you do it stage*". This is accompanied by disbelief that the other members of the team could be quite so stupid in carrying on like they do. The second is accompanied by the recognition that other disciplines do have something valuable to offer, the "*these are my strengths and weaknesses what are yours*" stage.

The final stage involves abandoning some of the assumptions of the discipline in the search for solutions, the "*OK so it doesn't work but if you ...*" stage. Psychology reached this last stage when founding fathers such as Landauer (1987) and Carroll (1990) started redefining the relationship between psychology and human-computer interaction (HCI). It is reasonable to argue that interdisciplinary HCI research is now making a major contribution to psychology. For example, Howes and Young's (1991) work producing models of users learning menu driven systems pinpoints an essential weakness in current "pure" cognitive theory. This weakness, that has been emphasised repeatedly by investigators from other less cognitive disciplines, is that human skill is predominantly display-based. Actions are generated primarily on the basis of how the current state of the environment is perceived and only secondarily on the basis of goals and plans.   This means that, to be complete, a model of the behaviour of an organism has to contain a model of the behaviour of its world.   Their work has put these ideas on a sound basis by showing how they can be thought about in a cognitive framework.   Returning to the analogy we started with, travel not only broadens the minds of the individual travellers, it enriches the culture they return to.

References

Carroll, J. M. (1990). Infinite detail and emulation in an ontologically minimised HCI. In: J. C. Chew & J. Whiteside (Eds.), *CHI'90: empowering people,* ACM, pp. 321–327.

Carroll, J. M., Kellogg, W. A. & Rosson, M. B. (1991). The task-artifact cycle. In: J. M. Carroll, (Ed.), *Designing interaction: psychology at the human-computer interface,* Cambridge University Press, pp. 74–102.

Dix, A. (1992). Pace and Interaction. In: A. F. Monk, D. Diaper & M. D. Harrison (Eds.) *People and computers 7,* Cambridge: Cambridge University Press.

Gilbert, N. & Monk, A. F. (1995). *Disciplines for the study of human-computer interaction.* Academic Press, in preparation.

Howes, A. & Young, R. M. (1991). Predicting the learnability of task-action mappings. In: S. P. Robertson, G. M. Olson & J. S. Olson (Eds.), *Human factors in computing systems: reaching through technology, CHI'91,* ACM, pp. 113-118.

Landauer, T.K. (1987). Relations between cognitive psychology and computer system design. In: Carroll, J.M. (Eds.), *Interfacing thought: cognitive aspects of human-computer interaction,* MIT Press, pp. 1-25.

Williams, E. (1977). Experimental comparisons of face-to-face and mediated communication: a review, *Psychological Bulletin,* **84,** pp. 963-975.

Index

Printed and bound by CPI Group (UK) Ltd, Croydon, CR0 4YY

03/10/2024

01040418-0016